# Music, Communities, Sustainability

# Music, Communities, Sustainability

## Developing Policies and Practices

*Edited by*

HUIB SCHIPPERS AND ANTHONY SEEGER

OXFORD
UNIVERSITY PRESS

# OXFORD
## UNIVERSITY PRESS

Oxford University Press is a department of the University of Oxford. It furthers
the University's objective of excellence in research, scholarship, and education
by publishing worldwide. Oxford is a registered trade mark of Oxford University
Press in the UK and certain other countries.

Published in the United States of America by Oxford University Press
198 Madison Avenue, New York, NY 10016, United States of America.

Library of Congress Cataloging-in-Publication Data
Names: Schippers, Huib, 1959- editor. | Seeger, Anthony, editor.
Title: Music, communities, sustainability : developing policies and
practices / edited by Huib Schippers & Anthony Seeger.
Description: New York : Oxford University Press, 2022. |
Includes bibliographical references and index.
Identifiers: LCCN 2022002580 (print) | LCCN 2022002581 (ebook) |
ISBN 9780197609118 (paperback) | ISBN 9780197609101 (hardback) |
ISBN 9780197609132 (epub)
Subjects: LCSH: Convention for the Safeguarding of the Intangible Cultural
Heritage (2003) | Cultural property—Protection. | Cultural policy. |
Intangible property. | Sustainability. | Music—Social aspects. |
Applied ethnomusicology.
Classification: LCC ML3916 .M8739 2022 (print) | LCC ML3916 (ebook) |
DDC 306.4/842—dc23
LC record available at https://lccn.loc.gov/2022002580
LC ebook record available at https://lccn.loc.gov/2022002581

DOI: 10.1093/oso/9780197609101.001.0001

3 5 7 9 8 6 4 2

Paperback printed by Marquis, Canada
Hardback printed by Bridgeport National Bindery, Inc., United States of America

# Contents

# Foreword

*Jeff Todd Titon*

In June 1999, experts in music from all over the world gathered at the Smithsonian Institution in Washington, DC, to discuss efforts to ensure the vitality and diversity of music on this planet. One of its main outcomes was the 2003 UNESCO Convention for the Safeguarding of the Intangible Cultural Heritage. Twenty years later, in September 2019, the Smithsonian Center for Folklife and Cultural Heritage invited another group of experts—some of whom also attended the 1999 meeting—to reflect on the consequences and impact of declaring music an intangible cultural heritage, as well as the framework surrounding it. While I was sadly unable to attend this meeting, it is a pleasure to offer some reflections in this Foreword to the important volume that emanated from it, critically assessing cultural policy and practice in regard to music.

In this book, 15 authors from three continents who have been deeply involved in these efforts review successes and failures of UNESCO and other cultural institutions in working to ensure future continuity in musical traditions. This book is about music-making communities, cultural policy, and sustainability. Music-making communities are social groups that participate in music through exchanges of sound, information, behavior, social solidarity, and at peak moments, exchanges not only of expression, but also emotion and feelings of flow. The community's total involvement with music is termed its music culture: ideas, actions, institutions, material objects—everything that has to do with music. We can identify music cultures with Indigenous peoples, with ethnic groups, with religious communities, with geographic communities, and with occupational communities, among others; we can also identify musical communities clustered around musical genres and sub-genres such as bluegrass, taiko, reggae, hip-hop, *guqin*, Afro-pop, jazz, and classical music.

Consider the two following vignettes, each focused on a different music-making community in the United States. One: Ralph Stanley, a renowned bluegrass musician and winner of a Heritage Award from the US National

Endowment for the Arts, performs with his band at a county fair. After the performance is over, he sits behind a portable table, with dozens from the audience queued up waiting to buy an autographed copy of his latest CD. A fan thanks him, saying if it weren't for her stumbling on one of his record albums 40 years ago, she'd not have become a bluegrass musician herself. Two: a half dozen members of the Indian Bottom Association of Old Regular Baptists, an obscure religious denomination in Kentucky with a singing tradition five centuries old, demonstrate their musical heritage for tourists at a folk festival, unwilling to think of it as a performance. Although CDs of this music happen to be available in a festival sales tent, they did not bring them and are not interested in marketing their music. These contrasting attitudes toward music commodification are expressions of two different music communities. The bluegrass community is presentational; that is, performers present music to an audience that pays to hear it. This religious community is participatory; that is, everyone in a worship service sings; there is no separate audience. The music is intended as worship, not entertainment; no one pays to make it or hear it. We can find examples of presentational and participatory musics all over the world.

Bluegrass music is secure through at least the next generation, with a professional organization (the International Bluegrass Music Association, or IBMA), an industry, and an international reach. Bluegrass music-making communities exist in many nations, including the Czech Republic, Sweden, and Japan. The religious community had considered its musical tradition endangered. Now it too is secure in its original context of church worship through at least the next generation, in part because of the community's partnership with applied ethnomusicologists, public folklorists, arts organizations, museums, and colleges and universities. No cultural policy is directed at the bluegrass music community today and none is needed; a network of supporters, some well-connected in the music industry, boosts the music through recordings, concerts, festivals, music instructions camps, and a presence on the internet.

On the other hand, the religious music community was the recipient of attention from historians, ethnomusicologists, folklorists, and musicologists, as well as arts administrators with their own connections to the music industry. This was the oldest, continuous English-language religious music in oral tradition in the United States. It had been thought to have become extinct, but 50 years ago it was found to have survived here. In the years since, these sympathetic outsiders visited and got to know community members, each group gaining the others' friendship and trust. The visitors marked the music as cultural heritage, and they arranged for its recognition outside of its region in demonstrations at museums, colleges, and festivals. Singers from this community were invited to academic conferences on the history of their music and its international kin. Community members shared their music and talked about its meaning. They also learned things about their music they had not known before. They had already known its value in worship; now they realized its historical import. They had already known that this music belonged to them; now they understood that they were its stewards. This musical community benefited from cultural policies at the national level in the United States that arose in the 1970s, policies that were directed at music and other folk arts among marginal social groups, with the goal of promoting cultural diversity and equity.

These two vignettes raise issues that confront the contributors to this book: How do differences in music-making communities impact the cultural policies directed at them? When should culture workers, such as arts administrators, museum specialists, ethnomusicologists, folklorists, sociologists, community scholars, and practitioners, attempt to intervene in musical life, and when should they leave music-making communities alone? How should cultural policymakers assess the health of music-making communities and their traditions, and with what inputs from and partnerships with the communities themselves? How should policymakers and culture workers define and carry out their roles? What are the cultural values that a given community assigns to its various musical activities, and how do cultural values determine economic value, and vice versa? If sustainability is a goal, what strategies may best be adopted to achieve it? What are the factors that enable a music-making community to be resilient in the face of disturbance and change, and how may a pragmatic, adaptive management strategy work toward sustaining cultural and musical integrity?

Moreover, underlying these particular issues is a broader consideration: Why is it the business of cultural policy to promote diversity and equity? Chiefly for two reasons: the belief, shared by many, in cultural equity; and the survival value of diversity, whether cultural diversity or biodiversity. Post–World War II decolonization and establishment of new nation-states, the growing influence not only of the United Nations but also of UNESCO, and a series of declarations of human rights and cultural sovereignty have led to a gradual acceptance of cultural democracy. Cultural democracy embodies cultural justice on the basis of the principles of human dignity and the rights of all to life, liberty, and self-realization. Every music tradition of every social group has cultural rights, just as all peoples throughout the world have the right to physical and cultural survival. Today sweeping social, political, and economic changes induce sweeping cultural changes that have profound effects upon music throughout the world. Modernization, development, political and cultural conflicts, refugee resettlements, industrial and technological revolutions all have subjected musical traditions to culture change, sometimes rapid and sometimes less so but no less profound. Ecology teaches that diversity itself has survival value in the face of profound change. An analogy between cultural and biological diversity was on Alan Lomax's mind in his influential "Appeal for Cultural Equity": "[At the same time that] folklorists and musicologists were studying the varied traditions of the peoples of the earth their rate of disappearance accelerated." With the loss of these communicative systems, "the human species not only loses a way of viewing, thinking and feeling but also a way of adjusting to some zone on the planet which fits it and makes it liveable" (Lomax, 1972, pp. 4–5). Cultural democracy thus couples with sustainability to provide a philosophical basis for inclusion and cultural pluralism initiatives in cultural policy, and especially for the more recent efforts, including those from UNESCO, in cultural conservation, heritage, and safeguarding.

*Cultural conservation* was the umbrella name that public folklorists and ethnomusicologists in the United States gave to their efforts since the mid-1970s in partnering with communities to encourage their traditional arts and expressive culture as heritage, music prominent among them, by identifying, documenting, and presenting them in museums, festivals, fairs, on recordings, and in film and other media (Loomis, 1982; Feintuch, 1988; Hufford, 1994). But the focus of this volume is on the international arena and UNESCO, which came to this practice late in the last century. UNESCO drew upon American public folklorists' and applied ethnomusicologists' experiences, but also on the 1950 Japanese Law for Protection of Cultural Properties, which included music and other "important intangible cultural properties" of utmost value (Article 71, Section 1), as well as conservation efforts in Korea (Howard, 2006). The concept of intangibility is meant to distinguish music and other ephemeral cultural performances from the tangible heritage embodied in material objects such as historically important architecture. International efforts in archiving and preservation and the activities of the International Council for Traditional Music (ICTM, a UNESCO-affiliated NGO) also influenced UNESCO when it constructed its more far-reaching and ambitious version of cultural conservation, its Convention for the Safeguarding of the Intangible Cultural Heritage (2003). Rejecting the term *folklore* in favor of the phrase *intangible cultural heritage* (ICH), UNESCO adopted the goal of what it termed "safeguarding" in its efforts to encourage member nations to identify, document, set aside, and care for their people's ICH, particularly those thought to be endangered. Often this exemplary heritage is carried by minority and Indigenous populations, themselves at risk as well as their traditions—populations that are already committed to and often struggling to maintain their way of life insofar as possible.

The concepts of cultural and musical sustainability arrived only a few years after the 2003 UNESCO safeguarding Convention. Unlike conservation, preservation, and safeguarding, which "put applied ethnomusicologists and public folklorists in a defensive posture of safeguarding property assets . . . with tourist commerce [and] staged authenticities," sustainability partnerships are targeted "interventions aimed directly inside music cultures" (Titon, 2009, p. 119). The sustainability principles that guide them do not come from developmental economics (sustainable development) but, rather, from "conservation ecology—diversity, limits to growth, interconnectedness, and stewardship" (Titon, 2009, p. 119). Sustainability quickly gained prominence in the worlds of public folklore and applied ethnomusicology in the United States, largely replacing the earlier concept of cultural conservation (see Cooley, 2019). Acknowledging its currency, the American Folklore Society themed its 2013 annual conference on cultural sustainability. Sustainability entered UNESCO's rhetoric not as cultural sustainability, however, but in the older sense of sustainable development, as popularized in the Brundtland Report (1987) and later reiterated in the 17 goals formulated in the 2030 agenda for sustainable development (UN 2015), which significantly lack a clear reference to culture, in spite of lobbying efforts by international cultural organizations to the contrary. Translated to the cultural sector, sustainable development seems to be limited primarily to a collateral economic benefit that may accrue from safeguarding ICH: namely, that ICH may also be regarded as a cultural asset that will generate income for the tourist industry. Heritage tourism depends on a local creative economy, that portion of the economy that relies primarily on arts and innovation (Howken, 2001).

If the traditional arts potentially do confer an economic benefit, then instead of their usual role as beggars at the policymaking tables, arts organizations become power brokers. Yet innovation and marketing are not always a good match for traditional expressive culture. As the second of the vignettes above shows, not all intangible, community-based cultural heritage is easily commodified; and sometimes the result is a confusion of cultural values with economic value (Titon, 2013a; see also van Zanten, Chapter 4, and Clark, Chapter 9, in this volume). The demands of the tourist market may come to take precedence over those of the original, tradition-bearing community and affect both the content and delivery of the "cultural asset." Moreover, targeted interventions to support one component of a music culture have sometimes had unpredicted negative consequences for other components and processes. It is ironic to consider cultural heritage tourism as an example of sustainable economic development if modernization and presumably un-sustainable economic development endangered the cultural traditions in the first place. In addition, scholars from a critical heritage perspective have pointed out that just as traditions are social constructions of the past in the present, so heritage is made, rather than discovered. This is especially true when traditions are subject to revivals, as for example during the 1960s when blues revivalists thought we had discovered something called "blues," but in our acts of discovery we constructed the object we thought we had discov-ered (Titon, 1993). Finally, a few scholars have critiqued the sustainability discourse within applied ethnomusicology for diverting attention from so-cial justice concerns that are central in feminist, Marxist, and Indigenous approaches to music and culture (Keogh & Collinson, 2016; Diamond & El Shawan, 2021, p. 3). Yet social justice concerns are paramount in many applied ethnomusicology projects targeted at sustainability (e.g., Summit, 2015; see also Haskell, 2015).

Cultural policies are the subject that the contributors to this book con-sider. The authors are themselves practitioners and contributors to these cultural policies, and their chapters are themed about music communities, commodification, heritage, cultural tourism, and best practices for musical diversity, inclusion, and equity. Taken as models, successes as related in this volume may succeed elsewhere. Or they may not. Failures, moreover, lead us to question even the fundamental assumptions behind our work, as well as the reasons for the difficulties in their implementation and the consequences of their outcomes. As Svanibor Pettan and I realized more than a decade ago, applied ethnomusicologists in one part of the world were unaware that they were developing and putting into practice models that had already been the-orized, practiced, thoroughly critiqued, and either modified or abandoned in other parts of the world (Pettan and Titon 2015, p. 10). Among the for-tunate consequences of *Music, Communities, Sustainability* will be a better understanding of the development of the 2003 UNESCO Convention, some of the influences of its ratification on communities and nation-states, the continuing exchange of ideas among professionals of sustainable cultural policies, and recommendations for improvements.

# References

Brundtland, G. H. (Chairman). (1987). *Report of the World Commission on Environment and Development: Our common future.* Oxford University Press.

Cooley, T. J. (Ed). (2019). *Cultural sustainabilities: Music, media, language.* University of Illinois Press.

Diamond, B., & El-Shawan Castelo Branco, S. (2021). Ethnomusicological praxis: An introduction. In B. Diamond & S. E. Castelo Branco (Eds.), *Transforming ethnomusicology,* Vol. 2: *Political, social, and economic issues* (pp. 1–25). Oxford University Press.

Feintuch, B. (Ed.). (1988). *The conservation of culture: Folklorists and the public sector.* University Press of Kentucky.

Haskell, E. (2015). The role of applied ethnomusicology in post-conflict and post-catastrophe communities. In S. Pettan & J. T. Titon (Eds.), *The Oxford handbook of applied ethnomusicology* (pp. 453–480). Oxford University Press.

Howard, K. (2006). *Preserving Korean music: Intangible cultural properties as icons of identity.* Ashgate.

Howken, J. (2001). *The creative economy: How people make money from ideas.* Penguin Global.

Hufford, M. (Ed.) (1994). *Conserving culture: A new discourse on heritage.* University of Illinois Press.

Keogh, B., & Collinson, I. (2016). "A place for everything, and everything in its place": The (ab)uses of music ecology. *MUSICultures, 43*(1), 1–15.

Lomax, A. (1972). Appeal for cultural equity. *The World of Music, 14*(2), 3–17.

Loomis, O. (Coordinator). (1982). *Cultural conservation.* Library of Congress, the American Folklife Center.

Pettan, S., & Titon, J. T. (Eds.) (2015). *The Oxford handbook of applied ethnomusicology.* Oxford University Press.

Summit, J. A. (2015). Advocacy and the ethnomusicologist: Assessing capacity, developing initiatives, setting limits, and making sustainable contributions. In S. Pettan & J. T. Titon (Eds.), *The Oxford handbook of applied ethnomusicology* (pp. 199–228). Oxford University Press.

Titon, J. T. (1993). Reconstructing the blues: Reflections on the 1960s blues revival. In N. V. Rosenberg (Ed.), *Transforming tradition* (pp. 220–240). University of Illinois Press.

Titon, J. T. (2009). Music and sustainability: An ecological approach. *The World of Musi,c 51*(1), 119–137.

Titon, J. T. (2013a). Music is not a cultural asset. https://sustainablemusic.blogspot.com/2013/03/music-is-not-cultural-asset-2.html.

United Nations. (2015). *The 17 goals for sustainable development.* United Nations Department of Economic and Social Affairs. https://sdgs.un.org/goals.

# Acknowledgments

Many people contributed directly and indirectly to the realization of this volume. First, we would like to thank the Smithsonian Institution, particularly the Center for Folklife and Cultural Heritage and its former Director Michael Mason. They supported the idea of organizing the working conference that spawned this book in the context of the Smithsonian Year of Music 2019, providing funding, space, and administrative support. We particularly thank Folkways Executive Assistant Logan Clark and her assistants, who shone in arranging many aspects of the gathering, making travel, technology, accommodation, and sustenance seem effortless.

Second, we would like to express our gratitude for the people at Oxford University Press, starting with former Editor of Arts and Humanities Suzanne Ryan, who immediately embraced the idea, attended the meeting, and made all the authors feel valued and at ease with the process. Her successor Norman Hirschy, Sean Decker, and Koperundevi Pugazhenthi were highly supportive and responsive as they steered the volume through peer review, edits, and into production. We'd also like to thank the anonymous peer reviewers for the support and suggestions for the volume. Queensland Conservatorium Research Centre at Griffith University kindly supported the indexing of the book.

Third, we would like to thank the authors for embarking and staying on this three-year journey with us: from agreeing to prepare a first draft of their chapters before we met, so that we could plunge *in medias res* when we gathered, to refining their papers on the basis of the discussions and reviewer feedback into the final versions presented here. We are also grateful for the frank and open discussions that characterized all our interactions, which makes this volume an important and honest historical document chronicling the rise of music as intangible cultural heritage, with all its intended and unintended consequences.

Finally, we would like to acknowledge the thousands of educators, scholars, policy workers, and other music industry professionals, the millions of musicians, and the billions of people who help create, develop, hand down, sound, support, and sustain music as an essential part of their lives and communities, often in challenging circumstances. They are the true heroes of this book; they have kept music strong and will keep it strong, long before and long after these words fade.

# Companion Website

**www.oup.com/us/musiccommunitiessustainability**

Oxford has created a website to accompany *Music, Communities, Sustainability*. Material that cannot be made available in the book is provided here, including two full-length additional chapters, a documentary, videos and photographs. We encourage you to consult this resource in conjunction with the chapters as you read this volume. Examples available online are indicated in the text with Oxford's symbol ⊙.

# Contributors

**Noriko Aikawa-Faure**

*Noriko Aikawa-Faure is the former Chief and Director of the Intangible Cultural Heritage Unit of UNESCO. Currently, she serves on the advisory committee of the International Training Centre for Intangible Cultural Heritage (China).*

**Salwa El-Shawan Castelo-Branco**

*Salwa El-Shawan Castelo-Branco is Professor Emerita of Ethnomusicology, founder and former director of the Institute of Ethnomusicology—Center for the Study of Music and Dance at the Universidad Nova de Lisboa in Portugal, and a former President of the International Council for Traditional Music (ICTM).*

**Naila Ceribašić**

*Naila Ceribašić is a scholarly advisor at the Institute of Ethnology and Folklore Research and Adjunct Professor of Ethnomusicology at the University of Zagrab, who from 2012 to 2021 represented the ICTM in the ICH Convention.*

**Logan Elizabeth Clark**

*Logan Elizabeth Clark is an ethnomusicologist with a focus on marimba music in contemporary Mayan migrant communities, and Executive Assistant at Smithsonian Folkways Recordings, Center for Folklife and Cultural Heritage, Smithsonian Institution.*

**Rebecca Dirksen**

*Rebecca Dirksen is an ethnomusicologist with a focus on Haiti, and an Associate Professor in the Department of Folklore and Ethnomusicology at Indiana University, Bloomington.*

**Catherine Grant**

*Catherine Grant is a music researcher with interest in cultural sustainability, and a Senior Lecturer in Music Literature and Research at Queensland Conservatorium Griffith University, Brisbane, Australia.*

**Richard Kurin**

*Richard Kurin is the Smithsonian Institution's Distinguished Scholar and Ambassador at Large, having previously served as Smithsonian Undersecretary, 2007–2017, and for the prior two decades as Director of its Center for Folklife and Cultural Heritage.*

**Xiao Mei**

*Xiao Mei is Professor of Music at Shanghai Conservatory of Music, Director of the Research Institute of Ritual Music in China, Director of Asian-European Music Research Center, and president of the Association for Traditional Music in China.*

**Olcay Muslu**

*Olcay Muslu is a former professional dancer and applied ethnomusicologist, currently involved in developing new degrees in traditional Turkish music as Assistant Professor of Music at Antioch State Conservatory, Hatay Mustafa Kemal University, Turkey.*

**Huib Schippers**

*Huib Schippers is Adjunct Professor at Griffith University, former Director/Curator of Smithsonian Folkways Recordings, and freelance consultant to organizations in the arts and academia.*

**Anthony Seeger**

*Anthony Seeger is Professor Emeritus at University of California, Los Angeles, and Director/Curator Emeritus of Smithsonian Folkways Recordings.*

**Gao Shu**

*Gao Shu is actively involved in work to preserve the vitality and diversity of Chinese performing arts, and an Associate Professor at the China National Center for Safeguarding Intangible Cultural Heritage, Chinese National Academy of Arts, Beijing.*

**Tan Sooi Beng**

*Tan Sooi Beng is actively engaged in the practice of community theatre for young people and in the rejuvenation of local heritage in Penang. She is Professor at Universiti Sains Malaysia and a vice president of the International Council for Traditional Music (ICTM).*

**Jeff Todd Titon**

*Jeff Todd Titon is Professor of Music, Emeritus, at Brown University and author/editor of nine books, including the popular introductory textbook Worlds of Music, as well as the Oxford Handbook of Applied Ethnomusicology.*

**Yang Xiao**

*Specializing in the music of the Dong people, Yang Xiao is Professor at Sichuan Conservatory of Music, standing director of the Chinese Minority Society, and Council Member of the Association for Traditional Music in China.*

**Wim van Zanten**

*Wim van Zanten is a Cultural Anthropologist Emeritus specialized in Indonesian music at the Universiteit Leiden, the Netherlands, who was involved in developing the Glossary of Terms for the ICH Convention.*

# 1

# Introduction

## Approaching Music as Intangible Cultural Heritage

*Anthony Seeger and Huib Schippers*

The support for certain musical practices to ensure their viability, development, transmission, and enduring significance to communities has always been almost exclusively a local, regional, or national concern. In many societies, this has led to intricate systems of support, from philanthropy to government subsidies, from grants for productions to paying living national treasures, from infrastructure for performance to elaborate education systems. Often, these are linked to a sense of identity and/or prestige. That is why the 2003 UNESCO Convention for the Safeguarding of the Intangible Cultural Heritage (hereafter ICH Convention) was a revolutionary document for those of us working in music and the performing arts: It was the first *global* effort to "keep our songs strong"—as a group of Australian Aboriginal women expressed it succinctly and eloquently in discussion with Barwick and Turpin (2016).

Whereas the 1972 UNESCO Convention Concerning the Protection of the World Cultural Heritage had largely focused on the celebration and preservation of buildings, monuments, and landscapes, the ICH Convention targeted the knowledge and enactment of ideas and skills by communities, groups, and individuals, inclusive of many kinds of knowledge and activities, rather than limited to predefined Eurocentric categories such as "music" and "folklore." In so doing, it courageously confronted a number of conceptual and practical challenges. As the contributions to this volume show, UNESCO's lofty goals came with many complicated choices. These ranged from defining what constitutes ICH and how it functions in various contexts to how to execute precise rules needed to implement a convention of this level of abstraction and global scope.

While it is unlikely that it will ever be turned into a Hollywood—or Bollywood—script, the story of how the ICH Convention developed and was

Anthony Seeger and Huib Schippers, *Introduction* In: *Music, Communities, Sustainability.*
Edited by: Huib Schippers and Anthony Seeger, Oxford University Press. © Oxford University Press 2022.
DOI: 10.1093/oso/9780197609101.003.0001

implemented is a riveting tale: a story of ideas, ideals, actions, people, and power (e.g., Seeger, 2015, and this volume). After I (Seeger) had attended several regional meetings as president of the International Council for Traditional Music, I was asked by Noriko Aikawa if I thought it would be possible to organize a global meeting in the United States to consider the 1989 UNESCO Recommendation on the Safeguarding of Traditional Culture and Folklore. Aikawa was brilliant, eloquent, strategic, and convincing, moving through crowds of scholars with a smile on her face and purpose in her step. Although I was concerned about the potential expense, as director of Smithsonian Folkways Recordings I took the suggestion to my supervisor at the Smithsonian, Richard Kurin, who welcomed the idea and threw himself into making it happen. As director of the Smithsonian Center for Folklife and Cultural Heritage, a dynamic administrator, trained social anthropologist, and folklorist, Kurin became one of the driving forces behind the realization of a conference focusing on a global assessment of the 1989 Recommendation. This meeting was held in Washington, DC, June 27–30, 1999, and produced key recommendations for the 2003 ICH Convention, in which Aikawa played a decisive role as director of UNESCO's Intangible Cultural Heritage Program (Seitel, 2001).

Twenty years after that gathering at the Smithsonian, as the next director of Smithsonian Folkways Recordings, I (Schippers) suggested a working conference to critically evaluate the first two decades of approaching music as ICH, featuring some of the people who were at its inception, and others who have worked with various nation-states, institutions, and communities since. At the time of this writing, the ICH Convention has influenced national policies, community arts, and opportunities for enabling people to continue to practice and develop traditions they value in many of the 180 nations that have ratified it, and even in some countries that have not yet done so. Participants of the second meeting, which took place on October 23–25, 2019, again at the Smithsonian Center for Folklife and Cultural Heritage, were asked to send their papers beforehand, so we could focus on discussions rather than presentations, which were open, honest, often critical, but ultimately optimistic.

This volume is the outcome of those discussion, divided into three parts: Part I presents a unique inside view of how the ICH Convention came about and operates, told by four people who were present when key aspects of the Convention and its implementation were discussed and decided. Part II offers profound reflections on how the Convention worked (and didn't work) on four different continents. Part III offers possible pathways to improve or develop new strategies to realize the objectives of the Convention in the ever-changing realities of the twenty-first century.

For reasons of space, two of the papers are summarized in this volume but appear in full on the book's website. Anthony Seeger and Wim van Zanten volunteered to do this since they no longer need to be concerned about institutional evaluations of their scholarly production. For the same reason, media examples have been placed on the website. We encourage readers to consult the website while reading the chapters here ⊙.

## The Genesis of the ICH Convention

In Chapter 2, Richard Kurin begins by reviewing some of the efforts to preserve what has been variously labeled "traditional," "folklore," "folklife," and "heritage" in different parts of the world during the past 150 years. Next, he discusses the changes from the 1989 UNESCO Recommendation to the 2003 ICH Convention, with special attention to the 1999 global meeting at the Smithsonian Institution. He notes the influence of both previous and contemporary UNESCO instruments on the development of the ICH Convention, among them the UNESCO Universal Recommendation on Cultural Diversity and the Masterpieces program (2001), and the Convention on the Protection and Promotion of the Diversity of Cultural Expressions (2005). He writes, "Participants concluded that a new instrument should contain certain additional features lacking in the Recommendation, such as a code of ethics for principles of respect; the inclusion of customary owners of traditional culture and folklore as the principal participants in and beneficiaries of the process of documenting and disseminating their knowledge; recognition of the collaborative role of NGOs and other institutions that could assist in preserving this cultural heritage; and widening the scope of the Recommendation to include the evolving nature of traditional culture and folklore—not 'freezing' it in some idealized past form." Tracing the writing of the Convention, he notes some aspects that make sense within the UNESCO context but subvert the objectives of the document, among them the necessity for ICH to conform to the Declaration on Human Rights, the definition of sustainability (which we will return to later), and the non-binding nature of the obligation of nations to consult the culture bearers in the safeguarding of their traditions.

Rich in detail and inside perspectives, Noriko Aikawa-Faure's Chapter 3 focuses on one of the core issues of this book: the changing nature of the participation of communities during the writing of the Convention. She describes the very strongly community-based, bottom-up recommendations that emerged from the 1999 Global Evaluation at the Smithsonian, which emphasized the importance of community initiative and control over their ICH and the steps taken to safeguard it. Noting how that strong community-based wording was weakened in the writing of the Convention and particularly in the development of the Operational Directives that transformed the general statements of the Convention into practice (and which can be altered without requiring the complex process of making changes to a Convention), she insists that "empowering communities should be one of the most powerful tools in ensuring an 'endogenous' participatory approach to the safeguarding of the ICH." She documents a steady erosion of the importance of communities and an increasing presence of top-down decisions in ICH policies.

UNESCO conventions are the final result of years of discussions, negotiations, and interventions. Even a single word can be important. The change of a single phrase can have major implications for what is included and excluded and for the implementation of the Convention by the countries that sign it. As anthropologist Wim van Zanten notes in Chapter 4, "conventions are constructions of words, and words are tricky things." He participated in meetings of specialists who endeavored to define essential concepts as the Convention was being written. He and his colleagues prepared a Glossary of Terms, which was eventually not included in the Convention itself. His chapter examines issues surrounding the definitions of two essential words in the Convention that are also the subject matter of this book: "community" and "sustainability." He addresses some of the complexities of the word "community" in relation to the Dutch tradition of Sinterklaas and Black Pete, and then traces the changing nuances of the word "sustainability" from the text of the Convention to its use in the Operational Directives. He concludes with an examination of a related concept referred to in the Convention, "sustainable development" (as distinct from the sustainability of music practices) and whether it can be applied to tourism, referring to his work with the Indigenous Baduy in western Java. The full chapter is available on the book's companion website⊙.

With her characteristic frankness, Naila Ceribašić's Chapter 5 moves from the genesis of the Convention to critiquing the lack of community agency in the nomination process for the Convention lists. She writes "based on my experience, ranging from very local to international levels, I can hardly recall cases of implementation under the 2003 Convention where culture bearers and their communities were truly empowered to have a decisive influence on the nature, representation, and actions relating to their ICH." She reveals how the vagueness of the definitions of the words "communities, groups, and some individuals" in the Convention arises repeatedly in the meetings of the 24 states in both the Intergovernmental Committee for the Safeguarding of the Intangible Cultural Heritage and the Operational Directives. Ceribašić also notes the disconnect between paper statements and on-the-ground realities, and the tendency of UNESCO to increasingly rely on paper statements alone, while excluding contributions by the public. The on-site descriptions are more often made by non-governmental organizations (NGOs) and ethnomusicologists (for example, Xiao Mei, Olcay Muslu, Tan Sooi Beng, Logan Elizabeth Clark, Salwa El-Shawan Castelo-Branco, and Rebecca Dirksen in this volume), and there is no mechanism for incorporating their findings through UNESCO channels. She suggests that one solution might be the creation of an ICH NGO monitoring center to integrate expertise into the process, and to operate more like the World Heritage Convention.

\* \* \*

These four chapters, told from the vantage point of active participants in key discussions, jointly form a unique document of the story behind the ICH Convention: the worldviews, the ideas, the words, the idealism, the pragmatism, the politics, the compromises, the concessions, the individual and joint efforts to turn a mind-bogglingly complex concept and massively diverse realities into a more or less workable global policy. As they illustrate, empowering musicians and communities was at the center of the planning for the ICH Convention. But once approved and operational, that was tested against the harsh realities of institutional and national ways of doing things. That is hardly surprising: UNESCO is a large and complex institution with over 195 member states, hundreds of NGOs as partners (including five in music), about 65 field offices and institutes reporting to headquarters in Paris, and an underfunded and overworked staff of about two thousand. Its officers pursue many initiatives simultaneously in different branches of the organization. What is being developed in one part of the organization can have an effect on what happens in another part. UNESCO also has National Commissions in most countries, which are expected to act as liaisons between national governments and UNESCO. Because it is an organization composed of nations, UNESCO can formulate recommendations and conventions for ICH, but it has little control over how these are implemented by the States Parties, so what actually happens varies widely.

## The ICH Convention in Action

In terms of positive effects, building on the reputation UNESCO had gained with similar instruments for tangible cultural and natural heritage, the ICH Convention powerfully increased awareness of the value of intangible cultural heritage across the world, and sparked a lively intellectual engagement with the concept. The value of this can hardly be overstated, with impact on musical performance, education, scholarship, economy, and tourism, to name but a few. More practically, it led dozens of countries to modify their cultural policies and inventory and celebrate elements of their cultural heritage, imbuing them with prestige (see, for example, Chapter 6 by Xiao Mei and Yang Xiao, Chapter 7 by Muslu, and Chapter 9 by Clark, in this volume), while some nation-states, most strikingly China, dramatically increased their funding for ICH as a result of the 2003 Convention.

On the negative side, there was a considerable amount of political negotiation around which form of which expression would get recognized, both within and between nation-states. And as anywhere with regulations, people tried to manipulate the system, for instance by misrepresenting ICH expressions and their histories to present newly created ICH, to the point that rumors circulated about bribing experts to recognize recently invented traditions as time-honored ones (cf. Hobsbawn & Ranger, 1983). Another issue raised by several scholars is the risk that ICH items come to be seen as just that: as objects, rather than parts of living culture (see, for instance, Gao Shu, Chapter 11 in this volume). Perhaps the biggest losers in these battles have been many of the communities themselves, who often found themselves without much agency in selecting, presenting, and planning for the ICH they created and owned (see Ceribašić, Chapter 5 in this volume; and for reflections on contemporary approaches to working with communities Bartleet & Higgins, 2018; Schrag & Van Buren, 2018; and Garcia Corona & Wiens, 2021.

Indigenous communities frequently have less power than other communities in the nation-states of settlers who displaced them from their territories and now surround them. In her critical examination of its provisions for Indigenous peoples, Henrietta Marie argued that the ICH Convention did not serve Indigenous people well because it failed to address issues of intellectual property, consultation, and mechanisms for protection, as well as some other UNESCO and UN instruments (2009, pp. 174–176). Perhaps the clearest statement regarding Indigenous control over their ICH is to be found in the 2007 United Nations Declaration on the Rights of Indigenous Peoples. It gives them far more control over their ICH than the ICH Convention grants to any other communities:

> Indigenous peoples have the right to maintain, control, protect and develop their cultural heritage, traditional knowledge and traditional cultural expressions [ ... ]. They also have the right to maintain, control, protect and develop their intellectual property over such cultural heritage, traditional knowledge, and traditional cultural expressions. (UNESCO, 2007, p. 23)

Even though specific protection of Indigenous rights was not granted in the ICH Convention, Indigenous peoples in many countries have become increasingly active agents for their own ICH, often using national ICH policies for their own ends (Stobart & Bigenho, 2018). Many nations that ratified the ICH Convention have nominated the ICH of Indigenous peoples within their national borders to the UNESCO lists in recognition of its importance for cultural diversity and national identity. Other nations that did not ratify the Convention for fear it would expose them legally or financially—including Australia, Canada, and the United States—in fact developed programs which could be considered in the spirit of the ICH Convention. For instance, the National Recording Project for Indigenous Performance in Australia has tried to counter the egregious loss of Aboriginal and Torres Strait Islander music by documenting music practices for future generations (Marett et al., 2005). The chapters by Clark and van Zanten reveal additional ways in which Indigenous communities make use of the ICH Convention and their Indigenous identities to negotiate their status within nation-states.

Other communities that are at peril of being underrepresented in nation-driven ICH exercises are those divided across national (often colonial) borders, diasporic communities, displaced people, refugees and other war victims, as well as censored, discriminated, persecuted, and incarcerated people. ICH in Africa frequently crosses national boundaries and is often misrepresented—the heritage of colonialism (e.g., Agawu, 2003). Diasporic cultures often present challenges in identifying and prioritizing what needs to be sustained (see, for instance, Dirksen, Chapter 14 in this volume). The culture of refugees and displaced people is supported erratically at best in their new and often temporary homes (Pettan, 2010), and culture is rarely a priority for incarcerated people (Balfour et al., 2019). Rebuilding meaningful engagement with music in post-conflict environments is a major challenge (Howell, 2018), and religious intolerance is a key reason for music actively "being disappeared" (Seeger in QCRC, 2008; see also Tan, Chapter 8 in this volume). There is a growing body of research and literature on many of these groups, but much works remains to be done in this realm.

With over 20 years of planning and implementing, it is fascinating to see the Convention's intended and unintended effects in specific nation-states, music traditions, and communities. Whereas the authors in Part I all participated in UNESCO committees related to the ICH Convention, the authors in Part II (and in Part III) have all done extensive research in the field, documenting the effects of the Convention and of approaching music as ICH in various settings. With the exception of Logan Clark and Rebecca Dirksen, who live in the United States, they all report on research projects conducted in their own countries, often after decades-long association with a particular genre. Each chapter reveals a different type of complexity in the relationships between musicians, communities, nation-states, and the UNESCO Convention.

In Chapter 6, Xiao Mei and Yang Xiao report on the largest comparative project described in this volume. The study on the impact of what they call the "ICH Movement" in China involved extended research on 11 "certified" practices over a period of 6 years. They write about multiple contexts for many of the traditions recognized as ICH, static state protection versus living state protection, the crystallization of five different forms of transmission, the recognition of inheritors, and the complex position of scholars between government and musicians in a system that is "led by the government, guided by scholars, and participated in by culture bearers." They conclude that the multiple gazes of government, institutions, academia, artists, the commercial world, and the population at large are a mixed blessing at best in the country that probably invests more in ICH than any other.

In Chapter 7, Olcay Muslu presents contrasting sustainability projects in two parts of Turkey: one both enabled and limited by the new approach of the government toward ICH since 2018, and the other one controlled by the community. She gives an insightful analysis of challenges in representation, expertise, and mixed motives, also noticing that "better visibility for elements of intangible cultural heritage and heighten[ing] awareness of their significance [ . . . ] can be a double-edged sword," as elements become "standardized and turned into stage performances and material for tourism." At the same time, she points out that "UNESCO-free" projects where the community truly has agency often suffer from lack of resources and visibility.

Tan Sooi Beng describes in Chapter 8 the complex relations between communities, state governments, the Malaysian nation, and the ICH Convention by comparing the treatment of Mak Yong theatre in Kelantan State and a multicultural heritage festival in George Town, in Penang State. Malaysia has its own nationalist cultural policies, but individual provinces have broad discretion over their implementation. The result, she argues, is that "the Convention does not offer protection against the misappropriation and cleansing of cultural forms to suit the requirements of political and religious elites, the suppression or exclusion of women in performance, and the dispossession of the tradition bearers, particularly in conservative Islamic states." She suggests possible improvements to the Convention, as well as the creation of regional centers for collaboration on ICH.

Logan Elizabeth Clark's Chapter 9 on the effect of a UNESCO listing on the Indigenous Achí-Mayan dance-drama in Guatemala provides an example of the ability of local communities to take advantage of the opportunities provided by UNESCO recognition. In this case, the participants valued the religious nature of the dance-drama, and the government valued the development of tourism in the rural region. Focusing on systems of value and the attitudes of the performers, Clark concludes, "UNESCO recognition resulted not in the replacement of local values, but rather in the translation of one type of value to another, and, consequentially, greater agency for the dance practitioners."

Salwa El-Shawan Castelo-Branco, in Chapter 10, examines the processes and legacies of heritagization of *Cante Alentejano* over a period of 90 years in southern Portugal. This unaccompanied two-part polyphonic singing was first institutionalized by Portugal's authoritarian regime (1933–1974), then was given new meanings during the democratic regime beginning in 1974, and in the twenty-first century has been shaped by the impact of the ICH Convention and its implementation in Portugal. In spite of the clear influence of different government policies over many decades, Castelo-Branco concludes that "the sustainability of *cante* has not depended so much on the politics of heritage, nor on recent attempts to package it as a value-added product for the tourist market, but rather on its central place in practitioners' lives, and the social intimacy created through the act of collective singing."

## The Future of Music as ICH

Part III moves from illustrating the complex relations of communities, nations, and UNESCO policies to considering some of the implications of these for future policies. No one expected the ICH Convention to be a perfect framework when it was launched (e.g., Kurin, 2004, and most contributors to this volume). A flawless system for safeguarding music practices worldwide may be impossible to devise. However, as with so many approaches to highly complex issues, while the ICH Convention and its implementation have probably raised more questions than the Convention answered, it has enabled more refined thinking and has led to better questions, suggesting ways forward to continue making this important work more effective. That is already evident from the authors in Parts I and II, but even more so in the final Part of this volume.

In Chapter 11, Gao Shu writes about the fascinating concept of experimental cultural ecological zones developed and implemented in China, with the stipulation that they abide by the adage "see people, see items, see life," protecting "both intangible cultural heritage and the human and natural environment[s] that foster the development of intangible cultural heritage." To the best of our knowledge, this is the only extensive nation-driven program that takes into account not only a single element of the tradition, but emphatically also the people and their social and natural environments. It also represents an important contrast with the item-focused sustainability efforts in China, which has led to a frequently critiqued system of public performances with high production values, but relatively little attention to cultural context.

Anthony Seeger notes in Chapter 12 that audiovisual archiving has been profoundly transformed in the twenty-first century by emerging technologies. The internet multiplied the number of archives, changed the relationships between archives and communities, and created an "archival multiverse" (Gilliland, 2018). The six basic functions of archives (relation to institutional mission, acquisition, organization, preservation, access, and dissemination) haven't changed, but the ways they are undertaken have. Many other features of ICH have also been transformed by the internet, which allows distant community members to work together. The isolation of the COVID pandemic forced further innovations in musical performances, human interactions, and creative collaborations: communities, individuals, and the usefulness of archives for serving, safeguarding, and creating music will all benefit from these changes. The full chapter is available on the book's companion website ▶.

In Chapter 13, Catherine Grant convincingly argues for carefully employing comparative approaches to gauge the vitality of specific practices and to assess changes over time, using three approaches that have proven their value in other arenas (cf. Grant, 2014). While cautioning against "applying positivist tools to something as rich, complex, and human as music," and aware of the "unruly tendency of music genres to mutate, and even migrate without human bearers," she presents three models that can provide useful references for the vitality of specific music practices, and any changes over time. These can contribute to the ongoing efforts toward monitoring the need for and efficiency of interventions over time.

Finally, Rebecca Dirksen's Chapter 14 addresses the full breadth of topics dealt with in the previous chapters. She begins with a description of Haiti's long history of national cultural policies. She notes that the activities of UNESCO have been marred by its insistence on the use of French in projects in Haiti, where most inhabitants speak only Kreyòl, by the reliance on geographic regions that placed Haiti with the Spanish-speaking countries of the Caribbean, and by a tendency to reproduce earlier colonial rhetoric about development. These have limited the participation of community activists and culture bearers. Contrasting two case studies—Haitian classical music and Vodou drums—she argues that Haiti is a place where the study of patrimony should be influenced by calls for restorative justice. The final third of her chapter is a critical reflection on the concepts of musical ecologies, sustainability, and the need to rectify pressing social problems. With its call for the study of what she calls the "frictions" between different parts of society and with international organizations, Dirksen provides a fitting coda to this collection.

\* \* \*

There are three more important and related critical issues we feel this Introduction should address in order to optimally frame the contributions that follow: (1) the emergence of Critical Heritage studies; (2) the impact of forces beyond the control of communities and nation-states on music; and (3) the discourse on music sustainability and its relationship to cultural ecosystems.

While this volume is firmly rooted in (applied) ethnomusicology, a related relevant body of scholarship is that of Critical Heritage Studies, some of the growth of which can be seen as a collateral development stimulated by the UNESCO heritage Conventions. Although Critical Heritage Studies has roots in the re-evaluation of folklore and its ties to nationalism and political movements, a large critical literature emerged at the turn of the twenty-first century that focuses on the social and political development of heritage and the implementation of the ICH Convention. Central to this literature is that "heritage" is not a thing from the past, but is created in the present through the process of "heritage-making" (also called heritagization), in which specific forms of ICH are selected as "heritage" for promotion and others are not (Kirshenblatt-Gimblett, 1998; Bendix, 2007; Bendix, Eggert & Peselmann, 2013).

Issues of power, social class, cultural appropriation, influence-peddling, and other social processes are part of heritagization. Their influence has been exacerbated by UNESCO being composed of nation-states, or "States Parties," who control the implementation of the ICH Convention in their respective countries. Many of the contributors to this volume refer to this tension; Kurin devotes several pages to the literature and calls attention to how communities themselves privilege certain parts of their musical lives. Castelo-Branco, Clark, Tan, Dirksen, and others also emphasize that heritage-making, or giving value to something, often appears and thrives at the local level. We hope this book can contribute to heritage studies both through its fine-grained analysis of how the 2003 ICH Convention was written, and examples of how issues of state power and local priorities interact with what local communities do with their heritage.

While it would be easy to conclude otherwise from our reflections on the importance of the ICH Convention for influencing global music diversity and vitality, it is essential to keep in mind that nation-states are not the only determining factors in whether specific music practices remain vital, nor are communities. It is safe to say that since the middle of the past century the music industry—and over the past 20 years or so the internet—have been much more powerful forces than any government policy or community initiative. They play a massive and constantly intensifying role in how music is created, heard, sustained, and transmitted. The ICH Convention was partly a response to many nations' concerns with the influence of global media on their countries. While it is probably true that more people have more access to more music now than ever before in the history of mankind thanks to the music industry, there are reservations about its role in determining *what* people hear: first by having a monopoly over the production of sound carriers (like LPs and CDs), and now that effectively virtually every type of music is accessible through the internet, through algorithms that determine much of what we are exposed to. Barring a number of independent labels (including the idiosyncratic non-profit Smithsonian Folkways, which we both ran at different times) and specialized online resources, these are usually not steered by concerns for cultural sustainability, a love of diversity, or a benevolent view of humanity, but rather by commercial imperatives (cf. Taylor, 2007), which does not always work in the favor of smaller and vulnerable music practices.

In this context, it is useful to be aware of the totality of factors that directly impact any music practice (we use that term as it is more specific than "tradition" or "genre," as any single genre may have different forms and contexts with different strengths and vulnerabilities). A dozen years ago, we started working on *Sustainable Futures for Music Cultures*, a large international research collaboration funded by the Australian Research Council. Using nine large case studies across the globe, we developed an approach to music sustainability that mapped out some 40 forces that impact the vitality of music practices (Schippers & Grant, 2016, companion website www.oup.com/us/music communitiessustainability). We clustered them into five domains: musicians and communities; regulations and infrastructure; system of learning music, contexts, and constructs (the latter referring to the values and attitudes that people bring to a music practice); media; and the music industry. This volume deals primarily with the first two domains, focusing on communities and public authorities (like UNESCO and nation-states who decide on regulations and infrastructure); but obviously communities have a major impact on contexts and constructs, and public authorities often control at least formal systems of learning of music in many nation-states. However, as stated above, the music industry and the internet are players that neither communities nor public authorities control significantly. An awareness of all these forces and the degree to which they can be influenced (cf. Grant, Chapter 13 in this volume) is crucial in supporting music. A striking example of this emerged during the preparation of this book: The COVID-19 pandemic has revealed itself as an unexpected and devastating force that transcends local communities and nation-states. While it is too early to draw any conclusions on the effect of the pandemic on ICH at large and music in particular, it will inevitably have a major impact on many community tradition bearers, national budgets, cultural policies, and the economic support of heritage projects.

We have chosen the word "sustainability" for the title of the book, rather than safeguarding, protecting, maintaining, or referring to vitality, stewardship, or resilience (cf. van Zanten, Chapter 4 in this volume, Titon, 2009, 2015; Keogh, 2013; Schippers & Grant, 2016, pp. 4–7). Most authors in this volume interpret sustainability to refer to a "culture's capacity to maintain and develop its music now and in the foreseeable future" (Titon, 2015, p. 157), but there is considerable room for interpretation. Some may feel that a tradition can be deemed preserved once it has been notated, recorded, documented, and deposited in an archive (cf. Seeger, Chapter 12 in this volume). Others opine that sustainability is best served by recognizing a particular item or practice as worthy of preserving (like on the UNESCO lists). Yet others will argue that any practice is part of a living culture, in which ongoing nurture by communities is paramount. Finally, there are those who feel it makes little sense to refer to sustainability without addressing wider agendas concerning humanity and the planet, especially social justice and the world's ecological challenges. Most authors in this volume gravitate toward the "living culture" approach; but there are important references to social justice issues (e.g., Dirksen) and holistic approaches to cultural ecosystems (Gao Shu).

A few authors explicitly refer to cultural ecosystems in the sense of the totality of forces working on the sustainability of a specific music practice (see above and Schippers & Grant, 2016), rather than ecosystems in the sense of the planet at large. The same goes for the word "ecological," which is only used in its metaphorical sense, while recognizing there is merit in "engaging the relationships to environmental crises and the non-human and abiotic contexts that are fundamental to ecological science" (Allen, 2018, p. 5; cf. Cooley, 2019), which can range from very direct links to materials like rare woods and protected animal parts for making instruments, to the disappearance of people's entire habitats (cf. Moyle, 2007; Titon, 2015; see also Dirksen and Gao Shu, this volume). But we are not focusing on "ecological" in that sense here.

In conclusion, we feel that every chapter in this volume contributes to the understanding of how policies related to cultural heritage are part of larger processes and how their implementation encounters specific issues in every case. They invite rethinking how to continue to improve the implementation of a bureaucratic instrument like the Convention. At the same time, there is a deep sense of appreciation of the work that has already been done and continues to be done quite apart from the Convention. Many of the chapters in this volume propose specific suggestions to address the frictions as evident in their specific case studies. Dirksen calls for transformative justice. Gao Shu suggests how ICH can be safeguarded better by addressing the larger ecosystem of which it is a part. Tan recommends regional centers to counteract nationalist heritage tendencies. Ceribašić proposes the creation of an ICH NGO monitoring center. Van Zanten advocates making glossaries of key terms part of Conventions. Muslu reveals that there are advantages and shortcomings to both government-controlled and community-controlled projects. Clark demonstrates how multiple value systems can operate simultaneously and independently. Castelo-Branco suggests that the embodied experience of practitioners and their audiences may be more important than shifting government policies. Seeger argues that safeguarding ICH will be transformed by the emergence of new Internet technologies that enable multiple opportunities for storing and retrieving information. Xiao Mei makes a compelling case for large, longitudinal research to investigate the effects of the ICH Convention on specific music practices, and Grant offers possible frameworks for measuring such effects.

Understanding the ICH Convention and the way it has been implemented around the world is imperative for members of communities, cultural workers, and policymakers, as well as ethnomusicologists, musicologists, and other scholars of music and heritage in the 21-twenty-first century. For all its drawbacks, the 2003 Convention has contributed to unprecedented global interest in local knowledge and creations, and to important changes in national cultural policies. Its weaknesses are primarily structural, procedural, political, and bureaucratic, as the contributors to this volume make abundantly clear. But behind their critical reflections lies an awareness of the strength of UNESCO in its ability to speak aspirationally and globally, and a conviction that musical diversity and cultural sustainability can be enhanced through both policy making and community action.

## References

Allen, A. S. (2018). One ecology and many ecologies: The problem and opportunity of ecology for music and sound studies. In Ecologies, *MUSICultures*, 45(1–2), 1–13.

Agawu, K. (2003). *Representing African music: Postcolonial notes, queries, positions.* Routledge.

Balfour, M., et al. (Eds). (2019). *Performing arts in prison: Creative perspectives.* Intellect.

Bartleet, B.-L., & Higgins, L. (Eds.). (2018). *The Oxford handbook of community music.* Oxford University Press.

Barwick, L., & Turpin, M. (2016). Central Australian women's traditional songs: Keeping Yawulyu/Awelye strong. In H. Schippers & C. Grant (Eds.), *Sustainable futures for music cultures: An ecological perspective* (pp. 111–143). Oxford University Press.

Bendix, R. (2009). Heritage between economy and politics: An assessment from the perspective of cultural anthropology. In L. Smith & N. Akagawa (Eds.), *Intangible heritage* (pp. 253–219). Routledge.

Bendix, R., A. Eggert, & A. Peselmann. (2013). *Heritage Regimes and the State.* Universitätsverlag Göttingen.

Bigenho, M., & Stobart, H. (2018) (Eds.). Dossier especial: Música e patrimonio cultural em América Latina. *TRANS: Revista Transcultural da Música 21-22 (2018).* https://www.sibetrans.com/trans/publicacion/24/trans-21-22-2018

Cooley, T. J. (Ed.). (2019). *Cultural sustainabilities: Music, media, language, advocacy.* University of Illinois Press.

Gilliland, A. K. (2018). *Conceptualizing 21st-Century Archives.* ALA Editions.

Garcia Corona, L., & Wiens K. (2021). *Voices of the field, pathways in public ethnomusicology.* Oxford University Press.

Grant, C. (2014). *Music endangerment: How language maintenance can help.* New York: Oxford University Press.

Hobsbawm, E., & Ranger T. (Eds.) (1983). *The invention of tradition.* Cambridge University Press.

Howard, K. (2006). *Preserving Korean music: Intangible cultural properties as icons of identity.* Ashgate.

Howell, G. (2018). Community music interventions in post-conflict contexts. In B.-L. Bartleet & L. Higgins (Eds.), *The Oxford handbook of community music* (pp. 43–69). Oxford University Press.

Keogh, B. (2013). On the limitations of music ecology. *International Journal for Music Research Online* 4. Retrieved December 16, 2013, from http://www.jmro.org.au/index.php/mca2/article/view/83

Kirshenblatt-Gimblett, B. (1998). *Destination culture: Tourism, museums and heritage.* Berkeley: University of California Press.

Kurin, R. (2004). Safeguarding intangible cultural heritage in the 2003 UNESCO Convention: A critical appraisal. *Museum International: Views and Visions of the Intangible Heritage, 221-222,* 66–76.

Marett, A., Yunupingu, M., Langton, M., Gumbula, N., Barwick, L. & Corn, A. (2005, September). *The national recording project for Indigenous performance in Australia: Year one in review.* Paper presented at Backing our Creativity: National Education and the Arts Symposium, Melbourne.

Moyle, R. M. (2007). *Songs from the second float: A musical ethnography of the Taku Atoll, Papua New Guinea.* University of Hawai'i Press.

Pettan, S. (2010). Music in war, music in peace: Experiences in applied ethnomusicology. In J. M. O'Connell & S. E. Castelo-Branco (Eds), *Music and conflict: Ethnomusicological perspectives* (pp. 177–192). University of Illinois Press.

QCRC. (2008). *Twelve voices on cultural sustainability* [video]. Queensland Conservatorium Research Centre.

Schippers, H., & Grant, C. (Eds.). (2016). *Sustainable futures for music cultures: An ecological perspective*. Oxford University Press.

Schrag, B., & Buren, K. J. Van. (2018). *Make arts for a better life: A guide for working with communities*. Oxford University Press

Seeger, A. (2015). Understanding UNESCO: A complex organization with many parts and many actors. In M. Foster & L. Gilman (Eds.), *UNESCO on the ground: Local perspectives on intangible cultural heritage* (pp. 131–142). Indiana University Press.

Taylor, T. (2007). *Beyond exoticism: Western music and the world*. Duke University Press.

Titon, J. T. (2009). Music and sustainability: An ecological viewpoint. *The World of Music, 51*(1), 119–138.

UNESCO. (1989). Recommendation on the safeguarding of traditional culture and folklore. http://portal.unesco.org/en/ev.php-URL_ID=13141&URL_DO=DO_TO PIC&URL_SECTION=201.html.

UNESCO. (2001). Declaration on the promotion of cultural diversity. Retrieved March 1, 2008, from www.unesco.org/education/imld_2002/unversal_decla.shtml.

UNESCO. (2003). Convention for the safeguarding of the intangible cultural heritage. Retrieved July 1, 2021, from https://ich.unesco.org/en/convention

UNESCO. (2005). Convention on the protection and promotion of the diversity of cultural expressions. Retrieved July 1, 2021, from passeport-convention2005-web2.pdf (unesco.org).

United Nations High Commission for Human Rights. (2007). Declaration on the rights of indigenous peoples. Retrieved April 6, 2021, from https://www.un.org/development/desa/indigenouspeoples/declaration-on-the-rights-of-indigenous-peoples.html.

# PART I
# THE GENESIS OF THE ICH CONVENTION

# 2

# Recognizing Intangible Cultural Heritage

*Richard Kurin*

The 2003 UNESCO Convention for the Safeguarding of the Intangible Cultural Heritage, an international treaty reaching almost universal acceptance—ratified by 180 nations at the time of this writing—has given tremendous lift globally among governments, scholars, cultural activists, and organizations, to efforts to preserve the diversity of the world's living traditions, including those involving the performance, production, and presentation of music. In this chapter, I offer a brief account of how and why this came about from my perspective as a cultural policy analyst as well as someone intimately involved in the development of the Convention. It supplements previous publications (Kurin, 2004a, 2004b, 2007, 2016, 2017), as well as perspectives offered by other participants and commentators (Aikawa, 2004; Aikawa-Faure, 2009, 2019; Bedjaoui, 2004; Blake, 2009; Duvignaud & Khaznadar, 2004; Hafstein, 2004; Ruggles & Silverman, 2009; Stefano et al., 2012, 2017; Stefano, 2019; Turgeon, 2014).

## Making Music Heritage

Music is found everywhere around the world, infusing every conceivable part of human life—at birth, in marriage, at death, in sickness and in health, in victory and defeat, in praise and in protest, in profound prayer, in entertainment uplifting and raunchy, and for every conceivable purpose. So granting its ubiquity, *when does music become musical heritage—and specifically, something improbably called "intangible cultural heritage?"*

A number of critical cultural theorists, Barbara Kirshenblatt-Gimblatt (1995, 1998, 2004, 2006) and Tony Bennett (1998, 2000, 2013) among them, argue that cultural expressions become *heritage* as they are named, valorized, and promoted as such. This, they assert, is not a matter of the mere existence

Richard Kurin, *Recognizing Intangible Cultural Heritage* In: *Music, Communities, Sustainability.*
Edited by: Huib Schippers and Anthony Seeger, Oxford University Press. © Oxford University Press 2022.
DOI: 10.1093/oso/9780197609101.003.0002

or persistence of a particular practice or expression or measure of its objective historical significance. Rather, what is important is heritage-making itself.

In this theoretical vein, heritage is regarded as a thoroughly modern phenomena whereby some authority—often the state, but it could be political leaders, tourism promoters, marketers or entrepreneurs, museum directors, authors, even scholars and protest organizers—seize upon a cultural form or practice and re-present it in some highlighted way that brings attention to its particular significance or importance. Specific forms of music, musical performances and productions, musical instruments, texts, and even venues and sites may be deemed as heritage, or alternatively denied that status, or just ignored.

In this view, heritage is a conscious, motivated process of selection toward a self-interested end. While heritage makes reference to history and may use historical events and circumstances as a way of justifying value, heritage is not just about history. It is more about contemporary life, the current time frame, and what is thought to be important to and by those doing the defining. It is a contemporary way of addressing relationships, like those between "tradition" and "modernity," "continuity" and "change," "native" and "newcomer," the "exemplars" and the "marginalized," the "privileged" and the "dispossessed."

Heritage-making screens out what might be regarded as the marginal or unimportant past. It may avoid or fail to recognize extant forms. Thus not all music becomes heritage. All sorts of ballads, lullabies, work songs, and musical performances may fail to rise to the level of recognized musical heritage because they are performed in private or are associated with lower classes or marginalized people. Some forms of musical production might not be recognized as worthy because they are perceived as counter to the state or other authorities. Would the drumming of Haiti's rebellious slaves under Napoleonic rule been recognized as heritage had France remained that country's ruler a century later? Would Soweto's protest songs have been accorded recognition as musical heritage in this century had not Nelson Mandela been freed from prison and led his countrymen to form a new, post-apartheid South Africa? Many forms of music—bawdy toasts, irreverent ballads, the chants and performances of defeated peoples and banished religious practices—may be explicitly recognized as part of the historical or ethnographic record—and not be accorded the status of heritage because they are thought unworthy of the designation.

At the same time, heritage-making gives more weight than history might otherwise accord to certain, select traditions. Some traditions, artistic practices, and specific expressions are highlighted, accentuated, propagated, and marketed. Some are transformed and reformulated with new meanings and prestige. "To Anacreon in Heaven" might have remained an obscure, idiosyncratic English drinking song had not Francis Scott Key used its tune in the composition of his new poem about the "Star-Spangled Banner" for what later became the US national anthem. Specific songs and performances are heralded, performed on stages, for ceremonies or through the media. Certain villages, towns, or regions become known as the "home" of or being "famous" for some genre, rite, or festival and performance venue. The designation of anthems, costumes, songs, dances, instruments, and plays as "national" is a typical example of this kind of heritage-making. Indeed, some forms of music may become explicitly identified as "heritage music."

Recognition of music and other cultural expressions as heritage has often, though not always, been accompanied by a parallel theme of endangerment and survival. This is not surprising. After all, "heritage," in the English derivation, references the idea of inheritance. Heritage is often seen as somewhat vulnerable. It may survive into the future, but it may not unless its purveyors are attentive to its continuity. This theme has typically been articulated as providing heritage with recognition, resource support, and legal protection, and encouraging transmission to a younger generation. Sometimes heritage is seen as having to be physically or socially defended against hostile opponents as well as external forces that may seek to suppress practices and expressions that typify the identity of a community, ethnic group, or nation—contestations over music in Taliban-controlled Afghanistan, between Saharan and sub-Saharan groups in Mali, and between Catholics and Protestants in Northern Ireland come to mind (Baily, 2004; Morgan, 2013; Cooper, 2009).

Issues of contestation and survival often illustrate a counterpoint to an over-reliance on critical culture theory views of heritage. It is not just heritage-making officials and scholars who construe the value of musical expression for a society. Communities themselves, all over the world, sing, chant, play music, and dance because they cherish those expressions as "traditions." The chanting of prayers in a synagogue, the singing of Christmas carols, the ritual dances at weddings, and even the musical cheers of football fans are all examples of traditionalized performances that would be meaningfully regarded as "heritage" by their performers, even if no scholar or official declared them to be so recognized. In many cases, music or song reflects the deeply felt beliefs and emotions of a community and its members and may become an expressive means of exuding joy and happiness, or overcoming disaster, travesty, fear, and loss. Such has been well documented for communities, like many Native American tribes for example, who consciously and explicitly sought to preserve their customary expressions in spite of officials and scholars disparaging them and actively seeking their demise. Songs and musics of survival often emerge from a compelling, felt need to give comfort, hope, or shape to despair—not from a desire for external validation. The most dramatic case I have ever witnessed was in Haiti, in the aftermath of the January 2010 earthquake, when some 200,000 of their family members, friends, and neighbors had been killed by collapsed buildings, virtually the whole population of Port-au-Prince—millions of traumatized people then camped on its streets with no food, no water, and dispossessed of shelter—lifted their voices in hymns and traditional songs in order to survive those first few perilous nights. They consciously called upon what they regarded as a heritage of resilience embodied in those songs (Kurin, 2011).

That sense of music rising up to meet the moment was recently felt by the global community. Amidst the COVID-19 pandemic, hundreds of millions were deeply moved by Andrea Bocelli's stirring solo "Music of Hope" concert on Easter Sunday 2020, broadcast from Milan's Duomo cathedral; millions more were heartened by the "One World Together at Home" concert organized by Global Citizen and Lady Gaga and featuring an incredible panoply of international stars singing familiar hit songs; many appreciated Yo-Yo Ma holding numerous Zoom concerts—"songs of comfort," he called them—with fellow professional and amateur cello players from around the world; and Manhattan residents repeatedly saluted first responders and healthcare workers from apartment balconies belting out the reassuring theme song, "New York, New York." The repetition of these performances, their replaying on YouTube and transmission via social media, and their rapid ritualization indicated a social process of traditionalization and heritage-making, one that joined artistic impulse with community need, rather than a politicized effort to gain official legitimation or external validation for a particular practice.

## Prelude to International Accord

Concern about the survival and recognition of various musical forms, and those in other genres of artistic activity—including crafts, storytelling,

culinary arts, occupational culture, adornment, ritual, and festive arts—
has motivated the work of many "song catchers," folklorists, and salvage
ethnomusicologists, particularly since the later part of the nineteenth century
and throughout the twentieth century. Some of these efforts, many of them in
Europe, grew out of larger projects to elaborate national identities and their
associated characteristics, customs, and artistic traditions. Other efforts,
such as those of Smithsonian anthropologists with the Bureau of American
Ethnology, for example, were focused on documenting living traditions of
native peoples who were thought to be inevitably "disappearing." Recording
technologies for sound and image, invented roughly around the same time,
made it possible to document these expressions in a new, lasting way and expose them to wider audiences for broader understanding and appreciation.

World War II provided an important benchmark in heritage recognition, support, and protection. Nazi Germany systematically looted the tangible cultural heritage of the countries it invaded and occupied. The United
States and allies formed the Monuments, Fine Arts, and Archives Section—
the famed "Monuments Men" (and Women)—to protect significant architectural and historical sites, and to identify treasured artworks, historical
artifacts, and archival collections, and to rescue and return them to rightful
stewards. In Japan, the United States made the decision to drop the atom
bomb on Hiroshima and not the traditional capital of Kyoto, as originally
intended, because it recognized the cultural significance of the latter and its
importance in not alienating and ultimately pacifying the population in a
postwar, occupational society. One of the consequences of cultural destruction and looting in the European theatre was the 1954 Hague Convention
for the Protection of Cultural Property in the Event of Armed Conflict. This
imposed obligations on parties in conflicts to identify and protect cultural
sites, collections, and resources.

In Japan, the government, while under occupation, contemplated the
loss and continuity of its traditions—largely associated with the elite,
courtly culture—and with US military support, initiated a state system of
documenting, classifying, and determining what exactly constituted officially recognized cultural heritage. Japan's 1950 Law for the Protection of
Cultural Properties and subsequent amendments defined tangible and intangible cultural heritage, living cultural treasures, properties of different
rank, and a regime of rights, rewards, and recognition, including tax relief,
to protect these forms of heritage for the future. In short, a system of valorization and an enacting bureaucracy was built up to manage heritage because

it was thought to be important for the identity, resilience, and well-being of a traumatized populace (Scott, 2003).

This general idea, albeit usually with less elaboration, became a model for several other nations—South Korea, Romania, Thailand, the Philippines—in the ensuing decades, and inspired a variety of initiatives that, while building upon the documentary research and archival collections established by previous generations of scholars, had a broader, more expansive advocacy and policy agenda. Some of the efforts for heritage-making resided in government or quasi-government bodies; in other cases it was in universities, museums, or through associations of scholars and artists, who took on what they viewed as socially and cultural responsible roles. A variety of heritage organizations were established in the 1960s, 1970s, and 1980s to encourage social and artistic recognition, resources for practitioners and scholars to document and present their work, and in some cases, legal protections. In the area of musical heritage, this led to performance series and festivals, recordings, radio and television shows, archives, publications, university classes and other educational initiatives, conferences, and awards.

In the United States, the national organization of musical heritage occurred largely in the period from the mid-1960s to the mid-1980s, building upon archival precedents at the Library of Congress and the Smithsonian and inspired by such seminal figures as Alan Lomax, Charles Seeger, Pete Seeger, Bascom Lamar Lunsford, and others. The movement toward national articulation and organization was led by cultural workers who were scholars and performers—my mentor Ralph Rinzler, Archie Green, Bess Lomax Hawes, and Alan Jabbour. They drew readily upon the knowledge of other scholar-performers like Ali Jihad Racy, Bernice Johnson Reagon, Jean Ritchie, Ethel Raim, Nazir Jairazbhoy, and Mike Seeger. The definitional thrust in the United States foregrounded grassroots and traditional music under the banner of "folklife" rather than "heritage," and included in relatively swift progression the founding of the Smithsonian's Festival of American Folklife in 1967, the Folk Arts Program of the National Endowment of the Arts in 1974, the American Folklife Center at the Library of Congress in 1976, the subsequent development of the National Heritage Fellowships, the Smithsonian Center for Folklife and Cultural Heritage, Smithsonian Folkways Recordings, the revitalization of the non-governmental National Council for the Traditional Arts, and the development of state folklorists and of non-governmental public sector folklife centers in New York, Philadelphia, Texas, and other regions.

Governments and cultural advocates developed regional, national, and even international programs to promote traditional music. The International Council for Traditional Music (ICTM) had been established in 1947 largely to promote scholarship. UNESCO initiated the Collection of Traditional Music of the World in 1961. The International Council of Folklore and Traditional Arts (CIOFF) was founded in France in 1970 by representatives from several European countries to promote folkloric dance and performance. The Kotharis founded the Rupayan Sansthan, or Rajasthan Institute of Folklore, in 1965; Uxi Mufti founded Lok Virsa, or Institute of Folk Heritage, in Pakistan in 1974; Chérif Khaznadar founded Maison des Cultures du Monde in Paris in 1982; the American Institute of Indian Studies established the Archives and Research Center for Ethnomusicology with the efforts of Nazir Jairazbhoy, Subha Chaudhuri, and Daniel Neuman in 1982, with Anthony Seeger joining soon after; the Gulf Cooperation Council established its folklife center, the Markaz al-Turāth al-Shaʿbī li-Duwal al-Khalīj al-Arabīya, in Doha in 1983; and Kevin Bradley developed the Oral History and Folklore Collection at the National Library of Australia in the mid-1980s (Anderson & McHenry, 1987).

While the 1886 Berne Convention and the 1952 Universal Copyright Convention applied legal protections to specific domains of artistic and musical publication and presentation internationally, they had limited implications for the broader support and encouragement of what many were defining as folklife, living cultural traditions, oral and musical heritage, and its purveyors as well. Calls for international policy treatment of heritage outside of an established copyright protection framework arose in the 1970s and 1980s. Initiated by threats to recognized cultural heritage sites, specifically the danger of a submerged Venice and the possible destruction of the ancient Egyptian site of Abu Simbel as a result of building the Aswan Dam, and strongly encouraged by the US Nixon administration, UNESCO took up the cause of preserving world heritage sites. The 1972 Convention Concerning the Protection of the World Cultural and Natural Heritage called for the recognition and preservation of nationally and internationally designated sites and encouraged expert cooperation and fiscal support for such efforts.

The World Heritage List, as it was quickly termed, gained global acceptance and popularity, and over the course of ensuing decades added hundreds of sites from around the planet. The Convention succeeded in providing legal protection for such sites, occasioning national recognition and international prestige. It gave countries cause to devote their own resources to supporting such sites and provided a means of drawing in resources in terms of expertise and funding for conservation, preservation, and restoration work—largely architectural and environmental—from outside sources. Educators made use of World Heritage Sites to promote local history and pride; tourism ministries promoted visitation and related commercial activity. Given the prominence of signature sites and the compelling issue of survival in the face of understandable challenges, the Convention was quickly and widely viewed as a very successful international, intergovernmental intervention in the cultural heritage arena.

Consideration of the Convention evoked thoughts about other forms of cultural heritage, particularly the living traditions practiced by communities. Bolivia early on, joined by others, suggested the international community address concerns about their encouragement and protection (Aikawa, 2004). However, UNESCO took little action for a decade as it concentrated on and devoted resources to World Heritage Sites.

## From Recommendation to Convention

In the 1980s, UNESCO held several meetings of experts addressing living cultural heritage. These were spurred on by and largely involved scholars and documentarians involved in folklife centers and archives. The meetings resulted in UNESCO issuing in 1989 a *Recommendation on the Safeguarding of Traditional Culture and Folklore*. This document identified practices that nations could put in place to preserve and encourage their living cultural heritage. In UNESCO and UN agency parlance, a recommendation is a type of "instrument." Conventions or treaties are international instruments that have the force of law, binding upon the nations that sign onto them. Declarations are instruments that are typically aspirational statements of rights, goals, and aims that do not convey legal obligations. Recommendations are the least weighty of international instruments. They are expressions of good or desired practices, with no legal requirement for their implementation.

The 1989 Recommendation defined *folklore* (alternatively, traditional and popular culture) as "the totality of tradition-based creations of a cultural community" and encouraged nations to develop national inventories, classifications, and typologies; to document those traditions; to store documentation in accessible archives and publicly present these traditions in museums, at festivals, in other venues, and through popular media; to train collectors and conservators and support research; to develop folklore materials for the schools; to provide support for folklore organizations; to provide intellectual property rights protections as appropriate; and to co-operate with other folklore efforts internationally (UNESCO, 1989; Honko, 1990; Sherkin, 2001).

Five years after the Recommendation was issued, UNESCO sought to ascertain its application and impact. UNESCO formulated a questionnaire that it sent to all of its member states, and less than half—83 nations—responded. UNESCO then sponsored eight regional conferences, holding meetings in the Czech Republic (June 1995) for Central and Eastern Europe; Mexico (September 1997) for Latin America and the Caribbean; Japan (February–March 1998) for Asia; Finland (September 1998) for Western Europe; Republic of Uzbekistan (October 1998) for Central Asia and the Caucasus; Ghana (January 1999) for Africa; New Caledonia (February 1999) for the Pacific; and Lebanon (May 1999) for Arab States. Each of these produced a report, with suggestions concerning the Recommendation's application, impact, and how it could be improved (Aikawa, 2001; Seeger, 2001).

During this time, Noriko Aikawa, who headed UNESCO's initiative for intangible cultural heritage, sought to hold an international meeting where the results of the survey and the regional meetings could be analyzed and discussed, and that could serve as a basis for moving ahead (Aikawa, 2001). UNESCO was under considerable pressure at the time to respond to a number of cultural currents of concern to its members. One was the lack of international programs to address how local, regional, and national cultures could remain robust and vital in the face of globalization, which in its cultural form was swamping diverse forms of expression through the mass promulgation of television, movies, recordings, and other products of a largely US-based commercial and entertainment industry. Culture ministers, directors, scholars, and workers from around the world bemoaned the fact that their youth were more interested in consuming and imitating American popular culture than investing their time and energy pursuing their more home-grown traditions. This was seen as a threat to the world's cultural diversity, a threat to national languages, societal norms, and institutions.

Cultural globalization was also seen as having economic consequences—limiting the growth and markets for homegrown culturally based industries, and thus retarding job growth, local skills development, creativity, and entrepreneurship (UNESCO, 1996; Appadurai, 1996). Another issue was that while the impact of the World Heritage List was positively felt in a number of countries—Italy, Greece, Egypt, China, Japan, India, Mexico, and Peru particularly—the emphasis on the renowned architecture of major empires left most countries wanting. Their heritage was underrepresented in the program, and was more evident in living cultural traditions. Yet aside from a rather perfunctory Living Human Treasures initiative in 1993—which led only a handful of nations to create a recognition program in their own countries—there was no major UNESCO program, no significant system of recognition, valorization, and support that recognized their cultural worth. Advancing the course of the Recommendation toward a more elaborate program and intergovernmental effort could address these issues.

The prospect of holding the conference in the United States was intriguing. The United States had been a strong, motivating force for the creation of UNESCO after World War II. Archibald MacLeish, former librarian of Congress serving as US assistant secretary of state, had drafted the preamble to UNESCO's charter, articulating its overarching purpose: "Since wars begin in the minds of men, it is in the minds of men that the defenses of peace must be constructed." UNESCO's work in education, science, culture, and communication was seen as a means of building that peace, and MacLeish had served as the first American member of UNESCO's governing board. Though it had been an active participant and leader of UNESCO, especially with the 1972 World Heritage Convention, the United States withdrew from the organization in 1984 during the Reagan administration because of asserted non-Western, non-democratic bias, bureaucratic bloat, and other related reasons. A series of UNESCO directors-general had sought US readmission, and the Clinton administration's Department of State seemed empathetic. It had active "observer" status and participated in numerous UNESCO discussions and programs. Some US organizations, such as the National Park Service and the Smithsonian, continued their involvement in UNESCO programs despite the lack of formal national membership.

Aikawa approached Anthony Seeger, the director of Smithsonian Folkways Recordings, who was then also serving as president of the International Council of Traditional Music—an NGO affiliated with UNESCO—about the possibility of holding the conference at the Smithsonian in Washington, DC. Given the Smithsonian's standing, this would provide prestige to the conference and import to its purpose, and also occasion American support for a UNESCO initiative (Aikawa-Faure, 2019; Seeger, 2019; Stefano, 2019).

Seeger thought the idea had merit and brought the proposal to me, given that at the time I was his supervisor at the Smithsonian and director of the Center for Folklife and Cultural Heritage. The concerns of the Recommendation were central to the work of the Center, which was engaged in the scholarly study and documentation of folklife traditions, and their presentation through its annual Smithsonian Folklife Festival held on the National Mall of the United States every summer, through recordings on Smithsonian Folkways, and through other educational programs. The Center had for several decades advocated for increased recognition and support of folk artists and practitioners and the continuity of their traditions. It was a good match thematically and a way of connecting what the Smithsonian, the National Endowment for the Arts Folk Arts Program, the Library of Congress American Folklife Center, and other organizations were doing in the United States to the goals and efforts of others across the globe.

We discussed the possible consequences of the Smithsonian co-hosting the meeting with UNESCO. While the Smithsonian was a US governmental organization, it was not an executive agency under the authority of the president. It had its own, independent governing board and a mission devoted to the "increase and diffusion of knowledge." The Smithsonian had periodically taken flak from some in Congress over its continuing collaborations with UNESCO, particularly with regard to the Man in the Biosphere Program. Smithsonian staff and leaders relished the fact that the institution had a strong well-earned reputation, and the political independence and legal status to pursue its research and educational mission—which certainly encompassed such an international conference in an area of long-term interest.

I informed colleagues in the Department of State, who embraced the Smithsonian's decision to move ahead, and even provided funding support. I sought and obtained additional funding from the National Endowment for the Arts and the Rockefeller Foundation. Aikawa secured funding from the UNESCO-Japan Funds in Trust.

Our team at the Center, staff members Seeger, Peter Seitel, James Early, Amy Horowitz, Diana N'Diaye, and research fellow Anthony McCann, quickly assessed the 1989 Recommendation and found that it was mainly oriented toward professional scholars, academics, and people managing archives, rather than on tradition bearers, and more focused on the documentation of culture than culture as a lived reality. We made a strategic decision to hold the conference at a time coinciding with the annual Folklife Festival. We thought that would be an appropriate context-setter because conference attendees would daily see living cultural traditions being performed, illustrated and demonstrated by cultural exemplars for an audience of about a million people outdoors on the National Mall between the US Capitol building and the Washington Monument. Programs at the 1999 Festival featured South Africa, Romania, and New Hampshire, represented by hundreds of musicians, performers, craftspeople, cooks, builders, and others drawn from a diversity of grassroots communities. This would put tradition-bearers at the center of the conference focus.

For the conference itself, we invited some 40 key representatives from around the world and dozens of observers. Participants included a mix of scholars, cultural officials, community cultural leaders from several continents, cultural advocates, representatives of UNESCO and the Smithsonian, and other agency experts (Seitel, 2001). We, as organizers, had a strong sense that we were engaged in not just crafting a better accord for folklife documentation, but rather addressing the serious business of how diverse cultures around the world could survive and flourish, and how those who exemplified and practiced those cultures could directly and meaningfully participate in that effort.

The conference was held in the Smithsonian Castle, with translation provided in several languages, and substantively covered the topics of the UNESCO Recommendation survey and the regional meetings. Most UNESCO nation members had been unresponsive, and many of the national commissions completing the survey lacked detailed knowledge of programs and initiatives in their countries; only a fraction were aware of the Recommendation. Overall, while some good work was being done with regard to documentation, educational efforts, public presentations, support programs, and legal protections, the scale and extent of effort seemed underwhelming and scattershot (Kurin, 2001).

The Recommendation was largely overlooked and irrelevant. Summaries from the regional meetings indicated many common concerns but with important regional differences. Arab States were concerned with the effects of globalization and the challenges it posed for preserving cultural identities. Western European countries also stressed the need to preserve cultural diversity in the face of global intellectual and creative forces. Eastern European countries were similarly concerned about the significance of traditional culture for their national identity, but particularly in the context of the transition from the communist system to a market economy. Asian countries noted the need to stress high court cultures but include as well the folklore of other, non-state traditional cultures. Latin America and Caribbean countries were quite concerned about cultural diversity and multiculturalism. African countries noted that expressions of cultural identity had been changing over the last decade, moving from an emphasis on nation-building to the recognition of multiple identities. Those from the Pacific region raised the difficulty of distinguishing tangible and intangible heritage from their cultural perspective—referencing the relevancy of international policies and accords to local and regional cultural realities (Seeger, 2001).

Discussions indicated that "folklore" was a problematic term, one rooted in European society and study that did not resonate globally. Indeed, many viewed it as pejorative. The term would have to be replaced in any future accord, though there was at the time no consensus over the appropriate replacement. Participants also found the Recommendation too firmly placed within the institutions of documentation and archiving, thus reflecting the protection of cultural products rather than the cultural producers. The balance of focus and concern had to shift from the need to document to the stronger need to protect the practices that create and nurture what is then documented—thus focusing attention more toward communities themselves than the scholars and organizations who studied them. The use of "fragility" in relation to traditional cultures was also questioned, as it implied that the goal was to document traditions before they inevitably died, instead of helping living people whose community-based forms of expression were being marginalized by specific forces and interests exerted by more powerful societal actors (McCann et al., 2001). Conference participants found that the responsibility for preserving and extending traditional heritage went well beyond government, and that cultural community members were the key agents in carrying their traditions forward (Seitel, 2001). This was summarized most elegantly by James Early with the refrain "there's no folklore without the folk" (Early and Seitel, 2002b).

Participants concluded that a new instrument should contain certain additional features lacking in the Recommendation, such as a code of ethics for principles of respect; the inclusion of customary owners of traditional culture and folklore as the principal participants in and beneficiaries of the process of documenting and disseminating their knowledge; recognition of the collaborative role of NGOs and other institutions that could assist in preserving this cultural heritage; and widening the scope of the Recommendation to include the evolving nature of traditional culture and folklore—not "freezing" it in some idealized past form. The conference considered the legal issues with regard to cultural property rights and protections (Prott, 2001), recommending that UNESCO ramp up action programs to achieve these objectives and also consider moving forward with a new, international convention (Seitel, 2001).

Aikawa was energized by the conference and now had a consensus of key international cultural figures to proceed toward a more elaborate vision. As she later shared, she and colleagues had envisioned the possibility of a new convention emerging from the serious, international assessment of the Recommendation (Aikawa, 2004; Aikawa-Faure, 2019). A few months after the 1999 conference, Japanese diplomat Koichiro Matsuura was elected as director-general of UNESCO. Matsuura was quite familiar with Japanese cultural heritage programs and the power of normative, legal instruments to drive governmental policy and practice. Matsuura had been chairing the World Heritage Committee and almost immediately found himself facing the desire of member states to address issues of cultural diversity and recognition in a changing world and through UNESCO programs.

Juan Goytisolo, a Spanish expatriate writer living in Marrakesh, had come to UNESCO with an issue that played right into these concerns. He was concerned about the fate of the city's central Jama el Fna square. Jama el Fna was on the World Heritage List. It was a massive, concrete-paved square surrounded by a great bazaar composed of hundreds of small shops and stalls. Every night people would set up hundreds of food stands to feed the massive crowds that would gather there. Jugglers, magicians, animal acts, singers, musicians, and all sorts of local and regional performers would fill the square with their artistry. The use of the square as a daily, festival-like space had persisted for perhaps centuries. Yet the tradition was currently under threat. Scores of buses filled with tourists would daily disgorge their passengers in the square and park there. The mayor and city leaders proposed discouraging the traditional use of the square and turning it into a parking lot for the buses. Goytisolo and others thought this would be a tragedy, and even counterproductive, as the food stalls and performances were indeed part of the touristic appeal and had economic benefit to the cultural purveyors. He asked UNESCO's help to address his concern.

Matsuura and UNESCO leaders took Goytisolo's concern seriously, as it resonated with other cases of endangered living cultural heritage. They knew that turning the Recommendation into a convention, as suggested by the Smithsonian conference, might take four or five years. But enacting a program was more discretionary, and did not require a new, legally binding treaty. Yet it could address the very issues at the forefront of the conference and of international and institutional cultural concern. Matsuura initiated

UNESCO's Masterpieces of Oral and Intangible Heritage program with the idea of designating living cultural traditions as worthy of international recognition and support (UNESCO, 2001; Aikawa-Faure, 2009; Hafstein, 2009). It would, in effect, parallel the World Heritage List, but allow for much broader inclusivity and include musical and performative traditions, ritual practices, craftsmanship and artistry, storytelling, and other intangible cultural traditions. Matsuura appointed an international jury to develop guidelines and criteria for selection, with Goytisolo as chair. I was appointed a jury member, along with Mali's president Alpha Konare, Jordanian princess Basma Bint Talal, Mexican writer Carlos Fuentes, Vanuatu cultural advocate Ralph Regenvanu, Bolivian singer Zelma Yugar, Moroccan ambassador Aziza Bennani, French anthropologist George Condominas, Ghanaian ethnomusicologist Kwabena Nketia, Jamaican folklorist Olive Lewin, and others. The jury was staffed by Aikawa and her colleagues. Paralleling the process for the World Heritage List, UNESCO member nations made specific nominations and compiled candidature files documenting the tradition, making the case for its quality and significance, and describing an action plan for enhancing its vitality. Expert associations of anthropologists, folklorists, and ethnomusicologists were asked to assess those nominations for jury consideration. Key representatives of these expert groups, including Seeger from the ICTM, joined sessions of the jury at UNESCO Paris in 2001 for the review of cases.

Though a number of us thought the terminology of "masterpieces" was misleading, and the underlying theme that the traditions were endangered or fragile—which many were not—the jury considered some four dozen traditions nominated and came up with a final selection of 19, ranging from Chinese *kunqu* opera to the balaphone tradition of Guinea, from Sicilian puppetry to the disappearing language and oral traditions of an Amazonian rainforest community. The selection involved some political wrangling, grappling with lack of representation from some world regions, and a few cases of possible conflict of interest among jury members. Director-General Matsuura then publicly announced the results in a ceremony at UNESCO headquarters, handing out certificates to ambassadors from the countries of the selectees. The proclamation was well received by country representatives, media back home, and more generally. While the program could bring public attention to the diversity of the world's cultural traditions and respect for them, I and several members of the jury expressed concerns about the program. The candidacies generally lacked viable action plans that might actually benefit the traditions. The involvement of local communities and representatives of the traditions was typically passive and perfunctory. Without substantive impact, the designation as "masterpiece" could be a shallow, symbolic act to convey prestige on national governments and officials without helping or enabling the actual tradition to better survive (Nas, 2002; Kurin, 2002; Seeger, 2009).

In 2001, UNESCO also released its Universal Declaration on Cultural Diversity. This aspirational document resulted from a different developmental track within UNESCO that sought to address issues of globalization largely from a human rights and cultural economic perspective. Anthropologist Arjun Appadurai (2002)—who, like Seeger and I, had received his PhD from the University of Chicago's fabled department—provided much of the underlying social analysis and theory leading up to its formulation. It assumed a larger purview for culture than the track flowing from the Recommendation that focused on folklore and traditional culture, as it had within its scope commercial-scale production of cultural goods, media, entertainment, and so on. But it was consistent with the thrust of the Masterpieces program and the outcomes of the Smithsonian conference in that it sought to promote respect for the diversity of the world's cultures and to enable carriers of those cultures to continue to practice, extend, and benefit from their creative efforts.

In the wake of the perceived success of the Smithsonian conference and during the course of the development of the Masterpieces program, UNESCO moved aggressively toward a new convention to address traditional living cultural heritage. The effort was funded by Japan's voluntary contributions to UNESCO, which supported several meetings of international experts, first in Turin in March 2001, then in Rio de Janeiro in January 2002, to work on definitions and conceptualization of the convention's main ideas (Blake 2001a, 2001b; Early & Seitel 2002a, 2002b). The Smithsonian's Peter Seitel and James Early, Canada's Gerald Pocius, Vanuatu's Ralph Regenvanu, and others were key expert participants in this process.

At the Turin meeting, the group accepted the use of "intangible cultural heritage." This had precedent with the translation of Japanese terminology and had gained acceptance with the UNESCO General Assembly in its approval of Matsuura's Masterpieces program. The term was conveniently differentiated from the "tangible," and though emotionally bland, nonetheless avoided the cultural and conceptual baggage associated with terms such as "folklore" and "traditional," "popular," "expressive," "oral," "ethnographic," and/or "living culture or traditions." "Safeguarding" emerged as a more over-arching term than others and covered what would be regarded as study, con-servation, preservation, protection (typically meaning legal prescription), presentation, education, and cooperative activities.

The group, though, held true to the recommendations from the Smithsonian conference in terms of emphasizing the role, agency, and centrality of culture bearers and cultural communities over international agencies, national and local officials, relevant cultural institutions, scholars, and other experts. At the subsequent meeting in Brazil, the consulting group further refined the concepts in the developing convention and staved off what they took to be UNESCO's back-pedaling toward a more typical institutional and officially centered document. A third meeting scheduled for New York was canceled and UNESCO proceeded to draft a convention. What propelled UNESCO forward quickly was another convention of greater consequence to its advocates, particularly France, making its way forward.

That accord was the Convention on the Protection and Promotion of the Diversity of Cultural Expressions. While on the surface it may have had some of the same concerns as the intangible heritage convention, it was the formal follow-up to the cultural diversity declaration and more focused on supporting the world's cultural industries in the face of US-dominated ec-onomic globalism. It would offer a means of France protecting its cultural industries, from wine and champagne to publications. It had the strong sup-port of Canada, under the leadership of heritage minister Sheila Copps, who found her country's movie and television industries swamped by those in the United States. Other nations saw this treaty as carving out economic oppor-tunity, using culture as a vehicle for doing so. And while they were unlikely to a obtain a favorable, legally binding agreement through the World Trade Organization, they felt they could succeed through UNESCO. This strategy was known as "forum shopping" among treaty experts, and if countries rati-fied it, it could have major trade and economic consequences. French presi-dent Jacques Chirac apparently strongly encouraged Matsuura to take action on this proposed Convention, and in order to do so, UNESCO first had to dispose of the intangible cultural heritage convention by getting it approved.

A draft text for an intangible cultural heritage treaty was quickly drafted based closely upon the 1972 World Heritage Convention, but taking into consideration the deliberations of the expert roundtables (Aikawa, 2004; Aikawa-Faure, 2009; Blake, 2009; Zanten, 2004). It was distributed to UNESCO members and to observer delegations like the United States for comment. A meeting of experts was then called for Paris. In Washington, I, along with colleagues from the State Department, Library of Congress, National Endowments, and other agencies, reviewed and commented on the draft. Barry Bergy, director of traditional and folk arts at the National Endowment for the Arts, and I prepared to join State Department colleagues in Paris to deal with comments and issues, discuss and modify the draft. As we were doing so, President George W. Bush on September 12, 2002, a day after the one-year anniversary of 9/11, announced in New York, at the United Nations, that the United States would rejoin UNESCO in 2003. This was a wholly symbolic gesture of international solidarity as the United States was putting together a coalition in its War on Terror, rather than an act representing a renewed interest in UNESCO's programs. Nonetheless, the United States rejoining the organization heightened the stakes in our participation in the drafting of the convention. Over the course of three separate conclaves in the ensuing year, we participated fully in debating the final, consensus version of the Convention on the Safeguarding of Intangible Cultural Heritage, which came up for vote by the UNESCO General Assembly in October 2003.

## The Convention

As might be imagined, everything in the text of the Convention was subject to discussion and argument among the content experts (largely anthropologists, folklorists, and ethnomusicologists), cultural managers, lawyers and international legal scholars, diplomats, and officials who drafted, reviewed, and approved it (Stefano, 2019). The Convention defined "intangible cultural heritage" as

the practices, representations, expressions, knowledge, skills—as well as the instruments, objects, artefacts and cultural spaces associated therewith— that communities, groups and, in some cases, individuals recognize as part of their cultural heritage. This intangible cultural heritage, transmitted from generation to generation, is constantly recreated by communities and groups in response to their environment, their interaction with nature and their history, and provides them with a sense of identity and continuity, thus promoting respect for cultural diversity and human creativity. (UNESCO, 2003)

This was a much improved and more sophisticated statement than the essentializing definitions of folklore and oral tradition that preceded it. It recognized key social processes involved in the creation, distribution, and transmission of expressive culture. Some of us recognized the difficulty of defining complex social and cultural phenomena in such a succinct way. And while drafters still in the main assumed a focus on what would have been called folklore, oral tradition, community-based, or grassroots culture, it technically allowed a lot more room for inclusion. This was especially so given the Convention noted that intangible cultural heritage was "manifested in" oral traditions and expressions, including language as a vehicle of the intangible cultural heritage; performing arts; social practices, rituals and festive events; knowledge and practices concerning nature and the universe; and traditional craftsmanship." Given such, expressions such as avant-garde theatre, video games, posts on Facebook fan groups and social media chat sites, pop music, hip-hop, modern dance, karaoke, contemporary state rituals, fast-food recipes, American football, Thai boxing, Australian cricket, and the "war stories" of soldiers, civil rights activists, lawyers, and astrophysicists could all conceivably find a way of meeting many or most of the definitional criteria.

Also understandable, but ethnographically problematic, was the restriction the Convention placed on what it would consider intangible cultural heritage.

For the purposes of this Convention, consideration will be given solely to such intangible cultural heritage as is compatible with existing international human rights instruments, as well as with the requirements of mutual respect among communities, groups and individuals, and of sustainable development. (UNESCO, 2003)

This is a very high and, one might say, unrealistic and imposing standard. During the drafting and deliberations I noted, somewhat tongue-in-cheek, that this formulation represented the Disneyfication of culture, as it sanitized from consideration of human creativity a great deal of human heritage. Understandably, UNESCO didn't want to support or encourage practices inimical to human rights, such as slavery, infanticide, female genital mutilation, or torture (Zanten, 2004; Aikawa, 2004). Yet the standard is not without controversy. Could performance by Yemeni musicians accompanied by friendly kat-chewing be regarded as intangible cultural heritage given its acceptance by those within the community while being ill-regarded by cultural authorities and national officials? Indeed, such an issue had disqualified a Masterpieces candidature the first time around in 2001, but presented in a sanitized form, resulted in its inscription on the list in 2003. Is a Hindu ritual tradition that includes Brahmins, but excludes non-Brahmins, disqualified as intangible cultural heritage because of its discriminatory quality? —a question raised in response to the inscription of another tradition in 2001. Is a musical tradition where only men play instruments and only women sing inequitable, and thus a violation of human rights accords? Determining what is allowable or not as intangible cultural heritage under the Convention could, if taken seriously, present a difficult task for any committee of experts.

Similarly problematic is the "mutual respect" clause. Intangible cultural heritage is by definition something used for community self-definition. However, many cultural communities define themselves in opposition or resistance to others. Their very identity as a people or community relies on their victory over or defeat by others. Their defining songs and tales may celebrate the glory of empire, victorious kings, religious conversion, or alternatively, resistance to perceived injustice, martyrdom, and defeat—not the mutual respect of peoples. Thus again, if taken seriously, all sorts of songs, epic stories, and artistic depictions could be disqualified. The only saving grace on this point was that it could have been even more problematic. A provision in the penultimate draft of the Convention would have required intangible cultural heritage to be "consistent with principles of equity and justice."

The standard of "sustainability" was also problematic. Consider that the whole treaty is about safeguarding heritage thought to be endangered to some degree or other. The very fact that they are endangered means that they are not sustainable in their current forms or in their current contexts—hence the need for national or international intervention. Yet by definition, for a tradition to be recognized as intangible cultural heritage under the Convention, and thus worthy of safeguarding, it must itself also be sustainable.

As for the purpose of the Convention, "safeguarding" is defined as:

> measures aimed at ensuring the viability of the intangible cultural heritage, including the identification, documentation, research, preservation, protection, promotion, enhancement, transmission, particularly through formal and non-formal education, as well as the revitalization of the various aspects of such heritage. (UNESCO, 2003)

The Convention calls upon nations and communities to create inventories of their intangible cultural heritage and develop action plans for its safeguarding. Safeguarding activities include familiar support for research, archival documentation, institutional efforts, and international cooperation, as found in the 1989 Recommendation, but were expanded to be more explicit about integrating intangible cultural heritage into educational, economic development, and civic programs and providing more avenues and opportunities for the participation of cultural practitioners. Article 15 spells out most explicitly the role of culture bearers and their communities:

> Within the framework of its safeguarding activities of the intangible cultural heritage, each State Party shall endeavour to ensure the widest possible participation of communities, groups and, where appropriate, individuals that create, maintain and transmit such heritage, and to involve them actively in its management. (UNESCO, 2003)

Granted that "endeavoring to ensure" provides governments with a good deal of room between pro forma and substantive efforts to involve cultural communities in safeguarding efforts, and represented considerable backsliding from the major recommendation of the Smithsonian conference, this provision is nonetheless unique in UNESCO cultural treaties in calling for the active participation of those who are supposedly to benefit from the accord. For me, this was a promising provision, and the fact that it was included, albeit in qualified form, was an accomplishment given that UNESCO represents member governments—many of which are hierarchical or even authoritarian—committing to share power over culture with the governed (cf. Aikawa-Faure, van Zanten, and Ceribašić in this volume).

The Convention also established a general assembly of the signatories, as is typical, and an Intergovernmental Committee for the Safeguarding of the Intangible Cultural Heritage to monitor, carry out, and help support international and intergovernmental work. Additionally, the treaty called for the accreditation of appropriate NGOs to advise the Committee. A fund was established to accept voluntary member dues and donations. The Committee would oversee two international "lists." One will be a list of "representative"—one might have preferred the term "exemplary"—intangible cultural heritage. This incorporated the items already designated Masterpieces of Oral and Intangible Heritage by UNESCO, which by the time of the treaty coming into force in 2005 included some 90 designees. This would be comparable to the World Heritage List. The other list was that of endangered cultural heritage—those traditions recommended to UNESCO for immediate safeguarding work by the international community.

The issue of the lists was perhaps the most contentious of the debates in the drafting and consideration of the Convention. For most of the participating cultural heritage managers, government officials, and administrators, this seemed like a commonsensical tool for managing a national resource. An inventory would provide an account of cultural assets that could then be assessed, managed, and evaluated. For cultural scholars, this was a misguided effort to atomize cultural practices, to treat them like things rather than a complex of people, circumstances, and relationships. It would substitute the fiction of government management of culture for actual, thoughtful activities that in cooperation with communities might strengthen the particular cultural expressions and their purveyors. It could perpetuate one of the major problems with the Masterpieces list—providing just a hollow homage to national prestige (Hafstein, 2009; Brown, 2005). Scholars, joined by some cultural advocates and managers, argued instead for the elucidation of "best practices" that could help strengthen grassroots expressions. The managers and officials outnumbered the anthropologists, folklorists, ethnomusicologists, and cultural scholars—and the lists stayed in.

A number of other contentious issues attended the drafting of the Convention and agreement on a final text. Some cultural colleagues found problematic the "artificial" separation of intangible and tangible culture. Often, the tangible and intangible are conjoined. They pointed out that for many local and indigenous communities, particular land, mountains, volcanoes, caves, and other tangible physical features are endowed with intangible meanings that are thought to be inherently tied to their physicality. Safeguarding intangible heritage was more complicated in such cases, because it also meant preserving and protecting local, tangible sites and environments (see Gao Shu in this volume). Similarly, with regard to musical traditions, instruments, tangible textual scripts, costumes, props, and stage settings are part and parcel of performance traditions like Japanese Noh, Chinese opera, and many others. Action plans had to account for that.

Another issue was the Convention's obligation that signatory nations "take the necessary measures to ensure the safeguarding of the intangible cultural heritage present in its territory" (UNESCO, 2003). "Necessary measures" could be interpreted in an extreme way, especially by undemocratic and authoritarian governments. While the drafters certainly did not envision governments using coercion to force children to follow their parents' traditional occupation or avocation, the use of this terminology, rather than a more temperate "appropriate measures," left room for potential government mischief.

Additionally, the Convention did not really anticipate the possibility for unintended deleterious consequences of safeguarding activities. For example, elevating a tradition, giving it public attention, could invite all sorts of internal battles over prominence within a cultural community. Putting resources into a traditional practice might upset and realign the very social and economic relationships that enabled the practice in the first place. This would particularly be the case if the effort to make the tradition sustainable involved commercializing it, turning community-facing performances, for example, toward touristic presentations.

Finally, there was a general concern among several countries that the Convention as a whole was an attempt by many nations to have their government assert "ownership" or property rights over their cultural expressions. If nations were legally bound to take responsibilities for their intangible cultural heritage, the concern was that it gave them room to claim property rights. For some countries, like the United States, this was of overriding importance, and anathema to the Patent and Trade Office and various commercial concerns. It would require a regimen of copyright and patent law that did not exist—though it was separately being considered by the World Intellectual Property Organization and had been stalled there for years (Wendland, 2004; Aikawa, 2004). The Convention was seen as potentially restricting the ability of US cultural industries to use and appropriate cultural traditions around the world—and was thus viewed suspiciously as a forerunner to the diversity of cultural expressions convention moving toward UNESCO consideration. For several other nations—like Canada and Australia—which were supportive of the latter treaty, the intangible cultural heritage convention presented problems with regard to the possible and difficult assertion of government rights over and responsibilities for Native cultures. Though the intangible cultural heritage convention had in Article 3 a "savings clause" that declared the treaty would not affect rights and obligations under other treaties, officials of these nations were well aware and concerned about the apparent contradictions.

I drafted the brief for the Department of State to consider whether or not to support the treaty. While I pointed out many of the issues reiterated above, I recommended approval given that US cultural agencies and programs were already doing most of what the treaty required and that it did not impose upon us any new funding or legislative needs. I argued that if ineffective, the treaty would be harmless to US interests, and if accepted it would help forward values of respect and diversity that the United States had embraced. With US experience in the cultural heritage arena, our involvement and even leadership could actually help achieve the positive results envisioned in the Convention. My arguments failed to overcome two counter positions. One was a general reluctance of the administration to sign on to international treaties, especially ones that seemed inconsequential to US interests and priorities. The second was the specific objection of the Patent and Trade Office given what they saw was a slippery slope toward the use of cultural accords for economic and trade purposes (Kurin, 2014).

On October 17, 2003, in a meeting of the UNESCO General Assembly, some 120 nations voted for the Convention. Scores of others subsequently registered their approval. No nation voted against it. A handful—the United States, Australia, Canada, the United Kingdom, and New Zealand among them—abstained.

## Post-Convention Epilogue

Following passage at the General Assembly, nations went forward with the ratification process, which required formal approval by 30 States Parties. That was achieved in 2005, and the Convention came into force.

Though the Smithsonian's direct involvement in the work of the Convention was forestalled by the US failure to sign on, I and other colleagues continued to interact and advise UNESCO colleagues, particularly Assistant Director-General for Culture Mounir Bouchenaki, with whom we'd established a strong relationship that over the years resulted in a series of collaborative programs. Smithsonian staff continued to build on their professional ties, conduct field projects and educational activities, present papers at international professional meetings, publish articles, and attend specialized meetings, such as the Abu Dhabi conference on safeguarding music heritage coinciding with the meeting of the Convention's International Committee in 2009 (Kurin, 2017; Seeger, 2017). As UNESCO staffed up its office to implement the Convention, I was able to recommend Frank Proschan, a long-time staff member of the Smithsonian's Center for Folklife and Cultural Heritage, to take up a key post. Proschan served as program specialist in UNESCO's

Intangible Cultural Heritage Section from 2006 to 2015 and for the last two years as chief of program implementation. Proschan brought to the role a wealth of experience, mainly in Southeast Asia, and a keen awareness of community-based intangible cultural heritage and the complexities and challenges of safeguarding activities. Along with UNESCO colleagues, he helped organize national and regional meetings, produce a variety of training and capacity-building materials and programs, assess reports of safeguarding activities, manage the international lists, and aid NGO collaborations.

As Cecile Duvelle (2014), then head of the UNESCO section, reported in the decade following the UNESCO vote, the Convention was implemented with the required General Assembly of signatories, the international Committee, accredited NGOs, a fund, and processes for nations to report their activities and for promoting international cooperation. Among the key accomplishments of the Convention have been a large increase in the awareness among government cultural agencies, relevant NGOs, and scholarly and professional groups about intangible cultural heritage—certainly by orders of magnitude from the time of the 1989 Recommendation. There has also been a large increase in the number of governmental units, personnel, and resources devoted to intangible cultural heritage and conducting research, producing reports, conferences, and programs—though that remains unevenly distributed around the world. The number of countries participating in nominating traditions for the representational list has grown, and the number of listed traditions vastly expanded. As of early 2021, some 131 nations had successfully nominated "heritages," with the Representative List growing from the initially incorporated 90 "masterpieces" to 492. Another 67 heritages were on the Urgent Safeguarding List (UNESCO, 2021). Indeed, according to the UNESCO staff, the worry that the Convention would largely become a forum for seeking international prestige was well-founded. Many resources, much staff time, and most of the General Assembly's meeting time was taken up with managing the lists (Smeets & Deacon, 2007).

Early on, the staff developed the idea of encouraging best practices in safeguarding that had been floated during the Convention's drafting and deliberations. Growing from case studies of successful interventions in strengthening intangible cultural heritage in their countries, States Parties could also have their best practices listed—hopefully to inform and inspire others. Currently there are 25 best practice cases formally listed.

While there are cases where intangible heritage has been safeguarded, promoted, promulgated, preserved, and protected, and also integrated into educational, economic development, and civic projects, the documentation of such work and the achievement of such activities is still not to scale. The Convention has not solved the problem it sought to correct. Nor have nations and their institutions, save sporadically, engaged in developing the partnerships and relationships with cultural communities which was one of the aspirations of the Convention and the central critique of prior, top-down approaches. While UNESCO staff has encouraged community participation and agency in safeguarding activities, that has remained a largely unfilled methodology (Curtis & Proschan, 2009; Proschan, 2015). It is to some extent understandable. Most cultural communities are constituted informally. Cultural exemplars are more respected than they are elected. Identifying who speaks for the cultural tradition being safeguarded is not obvious, and a cultural community may be beset by factionalism and division. Developing a means of working together is also difficult. There are often great status differentials between public officials and experts, on one hand, and the practitioners of the tradition, on the other. Operationalizing community participation has been a great challenge for many cultural projects in the past, and continued to challenge even well-intentioned experts who worked to realize the Convention's aspiration.

In parallel fashion, the hope that NGOs, with mission, staff, and resources, presumably working closely with such communities, could play a positive role has not materialized on a large and broad enough scale. The lack of community participation which can help lead to substantive safeguarding results is a major lacuna in the implementation of the Convention (see also Ceribašić, this volume).

One of my great hopes was that the cultural involvement of some of the world's leading democracies, where traditions of citizen participation run long and deep, would help realize the goals of the Convention. For some of these countries, the historical failures to deal with Native or Indigenous people, immigrants, and marginalized groups had led to painful lessons, and, over time, corrections, at least by cultural institutions, to enable and aid community-level safeguarding activity. But that hope has remained unfulfilled. In the almost two decades after the initial vote, the treaty has now gained almost worldwide acceptance—but with the United States, Australia, Canada, the United Kingdom, and New Zealand still remaining exceptions. With changes in administrations, efforts, particularly in Canada and the United States, have been made to secure acceptance (Pocius, 2014). I again wrote the brief for the Department of State to consider accession during the

Obama administration. Since the diversity of cultural expressions convention had gained UNESCO approval in 2005—with strong US objection—the issue of the intangible heritage convention proving impetus to the assertion of cultural property rights over traditional culture was essentially taken off the table as an issue to overcome. The attempt to gain US approval for the intangible cultural heritage convention looked hopeful initially, but was ultimately derailed as a result of a UNESCO vote to grant membership to the Palestinian Authority (Kurin, 2014). In 2017, the Trump administration announced it would withdraw from UNESCO, and that formally took effect at the beginning of 2019, thus foreclosing formal reconsideration of the Convention.

With Joe Biden taking office in January 2021, UNESCO officials quickly took up the effort of persuading the United States to rejoin the organization and contacted a number of us who have been involved with its programs and initiatives over the years. The membership issue and the fact that the United States would owe about $700 million in back dues if it did rejoin make it difficult to determine the outcome of such efforts. Yet, even though it is not a member of UNESCO, the United States could still ratify the intangible cultural heritage treaty, become a State Party to it, and join its General Assembly. Thus, there is a route to US participation in the work envisioned in the Convention. While the Convention has flaws and its implementation has been skewed, it nevertheless recognizes in a fundamental way the value of a world with diverse cultural traditions and expressions, and where people have every right to practice, extend, continually modify, and elaborate them, as well as benefit from them spiritually, aesthetically, communally, civically, and economically. This seems quite in tune with America's democratic, creative, entrepreneurial, and forward-looking ideals, and invites our nation's participation.

## References

Aikawa, N. (2001). The 1989 Recommendation on the Safeguarding of Traditional Cultures and Folklore: Actions taken for its implementation. In P. Seitel (Ed.), *Safeguarding traditional cultures: A global assessment* (pp. 13–19). Smithsonian Center for Folklife and Cultural Heritage.

Aikawa, N. (2004). An historic overview of the preparation of the UNESCO International Convention for the Safeguarding of Intangible Cultural Heritage. In *Museum International: Views and Visions of the Intangible Heritage, 221–222*, 137–149.

Aikawa-Faure, N. (2009). From the proclamation of masterpieces to the convention for the safeguarding of intangible cultural heritage. In L. Smith & N. Akagawa (Eds.), *Intangible heritage* (pp. 13–44). Routledge.

Aikawa-Faure, N. (2019). Comment on Richard Kurin Keynote, at the Critical Developments in Cultural Sustainability: Sustaining Practice Conference, Smithsonian Center for Folklife and Cultural Heritage, October 23, 2019.

Anderson, H., Davey, G., & McHenry, K. (1987). *Folklife: One living heritage: Report of the Committee of Inquiry into Folklife in Australia.* Australian Government Publishing Service.

Appadurai, A. (1996). *Modernity at large: Cultural dimensions of globalization.* University of Minnesota Press.

Appadurai, A. (2002). Universal Declaration on Cultural Diversity: A document for the World Summit on Sustainable Development (pp. 9–16). Paris: UNESCO. http://www.arjunappadurai.org/articles/Appadurai_Cultural_Diversity_A_Conceptual_Platform.pdf.

Baily, J. (2004). Music censorship in Afghanistan before and after the Taliban. In M. Korpe (Ed.), *Shoot the singer: Music censorship today* (pp. 19–28). Zed Books.

Bedjaoui, M. (2004). The Convention for the Safeguarding of Intangible Cultural Heritage: The legal framework and universally recognized principles. In *Museum International: Views and Visions of the Intangible Heritage, 221–222,* 150–155.

Bennett, T. (1998). *Culture: A reformer's science.* Allen & Unwin.

Bennett, T. (2000). Acting on the social, art, culture and government. *American Behavioral Scientist 43,* 1412–1428.

Bennett, T. (2013). *Making culture, changing society.* Routledge.

Blake, J. (2001a). *Preliminary study into the advisability of developing a new standard-setting instrument for the safeguarding of intangible cultural heritage.* Report of the International Round Table "Intangible Cultural Heritage." Turin, Italy.

Blake, J. (2001b). *Developing a new standard-setting instrument for the safeguarding of intangible cultural heritage: Elements for consideration.* Paris: UNESCO.

Blake, J. (2009). UNESCO's 2003 Convention on Intangible Cultural Heritage. In L. Smith & N. Akagawa (Eds.), *Intangible heritage* (pp. 45–73). Routledge.

Brown, M. (2005). Heritage trouble: Recent work on the protection of intangible cultural property. *International Journal of Cultural Property, 12*(1), 40–61.

Cooper, D. (2009). *The musical traditions of Northern Ireland and its diaspora: Community and conflict.* Ashgate.

Curtis, T., & Proschan, F. (2009). Mobilizing communities to document their intangible cultural heritage: Information and networking for the safeguarding of intangible cultural heritage. *Discourses on ICH safeguarding issues.* 2009 Conference report. www.ICH Conventionap.org/.../E03-1_Mobilizing_communities_to_document_their_intangible_cultural_heritage.pdf

Duvelle, Cécile. (2014). A decade of implementation of the Convention for the Safeguarding of Intangible Cultural Heritage: Challenges and perspectives. In *Ethnologies: Patrimoine culturel immatériel/Intangible Cultural Heritage, 36*(1–2), 27–46.

Duvignaud, J., & C. Khaznadar. (2004). Le patrimoine culturel immatériel: Les enjeux, les problématicques, les pratiques. *Internationale de l'Imaginaire, nouvelle série, 17.*

Early, J., & P. Seitel. (2002a). UNESCO meeting in Rio, steps toward a convention. *Smithsonian Talk Story, 20,* 13.

Early, J., & P. Seitel. (2002b). No folklore without the folk. *Smithsonian Talk Story, 21,* 19–21.

Hafstein, V. (2004). *The making of intangible cultural heritage: Tradition and authenticity, community and humanity.* Unpublished PhD dissertation, University of California, Berkeley.

Hafstein, V. (2009). Intangible cultural heritage as a list: From masterpieces to representation. In L. Smith & N. Akagawa (Eds.), *Intangible heritage* (pp. 93–111). Routledge.

Honko, L. (1990). The final text of the Recommendation for the Safeguarding of Folklore. *Canadian Folklore Canadien, 12,* 11–20.

Kirshenblatt-Gimblett, B. (1995). Theorizing heritage. *Ethnomusicology, 39*(3), 367–380.

Kirshenblatt-Gimblett, B. (1998). *Destination culture: Tourism, museums and heritage.* Berkeley: University of California Press.

Kirshenblatt-Gimblett, B. (2004). Intangible culture as metacultural production. *Museum International: Views and Visions of the Intangible Heritage, 221–222,* 52–64.

Kirshenblatt-Gimblett, B. (2006). World heritage and cultural economics. In I. Karp et al. (Eds.), *Museum frictions: Public cultures/global transformations* (pp. 161–202). Duke University Press.

Kurin, R. (2001). The UNESCO questionnaire on the application of the 1989 Recommendation on the Safeguarding of Traditional Cultures and Folklore: Preliminary results. In P. Seitel (Ed.), *Safeguarding traditional cultures: A global assessment* (pp. 20–35). Smithsonian Center for Folklife and Cultural Heritage.

Kurin, R. (2002). UNESCO's Masterpieces of Intangible Cultural Heritage. In *Current Anthropology, 43,* 144–145.

Kurin, R. (2004a). Les problématicques du patrimoine culturel immatériel. In J. Duvignaud & C. Khaznadar (Eds.), *Le patrimoine culturel immatériel: Les enjeux, les problématicques, les pratiques. Internationale de l'Imaginaire, nouvelle série, 17,* 59–67.

Kurin, R. (2004b). Safeguarding intangible cultural heritage in the 2003 UNESCO Convention: A critical appraisal. *Museum International: Views and Visions of the Intangible Heritage, 221–222,* 66–76.

Kurin, R. (2007). Safeguarding intangible cultural heritage: Key factors in implementing the 2003 Convention. *International Journal of Intangible Heritage, 2,* 10–20.

Kurin, R. (2011). *Saving Haiti's heritage: Cultural recovery after the earthquake.* Smithsonian Institution.

Kurin, R. (2014). U.S. consideration of the Intangible Cultural Heritage Convention. *Ethnonologies: Patrimoine culturel immatériel/Intangible Cultural Heritage, 36*(1–2), 325–368.

Kurin, R. (2016). Conversation with Richard Kurin. In P. Davis & M. L. Stefano (Eds.), *The Routledge companion to intangible cultural heritage* (pp. 40–45). Routledge.

Kurin, R. (2017). Why safeguard our musical heritage for the future? In C. Khaznadar (Ed.), *Safeguarding music heritage* (pp. 10–20). Department of Culture and Tourism.

McCann, A., et al. (2001). The 1989 Recommendation ten years on: Toward a critical analysis. In P. Seitel (Ed.), *Safeguarding traditional cultures: A global assessment* (pp. 36–41). Smithsonian Center for Folklife and Cultural Heritage.

Morgan, A. (2013). *Music, culture and conflict in Mali.* Freemuse,

Nas, P. 2002. Masterpieces of oral and intangible culture: Reflections on the UNESCO World Heritage List. *Cultural Anthropology, 43*(1), 139–148.

Pocius, G. L. (2014). The government of Canada and intangible cultural heritage *Ethnonologies: Patrimoine culturel immatériel/Intangible Cultural Heritage, 36*(1–2), 63–92.

Proschan, F. (2015). Community involvement in valuing and safeguarding intangible cultural heritage. In K. V. Balen & A. Vandesande (Eds.), *Community involvement in heritage* (pp. 15–22). Garant.

Prott, L. (2001). Some considerations on the protection of the intangible cultural heritage. In P. Seitel (Ed.), *Safeguarding traditional cultures: A global assessment* (pp. 104–110). Smithsonian Center for Folklife and Cultural Heritage.

Ruggles, D. F., et al. (2009). From tangible to intangible heritage. In D. F. Ruggles & H. Silverman (Eds.), *Intangible heritage embodied* (pp. 1–14). Springer.

Scott, G. (2003). The cultural property laws of Japan: Social, political, and legal influences. *Pacific Rim Law & Policy Journal, 12*, 315–402.

Seeger, A. (2001). Summary report on the regional seminars. In P. Seitel (Ed.), *Safeguarding traditional cultures: A global assessment* (pp. 13–19). Smithsonian Center for Folklife and Cultural Heritage.

Seeger, A. (2009). Lessons learned from the ICTM (NGO) evaluation of nominations for the UNESCO Masterpieces of the Oral and Intangible Heritage of Humanity 2001–5. In L. Smith & N. Akagawa (Eds.), *Intangible heritage* (pp. 112–27). Routledge.

Seeger, A. (2017). Why safeguard musical heritage for the future: A view from an audiovisual archive. In C. Khaznadar (Ed.), *Safeguarding music heritage* (pp. 22–27). Department of Culture and Tourism.

Seeger, A. (2019). Comments in happy anniversary? The 1999 UNESCO-Smithsonian Conference and UNESCO's Intangible Cultural Heritage Convention discussion forum. October 17, 2019. Annual Meeting of the American Folklore Society.

Seitel, P. (Ed.). (2001). *Safeguarding traditional cultures: A global assessment.* Smithsonian Center for Folklife and Cultural Heritage.

Sherkin, S. (2001). A historical study on the preparation of the 1989 Recommendation on the Safeguarding of Traditional Cultures and Folklore. In P. Seitel (Ed.), *Safeguarding traditional cultures: A global assessment* (pp. 42–56). Smithsonian Center for Folklife and Cultural Heritage.

Smeets, R., & Deacon, H. (2017). The examination of nomination files under the UNESCO Convention for the Safeguarding of Intangible Cultural Heritage. In M. L. Stefano & P. Davis (Eds.), *The Routledge companion to intangible cultural heritage* (pp. 22–39). Routledge.

Stefano, M. (2019). Folklife at the International Level: Happy Anniversary to the 1999 UNESCO-Smithsonian Meeting. Library of Congress blog. https://blogs.loc.gov/folklife/2019/11/folklife-at-the-international-level-happy-anniversary-to-the-1999-unesco-smithsonian-meeting/

Stefano, M. L., & P. Davis (Eds.) (2017). *The Routledge companion to intangible cultural heritage.* Routledge.

Stefano, M., P. Davis, & G. Corsane (Eds.) (2012). *Safeguarding intangible cultural heritage.* Boydell Press.

Turgeon, L. (2014). Introduction: The politics and practices of intangible cultural heritage. *Ethnonologies: Patrimoine culturel immatériel/Intangible Cultural Heritage, 36*(1–2), 5–14.

UNESCO. (1972). Convention concerning the protection of the world cultural and natural heritage. https://whc.unesco.org/en/conventiontext/.

UNESCO. (1989). Recommendation on the safeguarding of traditional cultures and folklore. http://portal.unesco.org/en/ev.php-URL_ID=13141&URL_DO=DO_TO PIC&URL_SECTION=201.html.

UNESCO. (1996). Our creative diversity. Report of the World Commission on Culture and Development.

UNESCO. (2001a). Proclamation of the masterpieces of the oral and intangible heritage of humanity (2001–2005). https://ich.unesco.org/en/proclamation-of-masterpie ces-00103.

UNESCO. (2001b). Universal declaration on cultural diversity. http://portal.unesco.org/ en/ev.php-URL_ID=13179&URL_DO=DO_TOPIC&URL_SECTION=201.html.

UNESCO. (2002). Universal declaration on cultural diversity. Cultural Diversity Series No. 1. Paris: UNESCO.

UNESCO. (2003). Convention for the safeguarding of the intangible cultural heritage. Paris: UNESCO. https://ich.unesco.org/en/convention.

UNESCO. (2005). The convention on the protection and promotion of the diversity of cultural expressions. Paris: UNESCO. https://en.unesco.org/creativity/convention/ texts

UNESCO. (2021). Browse the lists of intangible cultural heritage and the register of good safeguarding practices. https://ich.unesco.org/en/lists

Wendland, Wend. (2004). Intangible heritage and intellectual property: Challenges and future prospects. *Museum International: Views and Visions of the Intangible Heritage, 221–222,* 97–106.

Zanten, W. van. (2004). Constructing new terminology for intangible cultural heritage. *Museum International: Views and Visions of the Intangible Heritage, 221–222,* 36–43.

# 3

# Modalities for Community Participation in Implementing the UNESCO ICH Convention

*Noriko Aikawa-Faure*

The UNESCO Convention for the Safeguarding of the Intangible Cultural Heritage (ICH Convention) is the first example of an international cultural heritage treaty that acknowledges the need for community involvement to such a high degree (Blake, 2019). This principle emerged from the landmark 1999 UNESCO/Smithsonian Institution Conference, *A Global Assessment of the 1989 Recommendation on the Safeguarding of Traditional Culture and Folklore: Local Empowerment and International Cooperation.* It was further endorsed by the Turin Round Table, where experts discussed the definition of the term "intangible cultural heritage" and by the Rio Expert Meeting that identified the priority domain to be included in the future instrument, which was fed finally into the ICH Convention. This chapter examines not only how this concept of community involvement in the safeguarding of the ICH was enshrined by the experts at their meetings, but also how it was subsequently watered down by the representatives of UNESCO member states at the intergovernmental meetings that drafted the ICH Convention and its Operational Directives (ODs) from 2005 to 2008.

The concept of "community participation" emerged within the framework of the emphasis on "endogenous development" developed under the Second UN Development Decade (1971–1981). The Mexico City Declaration, the conclusion of the World Conference on Cultural Policies held in Mexico City in 1982, was instrumental in the elaboration of subsequent UNESCO cultural programs. This Declaration included the principle of "Culture and Democracy,"[1] among eight

---

[1] Mexico City Declaration on Cultural Policies, World Conference on Cultural Policies (Mexico City, 26 July—6 August 1982), paragraph 17: "everyone has the right freely to participate in the

Noriko Aikawa-Faure, *Modalities for Community Participation in Implementing the UNESCO ICH Convention*
In: *Music, Communities, Sustainability.* Edited by: Huib Schippers and Anthony Seeger, Oxford University Press.
© Oxford University Press 2022. DOI: 10.1093/oso/9780197609101.003.0003

others,[2] as governing cultural policies. It affirms the role of communities in building cultural democracy[3] in line with the cultural rights deriving from Article 27 of the Universal Declaration of Human Rights. As a follow-up to the recommendations of the Mexico Conference, the World Decade for Cultural Development (1987–1997) was proclaimed by UN General Assembly in 1986, giving a mandate to UNESCO to achieve the following goals:

   (i)  to promote the acknowledgment of the cultural dimension of
        development;
  (ii)  to affirm and enrich cultural identities;
 (iii)  to broaden participation in culture; and
  (iv)  to promote international cultural cooperation.

The UNESCO Intangible Cultural Heritage Programme, launched in 1993 within a different framework and introducing new perspectives,[4] already included the concept of the participation of practitioners and communities in the safeguarding of ICH as one of the underpinning concepts of the program (Aikawa, 2007). However, the crucial event that impacted the implementation of this concept was the 1999 Washington Conference, which reviewed the implementation of the UNESCO 1989 Recommendation on the Safeguarding of Traditional Culture and Folklore and advocated the creation of a new legal instrument for the safeguarding of ICH.

The international Conference, entitled "A Global Assessment of the 1989 Recommendation on the Safeguarding of Traditional Culture and Folklore: Local Empowerment and International Cooperation," was

cultural life of the community, to enjoy the arts and to share in scientific advancement and its benefits." This intergovernmental conference was the concluding one of six regional intergovernmental conferences held since 1970.

   [2] These principles are: 1) cultural identity; 2) the cultural dimension of development; culture and democracy; 4) cultural heritage; 5) artistic and intellectual creation and art education; 6) the relationship of culture with education, science and communication, and planning; 7) administration and the financing of cultural activities; 8) international cultural cooperation and UNESCO's role.

   [3] *Mexico City Declaration on Cultural Policies, World Conference on Cultural Policies (Mexico City, 26 July–6 August 1982)*, paragraph 18: "Culture springs from the community as a whole and should return to it; neither the production of culture nor the enjoyment of its benefits should be the privilege of elites. Cultural democracy is based on the broadest possible participation by the individual and society in the creation of cultural goods, in decision-making concerning cultural life and in the dissemination and enjoyment of culture."

   [4] The new perspectives were defined during the International Consultation on New Perspectives for UNESCO's Programme: Intangible Cultural Heritage, UNESCO, Paris, June 1993.

organized by UNESCO together with the Smithsonian Institution in June 1999. Prior to the Conference, UNESCO conducted eight regional seminars[5] to discuss how the 1989 Recommendation had been received and implemented in each world region. Summaries of the reports of these seminars were presented by Anthony Seeger at the Washington Conference (Seeger, in Seitel, 2001a). It is worth noting that each region had different concerns and cultural priorities on the eve of the creation of the ICH Convention and that the question of the "participation of communities" was not a priority for every nation worldwide. Only the Latin American and Pacific countries argued for the community role. For the Latin American region, the prime concerns were multiculturalism and hybrid cultures. The countries of the region considered the role played by folklore creators and actors to be one of democratic development and integration. From the point of view of the Pacific States, there should be no boundaries between natural, cultural, tangible, and intangible heritage. For this region, customary law and traditional knowledge had a significant meaning.

Moreover, the participation of the communities in any actions relating to heritage preservation was crucial. The Asian countries wanted traditional high cultures to be considered, in addition to folk cultures, and expressed their concern at the lack of policy documents and training. They were worried about the distortion of traditional culture and folklore (hereafter TCF) in the event of excessive tourism development. The Central Asian countries underscored the significance of folklore as a way to form national identity in their newly independent states, and they deplored the weak research infrastructure for folklore. For the African countries, while the TCF had been considered as a means to express cultural identity during the nation-building period, at the time of the Conference, policies to promote multiple identities had become their priority. They were concerned about the misuse of the TCF by commercial entities. The Central and Eastern European countries deplored the weaker national infrastructure for the preservation of TCF following the introduction of market economies in the region. The Western European countries were concerned about the endangering of cultural diversity. They considered that the emphasis should be placed on protecting the TCF of minority groups. The Arab States expressed their concern

---

[5] Western Europe, Central and Eastern Europe, Latin-America and the Caribbean States, the Asian countries, Central Asian countries, Pacific States, Arab States and Africa.

about the loss of their TCF, and consequently their identity, due to growing globalization.

Based on the above-mentioned analysis of the eight regional seminars and the critical analysis of the 1989 Recommendation conducted by Anthony McCann together with members of the Center for Folklore and Cultural Heritage at the Smithsonian Institution (Seitel, 2001a, the Conference recommended action plans to UNESCO and to the governments of its member states. The preamble to these plans referred to a wide range of then-prevailing concepts relating to TCF[6], such as the primary role of communities, TCF's contribution to the assertion of cultural identity, its social role in bringing different groups of people together despite their diversity, and its contribution to sustainable human development and the right to culture, notably the protection of communities' traditional knowledge.

Out of the 21 action plans addressed to the governments of the member states of UNESCO, 11 referred to a respect for the primary role of local communities in dealing with the TCF. Finally, by way of action plan 12, the Conference recommended that the UNESCO member states request the Organization to undertake a feasibility study for the drafting of a new international normative instrument on the safeguarding of TCF. In response, the Czech Republic, Lithuania, and Bolivia, supported by Bulgaria, Côte d'Ivoire, Slovakia, and Ukraine, submitted a Draft Resolution[7] to the 30th session of the UNESCO General Conference (October–November 1999). UNESCO, following the positive decision of the General Conference, entrusted Janet Blake, who was the rapporteur of the Washington Conference, to draw up a feasibility study[8]. In developing this document, she advocated that in the new instrument cultural communities be recognized as principal agents in ensuring the viability of their ICH (Blake, 2001)

In what follows, I will first describe how the involvement of the communities was discussed throughout the preparatory meetings of ICH Convention, notably in Turin, Rio de Janeiro, and Istanbul. I will then observe which provisions of the ICH Convention reflect this principle and how the texts of the ODs relating to the participation of communities and practitioners developed through the four sessions of the Intergovernmental Committee (IGC) and how they were finalized by the Second General Assembly of States

---

[6] Prior to the creation of the Convention, the ICH was called as 'Traditional Culture and Folkore'.
[7] 30C/DR.84
[8] The study is entitled "Developing a New Standard-setting Instrument for the Safeguarding of the Intangible Cultural Heritage: Elements for Consideration."

Parties in 2008. Finally, I will look at what has been done since to improve the participation of communities in the safeguarding of the ICH.

## Participation of Communities: The Turin Round Table

The first preparatory expert meeting for the future international normative instrument took place in Turin in March 2001 to reflect upon its conceptual framework. The purpose of this meeting, entitled "International Round Table on Intangible Cultural Heritage—Working Definitions," was to clarify the definition, scope, and relevant terminology of ICH. The Round Table could be qualified as a follow-up meeting to the Washington Conference from a conceptual perspective. Some of the participants at the Washington Conference, such as Manuela Carneiro da Cunha, Janet Blake, Peter Seitel, and James Early, the last two of whom are from the Smithsonian Center for Folklife and Cultural Heritage, were key figures at the Round Table.

At the session on the working definitions of the ICH and terminology, three anthropologists, Lourdes Arizpe, Manuela Carneiro da Cunha, and Peter Seitel, presented papers. Lourdes Arizpe (2001) presented a paper entitled "Intangible Cultural Heritage: Perceptions and Enactments" using graphics. She first enumerated the obstacles that might be encountered in defining the scope and working definition of the ICH, and she then reflected on the elements to be treated under the future legal instrument.

Lourdes Arizpe emphasized that "enactment is an essential and defining aspect of the ICH in the sense that this heritage exists and is sustained through the acts of people" (UNESCO, 2001, p. 2). She argued that the emphasis should be placed on the ICH being viewed holistically and understood as a process of creation, comprising skills, enabling factors, products, meanings, impacts, and economic value. Arizpe, a former assistant director-general for culture at UNESCO, proposed a definition which could be acceptable to a majority of the organization's member states, since otherwise the legal instrument would not be adopted at the UNESCO General Conference.

She was concerned with the need for a necessary balance between a political consensus among the UNESCO member states and scientific rigor. She also suggested that UNESCO should identify within its new international instrument those areas which had not been dealt with by other international organizations, such as the World Intellectual Property Organization (WIPO) and the World Trade Organization (WTO), and which had a comparative advantage for UNESCO. She then suggested the following areas as the scope of the future instrument: (i) the area between nature and culture; (ii) areas concerning indigenous people's cultures; (iii) social cooperation and social cohesion; (iv) oral traditions; and (v) local arts and crafts (UNESCO, 2001). She therefore favored a limited number of areas for the new instrument in order not to overlap with those already covered by other international organizations and other bodies.

Manuela Carneiro da Cunha (2001) proposed a larger scope. She presented a paper entitled "The Notion of Intangible Heritage: Towards Working Definitions." Her presentation focused on the traditional knowledge of indigenous peoples. She argued that the protection of traditional knowledge was closely connected to the protection of the social and environmental context in which it exists (see also Gao Shu, Chapter 11 in this volume). It was, therefore, necessary to support the producers of cultural heritage as "participant agents in its protection and conservation," she said. Moreover, she noted that given that local and indigenous people's ways of life were closely linked with ecological knowledge and genetic resources, it was imperative to recognize equity in sharing benefits and to ensure control by the producers of cultural goods, as well as to grant them free, prior, and informed consent when registering their knowledge. She concluded that UNESCO should take a holistic view of protection and a wide-ranging definition of the ICH, including (i) folklore and crafts; (ii) bio-diversity; and (iii) indigenous knowledge.

After these presentations, the participants engaged in various debates, on the one hand supporting anthropological concerns regarding local practitioner communities, and on the other hand expressing political concerns of UNESCO member states. Of the 16 participants at the meeting, there were four anthropologists, two folklorists, three lawyers, one linguist, one ethnomusicologist, three diplomats, and two government officials. The participants agreed that the "utmost importance should be given to 'participatory democracy' rather than 'representative democracy,' and in this respect, a future normative instrument should emanate from a democratic process. . . ." (UNESCO, 2001, p. 6). The participants were reminded of the relevance of a leitmotif proclaimed at the Washington Conference, namely of the "centrality of traditional custodians as full partners and experts in the safeguarding of cultural heritage," confirming their strong support for this principle. They proclaimed that " 'community' should be considered [as] a keyword and carefully examined in defining the Intangible Cultural

Heritage" (UNESCO, 2001, p. 7; see also van Zanten, Chapter 4 in this volume). During the discussion on the significance of the active participation of the "makers of culture" in the protection of the cultural heritage, some participants questioned whether such "makers of culture" could be qualified as experts. In order to counter this doubt, the participants emphasized that a "legal instrument should work *with* people and not *on* people" (UNESCO, 2001, p. 7).

Peter Seitel (2001b) presented a paper entitled "Proposed Terminology for Intangible Cultural Heritage: Toward Anthropological and Folkloristic Common Sense in a Global Era," in which he underscored the role of communities in the safeguarding of the ICH. In his paper, he proposed definitions of terms that could be used in the future legal instrument, including "cultural process," "traditional knowledge," and "community." He expressed his opposition to the creation of a listing system in the manner of the UNESCO 1972 Convention and instead recommended setting up cultural registers of the ICH on the Web. He also noted that the "creation of such cultural registers would be useful for the legal defense of Intellectual Property Rights in support of WIPO efforts in this area" (Seitel, 2001b, p. 10).

Two legal papers concerning the "scope and definition of an instrument to be developed" were presented. First, Blake (2001), again assigned as the rapporteur of the Round Table as she was at the Washington Conference, introduced her "Draft Preliminary Study on the Advisability of Developing a Standard-Setting Instrument for the Protection of the Intangible Cultural Heritage" that was planned to be presented to the UNESCO Executive Board at its 161st session in May 2001. Among the areas which such an instrument might encourage, Blake included "enabling cultural communities to continue to create, maintain, and transmit it [the ICH] in the traditional context" (Blake, 2001, p. 80). She also referred to the inclusion in the instrument of customary rules and practices regarding the secrecy of certain forms of traditional knowledge and the involvement of tradition-holders in the preservation, planning, and management of the intangible heritage (Blake, 2001). Reacting to the emphasis placed by Blake on the involvement of practitioners, the participants then engaged in some contentious debate. The point was made finally that while priority should be given to the active involvement of local communities and civil society, agencies linked to UNESCO or its member states should also be consulted (UNESCO, 2001).

The chair of the meeting, Francesco Francioni, then presented his paper entitled "The Specificity of Intangible Heritage as an Object of International

Protection" (Francioni, 2001). Francioni[9] presented his view that the future legal instrument for ICH should encompass the concept of the "importance" or "significance" of Intangible Heritage for the cultural and social identity of the people, community, or group that are the creators or bearers of the heritage and, therefore, a reference should be made to the universal value of certain types of intangible cultural heritage. The paper provoked extensive debate, notably on Francioni's idea of referring to "the universal value of certain types of Intangible Cultural Heritage" inspired by the World Heritage Convention (UNESCO, 2001, p. 17). Finally, the Turin Meeting adopted 17 action plans, of which two[10] concerned the primary role of communities in the safeguarding of the ICH. The 14th action plan[11] concerned community involvement as a selection criterion for the ICH projects to be declared and disseminated.

The plans included a definition of the term "Intangible Cultural Heritage," as well as the areas to be covered by the proposed instrument. The adopted definition for the ICH ran as follows: people's learned processes along with the knowledge, skills and creativity that inform and are developed by them, the products they create, and the resources, spaces and other aspects of social and natural context necessary to their sustainability; these processes provide living communities with a sense of continuity with previous generations and are important to cultural identity, as well as to the safeguarding of cultural diversity and the creativity of humanity" (UNESCO, 2001, Appendix III, p. 6).

The scope of the proposed instrument included "oral cultural heritage; languages; performing arts and festive events; social rituals and practices;

---

[9] Francioni proposed also: i) a general, synthetic, and inclusive clause to be included in the proposed instrument encompassing all forms of Intangible Heritage with an indication of some essential typologies; and ii) that the definition used must reflect the intrinsic cultural values of the heritage as conceived and perceived by the people, group, or community to which it belongs.

[10] Action plans 3 and 4 of the Turin meeting were: "3. Ensure that the international legal instrument addresses primarily creators and custodian communities in addition to scholars, researchers and cultural workers, and that the dignity and relevant rights of creators and practitioners of intangible cultural heritage are respected and that further actions are taken to support their socio-economic well-being; 4. Ensure that the process of elaborating a new standard-setting instrument. is carried out with the full participation of all parties concerned, more particularly at the grass-roots level, i.e. cultural practitioners and custodian communities or communities at the national, regional and international level" (Turin meeting final report, UNESCO, 2001).

[11] The 14th Turin action plan concerned the criteria for selection in the proposed project on the proclamation and dissemination of projects selected as "Best Practices for the Safeguarding of ICH" and were "Encourage, disseminate and proclaim best practices for safeguarding intangible cultural heritage that: (i) were generated or involve members of the community; (ii) have shown in concrete achievements that they can successfully reach their goals; (iii) are exemplary for communities within the country or in other countries of the world;
    (iv) involve women to the fullest extent of their potential participation; (v) enhance the social and ecological sustainability of the group and region" (Turin meeting final report, UNESCO, 2001).

cosmologies and knowledge systems; [and] beliefs and practices about Nature" (UNESCO, 2001, Appendix III, p. 6). It should be noted that the above-mentioned action plans, together with the areas to be included in the proposed instrument and the definition of ICH, were drafted by a group chaired by Lourdes Arizpe during the Round Table (UNESCO, 2001). The adopted definition, which is substantively community centered, and the related scope of the instrument, became the underpinning elements of the ICH CONVENTION.

In October–November 2001, the 31st session of the UNESCO General Conference, after a heated and largely political debate, approved the legal instrument for the safeguarding of ICH as a "convention" (Aikawa-Faure, 2009). The debate on the creation of a convention on the ICH in the expert meetings then increasingly reflected governments' political views, while previous discussions focused on the experts' substantive views.

Another expert meeting[12] took place in Rio de Janeiro in January 2002 in order to identify the priority areas that the future Convention should encompass in the vast field of the ICH. Koichiro Matsuura, then director-general of UNESCO, decided[13] that this meeting should be of a more political nature than the Turin meeting. Mohammed Bedjaoui, a former president of the International Court of Justice, a former minister of foreign affairs of Algeria, and then a member of the UNESCO Executive Board, chaired the meeting. It should be noted that he then chaired all the subsequent expert and intergovernmental meetings that drafted the text of the Convention, including the last session (June 2003) that finalized the draft. Seven then members of the UNESCO Executive Board also participated in the Rio meeting.

The participants first discussed the "role of UNESCO in the field of ICH as compared with that of other international and regional intergovernmental organizations" and agreed that UNESCO should avoid overlaps with other agencies such as the WIPO whose specific competency lay in economic rights. UNESCO should maintain a cultural approach to the ICH and aim to enhance the awareness of the value of ICH and the need for its protection (UNESCO, 2002a, p. 3; see also Kurin, Chapter 2 in this volume and UNESCO 2002b).

---

[12] International Meeting of Experts: Intangible Cultural Heritage: Priority Domains for an International Convention, Rio de Janeiro, Brazil, 22–24 January 2002.

[13] UNESCO internal memo, 7 December 2001 (ADG/CLT/Memo/01.116).

The meeting then examined the impact of the "first proclamation of the 19 selected Masterpieces,"[14] the first result of a program entitled "Proclamation of the Masterpieces of the Oral and Intangible Heritage of Humanity" that UNESCO launched in 1998 (Aikawa-Faure, 2009). The experts recommended that a close link should be maintained between the Proclamation program and the drafting of the future Convention. They then underscored the need to ensure that the process of elaborating the Convention takes place with the full involvement of all the parties concerned, especially at the grassroots level. In this regard, Antonio Arantes suggested considering ICH as having two dimensions, an internal dimension, notably considering ICH from the perspectives of practitioners, and an external dimension, notably enhancing the value attributed to ICH by establishing a relevant normative instrument for it, such as an international convention. The participants agreed that an international convention should consider in parallel the perspectives of the interest of the communities and those of the obligation of the member states (UNESCO, 2002a).

The meeting then reviewed the question of terminology on the basis of a paper entitled "Terminology in the Field of the ICH" presented by Seitel. In it, he suggested that the scope of the term "Intangible Cultural Heritage" could be defined on two axes: (i) the different communities in which the ICH has been practiced, such as indigenous, ethnic, religious, etc.; and (ii) the scope of human activity within a society, such as traditional knowledge and practices. The participants unanimously agreed with Seitel, who reiterated that local agencies and NGOs should be granted a right of consultation in the drafting of the new Convention. The Rio meeting suggested that UNESCO should convene a restricted drafting group and an expert meeting to review questions of terminology in order to establish a brief operational glossary and develop an ethical framework for the safeguarding of the ICH. The Rio meeting thus endorsed politically and substantively the fundamental framework of the future Convention and designed a road map for its development.

Following the Rio expert meeting, UNESCO organized in Paris the first "select drafting group on the first draft of an international convention for

---

[14] "Impacts of the First Proclamation of the 19 Masterpieces proclaimed as the Oral and Intangible Heritage of Humanity—Critical Analysis" (working document at the Rio meeting, RIO/ITH/2002/ WD/7). This document reflected the results of a survey conducted by UNESCO in countries where ICH elements had been proclaimed.

Intangible Cultural Heritage" in March 2002. This meeting was the first step to preparing the Convention specifically from a legal perspective. A group of legal experts examined the preliminary draft of the Convention drafted by the chair, Bedjaoui, and endorsed the significance of the involvement of communities in all stages of the safeguarding of the ICH. The "First Preliminary Draft of an International Convention for the Intangible Cultural Heritage" drafted by the group included this principle in Chapter III as follows: "that the Intangible Cultural Heritage be fundamentally safeguarded through creativity and enactment by the agents of the communities that produce and maintain it."[15] Moreover, under the Chapter IV relating to the General Provision, it is mentioned that ". . . these processes provide living communities with a sense of continuity with previous generations and are important to cultural identity, including the safeguarding of cultural diversity and the creativity of humanity."[16] In Article 3: "Prerogatives of the States," it is also mentioned that "it is for each State to ensure the substantial and active participation of the practicing [practitioner] communities concerned" (UNESCO, 2002c).

As a follow-up to the recommendation of the Rio meeting, an expert meeting was held to establish a glossary for ICH in June 2002 (by the Netherlands National Commission for UNESCO). The term "community" was defined there as "people who share a self-ascribed sense of connectedness. This may be manifested, for example, in a feeling of identity or in common behavior, as well as in activities and territory. Individuals can belong to more than one community" (Zanten, 2002, p. 1; see also van Zanten, Chapter 4 in this volume).

The second "select drafting group on the first draft of an international convention for the ICH," held in June 2002 (UNESCO, 2002d), included the principle of the "association of the civil society and local communities in the process of the safeguarding of Intangible Cultural Heritage" as one of the fundamental principles of the future Convention. A point was raised on how to link the cultural communities to the work of the Intergovernmental Committee to be set up under the Convention, and in response the experts included mention in the text of the preamble of the primordial role of

---

[15] Chapter III. Objectives and Principles, Article 1, paragraph 2, The Basic Principles of the Present Convention, First Preliminary Draft of an International Convention for Intangible Cultural Heritage.

[16] Chapter IV. General Provision, Article 2 definition, paragraph 2, First Preliminary Draft of an International Convention for Intangible cultural Heritage.

communities in the enactment of the ICH, "noting that Intangible Cultural Heritage is fundamentally safeguarded through the continued creativity and enactment of agents of the communities that produce, maintain, and transform it" (UNESCO, 2002d, Annex p. 2).

In September 2002, UNESCO organized the Third Round Table of Ministers of Culture[17] in Istanbul to discuss the theme of "The Intangible Heritage: A Mirror of Cultural Diversity." It presented a paper entitled "Discussion Guidelines," which included a "brief analysis of the concept of Intangible Cultural Heritage," drafted by Arizpe (UNESCO, 2002e). In it, she eloquently described the interrelationship between the ICH and related communities as follows: "for intangible cultural products or expressions to be recognized as heritage there must be a group of individuals that acknowledge them as their common heritage" (UNESCO, 2002e, p. 11).

The culture ministers gathered in Istanbul declared a joint position that connected ICH closely with cultural identity, cultural diversity, creativity, and sustainable development in line with the UNESCO Universal Declaration of Cultural Diversity (2001). They also announced that governments should facilitate the democratic participation of all stakeholders in the safeguarding of ICH, because the safeguarding and transmission of ICH are essentially based on the will and effective intervention of the actors involved. However, they considered with some reservations that "it is appropriate and necessary, in close collaboration with the practitioners and bearers of all expressions of Intangible Cultural Heritage, to consult and involve all the stakeholders, namely the governments, local and regional communities, the scientific community, the educational institutions, the civil society, the public and private sector as well as the media" (UNESCO, 2002e. Referring to the UNESCO 31C Resolution adopted by the UNESCO General Conference, the ministers endorsed the actions of UNESCO by stating that developing "an appropriate international Convention [ . . . ] could be a positive step forward in pursuing our goal . . ." (UNESCO, 2002e).

---

[17] 74 ministers of culture and 36 other State representatives met in Istanbul under the auspices of UNESCO and at the invitation of the Turkish Government, to discuss the safeguarding of the intangible heritage in the light of its importance for cultural diversity.

## Participation of Communities: The Convention and Its Operational Directives

In the text of the ICH Convention, the principle of the "participation of communities and practitioners" is considered in four different ways: first, as an expression of principle in a general sense in the text of the Preamble and two following articles (Article 1b and 2-1); second, as an address to UNESCO member states as an obligation or encouragement for their ICH identification and safeguarding (Article 11 (b), Article 14 (a)-2, and Article 15); third, despite the absence of the words "with the participation of the communities," other articles concern communities and their members (Article 13 (d) (ii), and 21 (b)); and fourth, two articles (8.3 and 8.4) concern the ways in which community members, among others, may participate in the work of the IGC. The proposed inclusion of these references in the text of the Convention had not always been welcomed by some states during the Intergovernmental Meetings of Experts (IGME), and they had been confronted by a number of political obstacles (Blake, 2006).

In order to ensure that the principle was well understood, the Preamble of the Convention and the chapters concerning its purpose and the definition used for the ICH stipulate clearly the central role of the communities and practitioners. In the Preamble, the significant roles of communities, in particular indigenous communities, in the production, safeguarding, maintenance, and recreation of ICH is affirmed. In Article 1b, it is stipulated that one of the purposes of the Convention is "to ensure respect for the Intangible Cultural Heritage of the communities, groups, and individuals concerned." The description of ICH as being that "of the communities, groups, and individuals concerned" means there is a special link between the ICH and local communities (Blake, 2006).

The definition of the ICH given in Article 2-1 of the Convention indicates that it considers as ICH solely those practices, representations, expressions, knowledge, and skills that communities, groups and, in some cases, individuals recognize as part of their cultural heritage. This heritage, transmitted through generations, is constantly recreated by the communities and groups concerned and provides them with a sense of identity and continuity. This definition implies that the Convention considers as ICH elements apt for safeguarding only those that the community or group or individuals concerned recognize as such (Blake, 2006; see also Kurin, Chapter 2 this volume).

As an obligation or encouragement to the States Parties to the Convention, a further four articles referred to the ethical principle of "with the participation of communities and practitioners." Article 11 (b) obliges[18] States Parties to define their ICH elements with the participation of communities, groups, and relevant NGOs. The insertion of this policymaking paragraph into the text was not an easy task, as could be seen at the relevant IGME. For some States such as Vanuatu and Bangladesh, such participation was essential, while for others, such as Australia, Turkey, France, and India, it was argued that such a policy might erode the sovereignty of the states concerned to decide on the safeguarding of the ICH. Finally, it was decided to keep a balance between state-initiated safeguarding on one hand, and safeguarding taking place with community participation on the other (Blake, 2006). Article 14 (a)-2 encourages[19] States to ensure recognition of, respect for, and enhancement of the ICH in society, in particular through "specific educational and training programmes within the communities and groups concerned." This paragraph indicates that community members need to be trained so that they can recognize the value of their ICH and ensure its maintenance and transmission. The entire Article 15 is devoted to encourage States Parties to ensure the "widest possible participation of communities, groups, and, where appropriate, individuals that create, maintain, and transmit such heritage, and to involve them actively in its management." According to Blake, in the initial draft of the Convention discussed during the intergovernmental negotiations, this provision was included in Article 13(d) relating to appropriate legal, technical, administrative, and financial measures that States were encouraged to take, where it would have been enforceable. However, placing the Article in an independent provision meant that its effect was weakened (Blake, 2006).

There are two articles that concern communities without mentioning them as such. In Article 13(d)(ii),[20] States' roles are reduced to guaranteeing that the right of access to the ICH is respected, given that the ICH has a special relationship with a particular cultural community (Blake, 2006). It is

---

[18] The word "Shall" is prescriptive language.
[19] "Shall endeavour to" is non-prescriptive language.
[20] Article 13 on other measures for safeguarding reads
"To ensure the safeguarding, development and promotion of the intangible cultural heritagepresent in its territory, each State Party shall endeavour to: [ ... ]
(d) adopt appropriate legal, technical, administrative and financial measures aimed at:
(ii) ensuring access to the intangible cultural heritage while respecting customary practices governing access to specific aspects of such heritage."

worth mentioning that in the text of Article 13(d) in the "first preliminary draft"[21] of the Convention, reference was made to the "active participation of the relevant cultural communities." But India suggested replacing the phrase by "measures aimed at," which was endorsed by the majority of experts attending the IGME (Blake, 2006). The inclusion of the term "practitioners" together with experts in Article 21 (b)[22] as one of the forms of international assistance to be provided to States Parties under the Convention also demonstrates the recognition of the significant role of practitioners in the safeguarding of the ICH (Blake, 2006).

Article 8 refers to the "working methods of the Committee," and two following paragraphs, Article 8(3)[23] and (8)4,[24] grant concessionary possibilities to it. Article 8(3) provides the Committee with the possibility of establishing a temporary consultative body, while Article (8)4 allows the participation in meetings of "public or private bodies as well as private persons" that could include community/practitioners' representatives.

It is important to note how the Operational Directives for the implementation of the ICH Convention weakened the involvement of communities. Chapter III of the ODs of the Convention addresses "participation in the implementation of the Convention," of which Part 1 refers to the "participation of communities, groups, and where applicable, individuals, as well as experts, centres of expertise and research institutes," and Part 2 refers to "non-governmental organizations and the Convention." It is worth examining here when and how these provisions were drafted, and, notably, how the "experts, centres of expertise, and research institutes" were added to "communities, groups, and where applicable, individuals" as stipulated in the text of the Convention.

---

[21] Drafted by the restricted working group and presented to the first session of the IGME in September 2002 (UNESCO Doc.CLT-2002/CONF.203/3).

[22] Article 21 on forms of international assistance reads
"The assistance granted by the Committee to a State Party shall be governed by the operational directives foreseen in Article 7 and by the agreement referred to in Article 24, and may take the following forms:
(a) Studies concerning various aspects of safeguarding
(b) the provision of experts and practitioners;

[23] Article 21 on forms of international assistance reads
"The assistance granted by the Committee to a State Party shall be governed by the operational directives foreseen in Article 7 and by the agreement referred to in Article 24, and may take the following forms:
(a) Studies concerning various aspects of safeguarding
(b) the provision of experts and practitioners."

[24] Article 8(4) reads that "the Committee may invite to its meetings any public or private bodies, as well as private persons, with recognized competence in the various fields of the intangible cultural heritage, in order to consult them on specific matters."

At the first session of the Intergovernmental Committee in Algiers in 2006, the Committee adopted an outline[25] for the ODs in which "community involvement"[26] was included, in Chapter 2 relating to "safeguarding" among other activities. Chapter 6 of the outline concerning Advisory Organizations contained three paragraphs, which referred to "criteria for the accreditation of NGOs to act in an advisory capacity to the Committee [Article 9]," "procedure for the selection of Advisory Organizations to be proposed to the General Assembly for accreditation [Article 9]," and "function and working methods of the Advisory Organizations [Article 9]."

The Algiers meeting specifically discussed the theme of "advisory assistance to the Committee."[27] During this debate, the Secretariat[28] proposed to create an Umbrella Advisory Body, under which several specialized NGOs would be brought together, to give advice to the IGC such as on reviewing and recommending nominations for inscription and monitoring of the implementation of the Convention. In the same document, the Secretariat also proposed two optional mechanisms allowing community representatives to participate in the work of the IGC: either to create a separate body (rather than a subordinate body) composed of practitioners and tradition-bearers, who would, *inter alia*, give comments on the evaluations and recommendations made by an advisory body, or to include a number of rotating representatives of communities in the Umbrella Advisory Body (UNESCO, 2006a).

These proposals were discussed, with the Latin American countries upholding the view that the mechanism of an Advisory Body would provide opportunities for indigenous people and community representatives to express their views. On advisory assistance to the Committee, India insisted that the NGOs bearing advisory functions should be chosen according to geographical balance, instead of being Euro-centered NGOs that have privileged links with UNESCO. Algeria and Senegal said that centers of expertise and research institutions in developing countries were not necessarily organized as NGOs and advocated that "centers of expertise and research institutions" should be added to NGOs, practitioners, and communities to constitute the advisory mechanism instead. The Committee finally suspended a decision concerning the proposal of the Secretariat, and instead

25 ITH/06/1.COM/CONF.204/Decisions (Algiers session), p.14.
26 Article 2.3 on community involvement [Articles 1, 2.1, 11, 12, 13 (d)(ii) and 15] (ITH/06/1.COM/CONF.204/Decisions, decision 5)
27 ITH/06/1.COM/CONF.204/6.
28 ITH/06/1.COM/CONF.204/6, paragraph 7

invited States Parties to propose, in written form, accreditation criteria for practitioners of intangible cultural heritage, non-governmental organizations, experts and centers of expertise, and requested UNESCO to submit a new proposal based on the written contributions of the States Parties for submission to the subsequent session of the Committee (UNESCO, 2006b).[29]

At the following extraordinary session of the IGC held in Chengdu (May 2006), the UNESCO legal officer[30] advised that Article 9.1 of the Convention relating to the accreditation of advisory organizations implied that examination of the ICH would only be done by NGOs. The Committee decided to consider separately NGOs and those not having NGO status, such as practitioners, experts, and centers of expertise (UNESCO, 2007a). The Committee also established the criteria and modalities for the accreditation of NGOs[31] and requested the Secretariat to submit at its following session a document on the "participation of communities or their representatives, practitioners, experts, centres of expertise and research institutes[32] with recognized competence in the various fields of the intangible cultural heritage in the implementation of the Convention.

At the following session of the IGC held in Tokyo in September 2007, the Secretariat presented a document relating to the involvement of communities or their representatives, practitioners, experts, centers of expertise and research institutes. The document, while simply reaffirming the crucial role that communities play in safeguarding the ICH at the national level, emphasized the importance of their participation, as well as that of experts, centers of expertise, and research institutes in the implementation of the Convention (UNESCO, 2007b).

At the outset of the debate on this point, UNESCO's assistant director-general for culture proposed to withdraw the document, given that it did not reflect the primary principle of the Convention, namely the active participation of communities. Brazil and China also pointed to the insufficiency

---

[29] ITH/07/1.EXT.COM/CONF.207/12 (summary record of the Alger meeting); ITH/06/1.COM/CONF.204/Decisions, Decision 6

[30] The UNESCO legal officer's intervention read that "consequently, the discussion of the Committee should be limited to paragraphs 7 and 8 of the document under consideration, dealing only with accreditation of NGOs, without any mixture with the status of individuals or entities other than NGOs having the possibility to act in an advisory capacity on an ad hoc basis" (ITH/07/2.COM/CONF.208/3, paragraph 225).

[31] ITH/07/1.EXT.COM/CONF.207/Decisions, Decision 10.

[32] Item 8 of the provisional agenda: Participation of communities or their representatives, practitioners, experts, centres of expertise and research institutes (ITH/07/2.COM/CONF.208/8).

of the document presented. The Committee, however, discussed this point and decided to establish a working group to further reflect upon the question of how to involve communities, experts, centers of research, and research institutions. While Senegal and Algeria championed the significant role played by experts and centers of research in safeguarding the ICH, Peru raised a point referring to the draft decision[33], saying that embracing in a single decision two very different groups, namely practitioners, on the one hand, and researchers, on the other, did not reflect the text of the Convention and its reference to the involvement of communities. The Committee finally decided[34] to request the Secretariat to consult States Parties on this point through correspondence and to create a Subsidiary Body that would prepare a document for the following session on possible modalities for the participation of communities or their representatives, practitioners, experts, centers of expertise, and research institutes in the implementation of the Convention.

As members of the Subsidiary Body to the Committee, Algeria (Group V(b)), Belgium (Group I), Japan (Group IV), Peru (Group III), Romania (Group II) and Senegal (Group V (a)) were elected, and Senegal volunteered as chair (UNESCO, 2007b). It should be noted that the draft ODs adopted during the same session of the Committee also encompassed other paragraphs that required the participation of communities. These were: (i) Criterion 4 for inscription on the Urgent Safeguarding List, as well as on the Representative List, which requires the participation of communities for the process of nomination together with their free, prior, and informed consent, and Criterion 5 on "programmes, projects, and activities that best reflected the principles and objectives of the Convention for the purposes of promotion and dissemination"; (ii)"Draft Guidelines for the use of resources," according to which resources could be used to allow private persons such as community members, among others, to participate in the work of the Committee for specific consultations; and (iii) "Draft ODs for international assistance: eligibility and selection criteria," in which the involvement of communities in the implementation of proposed activities was the decisive condition for granting assistance (UNESCO, 2007c).

---

[33] Draft decision in ITH/07/2.COM/CONF.208/8.

[34] ITH/07/2.COM/CONF.208/Decisions 8, of which paragraph 4 reads "reaffirms and emphasizes the crucial role that communities, groups and, where appropriate, individuals play in the safeguarding of the intangible cultural heritage, as well as the importance of their participation and that of experts, centres of expertise and research institutes in the implementation of the Convention."

The Subsidiary Body met three times in Paris, Bucharest, and Vitré (France), and, taking into consideration the comments sent by the States Parties, prepared draft ODs concerning the involvement of communities, groups, and, where applicable, individuals, as well as experts, centers of expertise, and research institutes in the implementation of the Convention.

During the deliberations of the second session of the Subsidiary Body in Bucharest, members were in favor of discussing two categories of actors separately in accordance with the document drafted by the Secretariat[35]. For example, Bulgaria (an observer at the session) presented a text for future discussion in two parts: one entitled: "Modalities for the Participation of Communities or their Representatives and Practitioners" (paragraph 3.1); and the other entitled: "Modalities for the Participation of Experts, Centres of Expertise and Research Institutes" (paragraph 3.2). There was also some discussion on the treatment of NGOs composed of representatives of communities. Finally, the Bucharest session of the Subsidiary Body adopted a text separating the two categories of actors.

Prior to the third meeting of the Subsidiary Body held in Vitré, an expert meeting was convened to hear experts' experiences relating to the involvement of communities in their research. The Subsidiary Body members discussed and adopted a text drafted by the Secretariat reflecting the discussions held during the expert meeting that took place in the morning of the same day[36]. The adopted text treated the two groups of actors in one text, and this was submitted to the Second Extraordinary Session of the IGC in Sofia in 2008. During the debate relating to the draft prepared by the Subsidiary Body[37], Estonia commended it for providing a clear indication on how the research institutions should work with the governments and communities concerned, but regretted that the role and the participation of communities were missing. Brazil and Peru supported the view of Estonia. Conversely, Bulgaria, Romania, and Algeria said that the text reflected fully the participation of communities. Furthermore, China and Turkey proposed to replace the term "involvement" with "participation" (UNESCO, 2008a). The text of Chapter 3.1 of the draft ODs adopted by the Second Extraordinary

---

[35] Report of the Subsidiary Body (ITH/08/2.EXT.COM/CONF.201/INF.4) p.10.
[36] Ibid., p.6, paragraph 33.
[37] ITH/08/3.COM/CONF.203/5, summary record of the second (Sofia) and third (Paris) extraordinary sessions of the Committee, pp. 8–19.

Session of the Committee (held in Sofia) modified the Subsidiary Body's text[38] significantly, with these modifications being outlined below.

The most noticeable modifications attenuated the commitment of the Committee, as well as the States Parties, to the participation of communities in the safeguarding of the ICH. This could be seen in the seventh paragraph relating to "access by communities . . . to the results of research," where the Subsidiary Body version said that "States Parties shall encourage access by communities. . . ." The Sofia version also reduced the States Parties' engagement by saying that "States Parties shall endeavour to facilitate access by communities. . . ." In paragraph 10 relating to regional cooperation, the "involvement of communities" was also replaced in the Sofia version by the "participation of communities," which implies a lesser engagement than "involvement."[39]

The amendment to paragraph 11 also reduced the possibility of community participation. While the Subsidiary Body's text mentioned that "within the limit of available resources, the Committee shall invite communities . . . as well as experts . . . to its sessions in order to create forums for encounters between them and the Committee . . . ," the Sofia version stated that "within the limit of available resources, the Committee may invite communities . . . as well as experts . . . to participate in its meetings in order to sustain an interactive dialogue. . . ."

The text adopted in Sofia was then presented in June 2008 to the 2nd General Assembly of the States Parties to the Convention. During the debate[40] on Article 11(b), which reads "among the safeguarding measures . . . identify and define the various elements of Intangible Cultural Heritage present in its territory, with participation of communities . . . and relevant non-governmental organizations," Saint Lucia opened the discussion on whether to include NGOs, which could be community organizations, in paragraph 3.1 reserved for non-NGOs. The General Assembly then accepted the proposal made by a working group established specifically to reflect on this matter by creating two subchapters to 3.2, as paragraph 3.2.1,

[38] Both the text of paragraph 3.1 of the ODs drafted by the Subsidiary Body and adopted by the Sofia session of the IGC began by a preamble that was removed by the 2nd General Assembly Meeting.

[39] The Sofia version says that "States Parties are encouraged to participate in activities pertaining to regional cooperation including those of Category 2 centres . . . and with the participation of communities . . . as well as experts . . .," whereas the Subsidiary Body version says that "States Parties are encouraged to participate in the activities of Category 2 centres . . . and with the involvement of communities, . . . as well as experts, . . .

[40] ITH/10/3.GA/CONF.201/INF.1.1 (Summary record of the second General Assembly meeting)

"participation of non-governmental organizations at the national level" to cover Article 11(b), and paragraph 3.2.2, "participation of accredited non-governmental organizations," to cover the function of NGOs on the Convention level (UNESCO, 2008b)[41].

Referring to paragraph 82[42] of the document pertaining to the examination of nominations to the Urgent Safeguarding List, China requested the replacement of the term "shall" by "may" in order to reduce the probability of the Committee's consulting experts, centers of expertise, and research institutes (UNESCO, 2008b). The General Assembly approved[43] draft chapter 3.1. of the ODs after some amendments. The major amendments were the amendment "shall" to "may" in the paragraph relating to the examination of nominations for the Urgent Safeguarding List mentioned above, and paragraph 86 pertaining to the possibility of inviting public or private bodies (including centers of expertise) as well as private persons (including communities) to give their views.

The ODs relating to the participation of communities were finally drafted in June 2008 and inserted in paragraph 3.1. This does not address exclusively communities, but instead addresses both communities, groups, and individuals as well as experts, centers of expertise, and research institutes. Among 11 sub-paragraphs, only three (78, 79, and 82) exclusively address communities, groups, and, where applicable, individuals. Sub-paragraph 78 prescribes States Parties to take measures to sensitize communities on the importance and value of their ICH. Sub-paragraph 79, also prescriptive, requires States Parties to undertake capacity-building programs addressed to communities. Sub-paragraph 82, less prescriptive, though still a firm requirement, requests States Parties "to endeavour to facilitate access by communities and groups . . . to results of research carried out among them as well as to foster respect for practices governing access to specific aspects of their ICH in conformity with Article 13d (paragraph 82)." One sub-paragraph addresses solely experts and centers of expertise, "inviting them to establish a directory of experts and centres of expertise" (paragraph 80). The other seven sub-paragraphs address both experts and communities. Thus, the concept embedded in the ICH Convention of "with the participation of

---

[41] *Ibid.*, p. 25.

[42] ITH/08/2.GA/CONF.202/5.

[43] The text approved by the 2nd General Assembly meeting (ITH/08/2.GA/CONF.202/ Resolutions, resolution 2 GA 5) is identical to those appearing in the Operational Directives currently in vigor except for the number of paragraphs and a few words of precision.

communities" was marginalized both at the national level and the international level (as participation in the Committee meetings) in the ODs.

Notwithstanding the fact that, as an intergovernmental organization, UNESCO's sole official interlocutors are member states, the top-down approach demonstrated in the three sub-paragraphs addressing communities, examined above, seems to be in contradiction to what the experts at the Smithsonian Conference and the subsequent Turin and Rio meetings had recommended. Have these provisions been effective in ensuring the participation of communities in the work of safeguarding the ICH at the national level?

As mentioned in the last paragraph of the preamble to the draft Convention (and suppressed by the General Assembly), namely, "taking into account that the present Operational Directives are an important step forward in the reflection process," it thus seems important to take another step forward in the reflection process regarding paragraph 3.1 of the ODs. The IGC might further reflect on the creation of new tools to strengthen the participation of communities either within the framework of the ODs or beyond the ODs, for example. These new tools would give practical guidance to States Parties on how best to implement the principle of community involvement at all stages of the safeguarding of the ICH by providing them with examples of best practices.

There are some promising developments in creating a new chapter in the ODs. "Ethical principles for the safeguarding the ICH,"[44] providing guidelines for States Parties on how to address communities while safeguarding the ICH, were elaborated by the Committee in 2015. An "Overall Results Framework for the Convention for the Safeguarding of the Intangible Cultural Heritage"[45] was also set up in 2018. This serves as a tool to measure the impact of the ICH Convention at national and international levels, and one of its eight thematic areas is the "engagement of communities, groups and individuals as well as other stakeholders." These new tools could be effective in reinforcing appropriately the role of communities in the safeguarding of the ICH, notably the periodic reporting recently adapted in the Overall Results Framework.

[44] https://ich.unesco.org/en/ethics-and-ich-00866
[45] https://ich.unesco.org/en/overall-results-framework-00984

# Conclusion

The participatory approach by communities to the safeguarding of the ICH that emerged at the Washington Conference was developed further as the conceptual framework for the future UNESCO legal instrument at the Turin, Rio, and Istanbul meetings and became the underpinning principle of the ICH Convention. However, in the process of elaborating the Convention's ODs, expected to provide guidance to States Parties on how to implement it at the national level, this approach was progressively weakened.

The question of implementing community participation in the safeguarding of the ICH Convention at the national level is politically complex. As discussed above, many States Parties had reservations about the participatory policy stipulated in the ICH Convention because they thought that such a policy might erode the sovereignty of their decisions. At the very first session of the IGC of the Convention in Algiers in 2006, "communities, groups and individuals" were merged with "experts, centres of expertise, and research institutes." Since then, the possibilities for community participation encompassed in the provisions of the ODs have been gradually reduced at successive sessions of the IGC.

The modalities for community participation in implementing the ICH Convention included in the ODs (79–89), such as "establishing functional and complementary cooperation among communities . . . as well as experts . . . (79)," or to "create a consultation body or a coordination mechanism . . . (80)," under sub-paragraph 3.1, allow governments to take measures in a top-down manner. This raises the question of how to answer Kurin's questions regarding problems resulting from the formalization of the social relations of local agencies, difficulties in the identification of the representatives of a given cultural tradition, difficulties in developing a means of working together of fractional cultural communities, and other political and sociological problems in the safeguarding of the ICH, including even logistical ones (Kurin, 2004; also Chapter 2 in this volume). All of these questions are entrusted to governments to answer under the ICH Convention. Neither UNESCO, as an intergovernmental organization, nor the IGC has direct access to local communities. The IGC receives periodic reports from States Parties to the Convention on its implementation and in answer to five questions that they are required to report on regarding the participation of communities. Given that there is no monitoring system for the ICH Convention, as there is for the World Heritage Convention, this periodic reporting cannot function as an enforcement tool. Even if a monitoring system were to be established, it needs to be external monitoring and not monitoring from within (see Ceribašić, Chapter 5 in this volume).

Nevertheless, Deacon has presented an ambitious policy instrument to facilitate community involvement that could minimize conflict by defining clear channels of communication, providing dispute-resolution mechanisms, clarifying the question of ownership over intangible heritage and providing other sources of income from heritage, taking examples from the European Landscape Convention (2002), and Australia, New Zealand, and South Africa (Deacon, 2004, pp. 43–44).

Another possible way forward in ensuring community participation in the safeguarding of the ICH could be by encouraging governments to "take necessary measures to raise awareness of the communities, groups, and where applicable individuals regarding the importance and the value of their ICH as well as of the Convention" (paragraph 81 of the ICH Convention ODs) and "undertake necessary measures to ensure their capacity building of communities, groups, and where applicable individuals" (paragraph 82 of the ICH Convention ODs), both of which are the sole paragraphs in Part 3.1 addressed directly and exclusively to "communities...experts, [and] centres of expertise."

Empowering communities should be one of the most powerful tools in ensuring an "endogenous" participatory approach to the safeguarding of the ICH. Taking into account the long and meandering relationship between the 2003 Convention and communities, the question remains of how to convince governments to empower communities and groups so that they can take part in the safeguarding of their own ICH.

## References

Aikawa, N. (2007). The conceptual development of UNESCO's Programme on Intangible Cultural Heritage. In J. Blake (Ed.), *Safeguarding intangible cultural heritage: Challenges and approaches* (p. 56). Institute of Art and Law.

Aikawa-Faure, N. (2009). From the Proclamation of Masterpieces to the Convention for the Safeguarding of Intangible Cultural Heritage. In L. Smith and N. Akagawa (Eds.), *Intangible heritage* (pp. 14–20, 33–34). Routledge.

Arizpe, L. (2001). Intangible Cultural Heritage: Perceptions and enactments" (PTT presentation). International Round Table on Intangible Cultural Heritage—Working definitions. Turin, March 2001.

Blake, J. (2001). Draft preliminary study into the advisability of developing a new standard-setting instrument for the Safeguarding of Intangible Cultural Heritage

(Traditional Culture and Folklore. International Round Table on Intangible Cultural Heritage—Working definitions (pp. 79–80). Turin, March 2001.

Blake, J. (2006). Commentary on the UNESCO 2003 Convention on the Safeguarding of the Intangible Cultural Heritage (pp. 29, 31–38, 61, 71–72, 76–77, 94). Institute of Art and Law.

Blake, J. (2019). Further reflections on community involvement in Safeguarding Intangible Cultural Heritage. In L. Smith and N. Akagawa (Eds.), *Safeguarding intangible heritage: Practices and policies* (p. 17). Routledge.

Carneiro da Cunha, C. (2001). The notion of intangible heritage: Towards working definitions. International Round Table on Intangible Cultural Heritage—Working definitions. Turin, March 2001.

Deacon, H., et al. (2004). *The subtle power of intangible heritage: Legal and financial instruments for safeguarding intangible heritage.* HSRC Press.

Francioni, F. (2001). The specificity of intangible heritage as an object of international protection. International Round Table on Intangible Cultural Heritage—Working definitions. Turin, March 2001.

Kurin, R. (2004). Safeguarding intangible cultural heritage in the 2003 UNESCO Convention: A Critical Appraisal. *Museum International, 56*(221–222), 72.

Seitel, P. (Ed.). (2001a). *Safeguarding traditional culture: A global assessment.*: Smithsonian Centre for Folklife and Cultural Studies.

Seitel, P. (2001b). Proposed terminology for intangible cultural heritage: Toward anthropological and folkloristic common sense in a global era. International Round Table on Intangible Cultural Heritage—Working definitions (p. 10). Turin, March 2001.

UNESCO. (2001). *Final report: International Round Table on Intangible Cultural Heritage—Working definitions* (pp. 2–7, 15–19; Appendix III). March 14–17, Turin.

UNESCO. (2002a). *Final report: International Meeting of Experts, Intangible Cultural Heritage: Priority domains for an international convention,* January 22–24 (pp. 3, 11–14). Rio de Janeiro, Brazil.

UNESCO. (2002b). *Final report: An Extraordinary Session of the International Jury for the Proclamation by UNESCO of the Masterpieces of the Oral and Intangible Heritage of Humanity.* Elche (Spain), September 21–23, 2001.

UNESCO. (2002c). *Final report of the First Select Drafting Group on the first draft of an International Convention for Intangible Cultural Heritage.* Paris, March 20–22, 2002.

UNESCO. (2002d). *Final report of the Second Drafting Group on the first draft of an International Convention for Intangible Cultural Heritage.* Paris, June 13–15, 2002

UNESCO. (2002e). IIIrd Round Table of Ministers of Culture "Intangible Cultural Heritage—a Mirror of Cultural Diversity" (Istanbul, 16–17 September 2002): *Discussion guidelines: Part I: Brief analysis of the concept of intangible cultural heritage by Lourdes Arizpe.* Paris, September 2002.

UNESCO. (2006a). Document: *Item 6 of the Provisional Agenda: Advisory Assistance to the Committee,* ITH/06/1.COM/CONF.204/6, 2–3.

UNESCO. (2006b). ITH/06/1.COM/CONF.204/Decisions, 15–16.

UNESCO. (2007a). ITH/07/1.EXT.COM/CONF.207/Decisions, Decision 10.

UNESCO. (2007b). ITH/07/2.COM/CONF.208/8, 38–41.

UNESCO. (2007c). ITH/07/2.COM/CONF.208/Decisions 8, Decisions 6, 9, 11 (annex 7), 12.

UNESCO. (2008a). ITH/08/3.COM/CONF.203/5, summary record of the second (Sofia) and third (Paris) extraordinary sessions of the Committee, 8–14.

UNESCO. (2008b). ITH/10/3.GA/CONF.201/INF.1.1 (summary record of the second General Assembly), 22–28.

Zanten, Wim van. (2002). *Glossary of Intangible Cultural Heritage* (results of the International Meeting of Experts on Intangible Cultural Heritage: Establishment of a Glossary, organized by UNESCO and the Dutch National Commission for UNESCO, Paris, June 10–12, 2002, The Hague.

# 4

# Definitions Related to the Safeguarding
# of Living Culture

## Words Matter

*Wim van Zanten (summary; full text available on companion website)*

Discussions in international institutions, including the important June 1999 expert meeting at the Smithsonian Institution frequently referred to in this collection, resulted in the 2003 UNESCO Convention for the Safeguarding of the Intangible Cultural Heritage (ICH; see, for instance, Kurin, Chapter 2, and Aikawa-Faure, Chapter 3, in this volume).[1] This convention is generally seen as a significant step in the process of dealing with cultural heritage. But conventions are constructions of words, and words are tricky things. Academically sound definitions are no guarantee that in practice, safeguarding will be carried out in a proper way. My full chapter, available on the book website, addresses the challenge of defining three important words in the Convention—community, sustainability, and sustainable development—through an examination of the UNESCO process for defining them and their application in a national case in the Netherlands and an Indigenous case in Indonesia.

In my view, the 2003 ICH Convention is a valuable correction of the 1972 World Heritage Convention, which omitted the culture of oral traditions. That omission, reflecting an ethnocentric viewpoint, was corrected with the 2003 Convention, and with great support of nation-states in Asia, Africa, and South America. The difference between the 1972 and 2003 Conventions becomes even clearer when we look at the different terminologies used. These terminologies reflect different approaches to safeguarding heritage.

---

[1] This is a brief summary of the chapter; the full text appears on the companion website, www.oup.com/us/musiccommunitiessustainability.

Wim van Zanten, *Definitions Related to the Safeguarding of Living Culture* In: *Music, Communities, Sustainability.*
Edited by: Huib Schippers and Anthony Seeger, Oxford University Press. © Oxford University Press 2022.
DOI: 10.1093/oso/9780197609101.003.0004

In the 1972 Convention, the "protection" was mainly aimed at the products of human culture: monuments, buildings, and sites of "outstanding universal value from the point of view of history, art or science." In contrast, the 2003 Convention was aimed at safeguarding *processes* that were valued positively by communities and by supporting the idea that "culture can only have continuity if people enjoy the conditions to produce and re-create it" (van Zanten, 2004, p. 37). Further, the 2003 Convention requires States Parties to cooperate with "communities, groups and relevant nongovernmental organizations" when safeguarding ICH (article 11(b)).

One could say that the text of the 2003 Convention was more "anthropological" and less "legalistic" about heritage. This shift to a more "anthropological text" resulted in critical remarks from legal experts that the terminology was not clear enough. As someone closely connected to the construction of the Glossary for the Convention, and as editor of the final text, initially I felt that the absence of more definitions—in the convention text itself or as an Annex—was not a serious problem, as the definitions in the Glossary should be considered as a "work in progress" (van Zanten, 2004, p. 36). However, soon afterward, I started to regret this omission. Many participants in the discussions at UNESCO meetings had different views on what, for instance, concepts of "community" or "oral expression" meant in the more anthropological context of the convention.

In the Glossary (2002), the definition of "community" is given as: "People who share a self-ascribed sense of connectedness. This may be manifested, for example, in a feeling of identity or in common behaviour, as well as in activities and territory. Individuals can belong to more than one community." In the discussions leading to this definition, the participants to this expert meeting for making a Glossary noted that "[c]ulture is now looked at as a site of contestation and no longer of homogeneous agreement between all people in a community; it is continuously re-created by people" (van Zanten, 2004, p. 37). The case study of the Dutch Sinterklaas illustrates how nations are not always communities of shared opinions about ICH.

The concept of "sustainability" frequently appears in UNESCO documents since it was defined by the Brundtland Commission of the United Nations in 1987. However, the word "sustainability" was not used at all, and "sustainable" was only used twice in the text of the 2003 Convention. The Glossary (2002) contains a definition for "sustainability" that was based on the one given by the Brundtland Commission: "Meeting the needs of the present without compromising the ability of future generations to meet their own needs."

In contrast to the 2003 Convention text, the UNESCO ICH-Operational Directives (2018) of the 2003 Convention devote many pages to the concept of "sustainability." Chapter VI is entirely about "Safeguarding ICH and sustainable development at the national level" (paragraphs 170–197; about one-fourth of the pages of the Operational Directives). In this chapter the three main dimensions, with the sub-dimensions of "sustainability" (social, economic, environmental), are discussed, but also "ICH and peace." Sustaining nature is not necessarily the same as sustaining ICH.

"Sustainable development" for ICH is often equated with tourism. In my opinion, the balance between safeguarding ICH and financial gain has been a serious problem in the 2003 Convention for a long time. In my second example, I discuss the question of sustainable development and cultural tourism for the small Indigenous group of the Baduy in western Java. The Baduy want to live a simple ascetic life, according to rules of their ancestors. Since about 2000, Indonesian authorities have advertised the Baduy village for "ethnic tourism" or "cultural tourism." That very much influenced the lives of the 12,000 Baduy. Not all Baduy reacted in the same way to this governmental promotion of the tourist industry. Some of them were interested in this cultural tourism because it supplied them with some additional income. Others were very much against tourism, because too many visitors would influence the daily life of the Baduy in a negative way (van Zanten, 2021, pp. 44–55, 272–281.) The 2020–2022 pandemic has changed this profoundly; and it is too early to gauge the long-term effects.

Proper definitions are necessary for making us understand where we want to go. In the 2003 UNESCO Convention, the reports of the Intergovernmental Committee and its Subsidiary and Consultative Bodies are important sources for understanding the implementations of the more abstract texts. This "third source of guidance" should be studied carefully, along with the Convention text and the Operational Directives, when we want to understand the (fairly fast) developments in the 2003 Convention properly.

## References

Zanten, Wim van. (2004). Constructing new terminology for intangible cultural heritage. *Museum International, 221–222*, 36–44.

Zanten, Wim van. (2021). *Music of the Baduy people of western Java: Singing is a medicine.* [Verhandelingen series KITLV no 313; including audiovisual examples]. Brill Open Access. doi: 10.1163/9789004444478.

# 5

# Reclaiming Community Agency in Managing Intangible Cultural Heritage

## Paperwork, People, and the Potential of the Public Voice

*Naila Ceribašić*

This chapter aims to trace community agency as a prerequisite for the sustainability of intangible cultural heritage, and one of the pillars of the UNESCO Convention for the Safeguarding of the Intangible Cultural Heritage (ICH). Introduced at the conference held at the Smithsonian Institution in 1999, community agency has remained the subject of countless debates at all levels and in all aspects of the Convention's implementation. What follows is first and foremost a witness paper, based on my experience of representing the International Council for Traditional Music at the Convention. From one side, I shall examine how the centrality of community participation—its "agency"—has been addressed in the main statutory and relevant extra-statutory documents, also paying attention to on-topic debates in the process of the adoption of these documents (see also Kurin, Chapter 2, and Aikawa-Faure, Chapter 3, in this volume). From the other side, different understandings of community and its agency have vividly come to the fore in the discussions on international inscriptions of ICH elements, notably in cases of the Intergovernmental Committee for the Safeguarding of the Intangible Cultural Heritage's overturn of unfavorable recommendations by the Evaluation Body.

The majority of such cases indicate that communities concerned, after all, may not be limited to culture bearers and their immediate local communities, but encompass a much broader scope of stakeholders involved in safeguarding. The subject is also hotly debated on local, on-site levels (again, more often than not provoked by inscriptions coming back to communities of grassroots culture bearers), especially in terms of who is included and who is excluded from the recognition, and who is entitled to decide on that and other components, such as the nature, scale, and scope of the element, the

Naila Ceribašić, *Reclaiming Community Agency in Managing Intangible Cultural Heritage* In: *Music, Communities, Sustainability*. Edited by: Huib Schippers and Anthony Seeger, Oxford University Press. © Oxford University Press 2022.
DOI: 10.1093/oso/9780197609101.003.0005

forms and manner of its safeguarding, its funding, its promotion and representation in public, etc. Based on my experience, ranging from very local to international levels, I can hardly recall cases of implementation under the 2003 Convention where culture bearers and their communities were truly empowered to have a decisive influence on the nature, representation, and actions relating to their ICH.

Related to that is the issue that I will refer to as "paperwork"—ideas, principles, directives, criteria, reports, statements, etc., that exist in document form, contributing to an exponentially growing library, while how they relate to, reflect, or affect the dynamics on the ground is more often than not unclear. The system of international inscriptions is symptomatic for the overall program in this regard, too, even more so as it relies on a strict rule that examination and the subsequent decision to inscribe or not to inscribe pertain exclusively to the adequacy of information presented in the nomination file, and not to the element itself. The debate leading to the inscription of reggae music in 2018 provides a very illustrative example of the opposition between ICH as an insufficiently elaborated written text versus ICH as a complex living tradition.

The central questions today are not far from those posed in 1999. The questions of how to effectuate community agency, and concomitantly how to mitigate paperwork treatment of ICH, are still on the table. Instead of taking over the model of on-site monitoring by independent expert organizations that is used in the sister World Heritage (WH) Convention, it seems more appropriate to open the Convention to correspondence from the public, as it is called, i.e., to devise an inclusive mechanism that would allow, or even encourage, bearers of ICH and their communities, various other stakeholders, and public society at large to take part in (text-based) debates on safeguarding ICH under the 2003 Convention, especially as regards monitoring of elements included in the lists, registers, and inventories on national and international levels. This could help to mitigate multiple discrepancies in the operation of the Convention, and thus actually strengthen the sustainability of ICH.

## Community Agency as a Guiding Principle

Apart from the question of intellectual property rights, which was initiated by Bolivia in the early 1970s, and the question of processual and intangible aspects of heritage, which was put forward by several African and East Asian countries, in particular Japan, the third key idea in the genealogy of the Convention, the idea of community agency, was introduced at a conference held in cooperation with the Smithsonian Institution and UNESCO in Washington, DC, in 1999 (see also Kurin, Chapter 2, and Aikawa-Faure, Chapter 3, in this volume). Based on an analysis of the publications from that conference (Seitel, 2001), I have described elsewhere a long and extensive process of consultations that preceded the conference, as well as discussions and negotiations at the conference regarding the issue of community participation and agency versus top-down administrative and expert authority (Ceribašić, 2017, pp. 157–168). For this occasion, suffice it to say that final recommendations to States Parties and UNESCO, as they ought to be respective of different perspectives, operated on the terrain of shared authority between communities and other actors of safeguarding, while arguing for the inclusion of communities in various aspects of safeguarding (cf. Seitel, 2001, pp. 302–306). Nevertheless, it was a crucial step forward in relation to the initial 1989 *Recommendation on the Safeguarding of Traditional Culture and Folklore*, which was based on authoritative expert knowledge, without recognizing the role of communities, not to mention advocating their agency.

The importance of communities and community participation is integrated in several articles of the Convention. Most importantly, ICH is defined from a community perspective, namely as phenomena "that communities, groups and, in some cases, individuals recognize as part of their cultural heritage" (Art. 2). The remaining stipulations are rather ambiguous in this regard, however. Thus, it is the role of States Parties to "identify and define the various elements of the intangible cultural heritage present in its territory, with the participation of communities, groups and relevant non-governmental organizations" (Art. 11.b), which no doubt deliberately leaves room for various interpretations regarding who is the main force in the identification and definition of ICH: communities (following Art. 2) or States Parties (as appears to be more likely according to Art. 11.b). Similarly, in the article dedicated to the "participation of communities, groups and individuals," it is stated that "each State Party shall endeavour to ensure the widest possible participation of communities, groups and, where appropriate, individuals that create, maintain and transmit such heritage, and to involve them actively in its management" (Art. 15). If each State Party "shall endeavour to ensure" (instead of "shall ensure"), it means that the widest possible participation of communities is strongly recommended, yet not compulsory.

Another possible interpretation is that the mentioned endeavor relates to the "widest possible participation," implying that some degree of community participation is compulsory.

A clause from the Preamble—"*Recognizing* that communities, in particular indigenous communities, groups and, in some cases, individuals, play an important role in the production, safeguarding, maintenance and recreation of the intangible cultural heritage"—brings three additional nuances. First, it is important to notice that communities play only "an important" role, implying that various other stakeholders outside of communities also can play important roles, which is, again, semantically closer to Articles Art. 11.b and 15 than to Art. 2. Second, it is worth noticing that management is lacking in the formulation, which implies that communities may (as explicitly stipulated in Art. 15) but also may not participate in the management of their ICH (as implied by this statement from the Preamble). Third, the mentioning of indigenous communities is significant. As one can learn from the report of the "Third Session of the Intergovernmental Meeting of Experts on the Preliminary Draft Convention for the Safeguarding of the Intangible Cultural Heritage" (document CLT-2003/CONF.206/4), this happened thanks to other international instruments (conventions and similar legally binding documents) that explicitly include indigenous communities. Otherwise, the opponents of the inclusion would probably have prevailed.

The issue of "communities, groups and, if applicable, individuals" and their "widest possible participation" recurs over and over again in all debates and decisions of the Intergovernmental Committee (composed of 24 States Parties, obeying the principles of equitable geographical representation and rotation) and the General Assembly of the States Parties to the Convention, which are the governing organs of the Convention, and in the documents they produce—in the Operational Directives (ODs), as the most important statutory document derived from the Convention and its implementation (first adopted in 2008 and periodically revised since then), followed by the Ethical Principles for Safeguarding ICH (adopted in 2015), and the Overall Results Framework for the Convention (adopted in 2018), as well as in lower-ranked documents such as the forms for nominations to the two lists, proposals for the register of good safeguarding practices and requests for international assistance, the Aide-mémoires for completing nominations and requests (developed in 2014–2015), the forms for periodic reporting, etc.

The Aide-mémoires incorporate "all lessons learnt, observations and recommendations" formulated through the years by the evaluation bodies and the Committee, with the purpose of "assist submitting States to benefit from the experience accumulated by the Convention [ . . . ] in previous inscription cycles," i.e., to assist them "in elaborating complete files" (para. 1 and 2 in the Aide-mémoires). As such, they are the most specific in the elaboration of community participation, suggesting actually what I call "community agency," that is, a profound participation of culture bearers and their communities in all aspects of heritage identification, safeguarding, and management.

Other instances of more specific elaboration of communities and their participation in the statutory documents were, more often than not, adopted thanks to higher-level and/or already existing stipulations. Such was the case with directives concerning the contribution of safeguarding ICH to sustainable development, which invite States Parties "to ensure that their safeguarding plans and programmes are fully inclusive of all sectors and strata of society, including indigenous peoples, migrants, immigrants and refugees, people of different ages and genders, persons with disabilities and members of vulnerable groups, in conformity with Article 11 of the Convention" (ODs 2018: para. 174; cf. also para. 194, 197). Of ultimate importance for the endorsement of these directives (see Decision 10.COM 14.a, approved at GA in 2016 by Resolution 6.GA 7) was the 2030 Agenda for Sustainable Development of the parent organization—the United Nations. Otherwise, judging from the discussion leading to the adoption of these directives, the subject, language, and meaning of these stipulations would hardly find their place in the ODs.[1]

The emphasis given to gender aspects of ICH and its safeguarding, which was introduced in 2013, had a similar genealogy. In that case, the recommendations of UNESCO's Internal Oversight Service were instrumental, based on the findings of its evaluation and audit of the Convention (8.COM 5.c, annex I–II). The recommendations were the subject of serious, long, and at times heated discussions at 8.COM; nevertheless, they were finally largely endorsed, primarily thanks to the authority of the Service as

[1] The recordings (audio, video, or both) of complete COM (sessions of the Intergovernmental Committee for the Safeguarding of the Intangible Cultural Heritage) and GA (sessions of the General Assembly of the States Parties to the Convention) are available on ICH UNESCO website under the menu of "events." The numbers in front of the abbreviation "COM" indicate to which session the quotation refers. This particular discussion is available at https://ich.unesco.org/en/10com (item 14.a) and https://ich.unesco.org/en/6.ga (item 7).

an independent expert body of UNESCO, i.e., "an independent consoli-dated oversight mechanism that covers internal audit, evaluation, investi-gation and other management support to strengthen the functioning of the Organization" (https://en.unesco.org/about-us/ios). Consequently, the role of gender and the principle of gender equality were integrated into the ODs (in the chapters on raising awareness, reporting, and sustainable develop-ment) and from there into the nominations and periodic reports, as well as in the two most recent statutory documents—the Ethical Principles and the Overall Results Framework.

## Paperwork versus On-site Dynamics

It is easy to argue that communities are too diverse and too complex to be specified in operationally binding documents, or to define the nature of their agency. A counter-narrative, however, could be that the non-specificity allows for stretching the concept beyond its recognizability.[2] Indeed, taking again the two international lists as significant domains of the Convention's implementation, there are cases of inscriptions where community is equated, for instance, with an entire nation or a total population, and/or where com-munity means all possible actors involved in safeguarding, away from and unrelated to bearers, custodians, and practitioners of the ICH in question. A case from the 2015 cycle of inscriptions can serve as an illustration re-garding "community participation and consent in the nomination process," which is one of five inscription criteria. According to the examination of the Evaluation Body and the decision of the Committee, "additional information is required to demonstrate a coherence between assertions and evidence, in particular since families of [bearers of the element] and non-governmental organizations that figure prominently throughout the file did not consent to the nomination, while those offering consent are little mentioned elsewhere; in addition, one of only three letters of consent refers to an element with a broader scope" (Draft decision and Decision 10.COM 10.b.34). On the other hand, to provide an opposite example, one nomination was commended by the Body and the Committee as "exemplary," among other reasons, because it "clearly demonstrates a very wide participation of communities, groups and

---

[2] For more on the process of defining community in the early days of the Convention see Van Zanten's Chapter 4 in this volume.

individuals concerned throughout a long, distinctly collaborative, gradually expanding, coordinated and demanding process of nomination; numerous representatives of the general population, relevant associations and local institutions provided a broad spectrum of attestations to their free, prior and informed consent to the nomination" (Draft decision and Decision 10.COM 10.b.3).

Such assessments are not necessarily in tune with actualities of communities and their agency on the ground. What is written—not only in nominations and their examinations, but also in the complete library of documents produced for and by actors involved in the program of safeguarding ICH under the 2003 Convention—may or may not reflect the actualities; likewise, it may or may not impact the actualities. There are three ways to learn more about on-site dynamics of elements and communities involved in the ICH program: through periodic reporting, from scholarly studies, and, up to now only potentially, through more direct engagement of communities and public society in text-based deliberations on a national and, especially, an international scale. Up to now, the periodic reports have not proved particularly useful. There is no specific mechanism for their assessment (such as the examination conducted by the Evaluation Body in the case of nominations), so whatever is reported by the States Parties is taken as acceptable, and even received with gratitude, because not a negligible number of States Parties simply do not respond to the obligation to periodically submit their reports as prescribed by the ODs. For the same reason, the requirement of the widest possible participation of communities, groups, and, if applicable, individuals concerned is much easier to neglect in the periodic reports than in the nomination files. As explained by the Secretariat at 13.COM, "[t]he periodic reporting mechanism encourages community involvement but remains state-driven" (agenda item 13.COM 9, document ITH/18/13.COM/9, para. 6). The Overall Results Framework and the introduction of regional reporting (starting with a regional report from Latin America and the Caribbean in 2020–2021) ought to overcome the weakness of the reporting mechanism in the years to come.

As for the scholarly studies dealing with on-site dynamics of ICH, the major shortage, similarly, is in the lack of a specific mechanism—apart from the mere fact of their public availability—that would bring their results (no matter how relevant they might be) to the attention of the Committee and the Assembly as decision-making organs (even though the national delegations that compose these two organs usually do include some ICH scholars), thus helping them to reduce the gap between textualities and actualities, and from there to intervene if needed in order to improve the program as regards the safeguarding of specific elements or in more general terms, for instance concerning the implementation of community agency. Taking into account that scholarship and scholarly expertise have been continuously (since the beginning of the program, from the 1999 Washington conference onward) pushed toward the margin in order to create room for communities and their agency, it is not likely that this would significantly change.[3] Therefore, the greatest potential is contained in the third option, to which I shall return below.

The system of international inscriptions is a paradigmatic arena demonstrating another problematic aspect of textuality versus actuality of ICH: the process from the submission of nominations to the moment of their inscription pertains strictly to files, but with the act of inscribing, the file automatically becomes (i.e., returns to being) an element, a living practice recognized by the mechanism of inscription. The Evaluation Body, composed of six individual experts and six accredited non-governmental organizations (NGOs) with "proven competence, expertise and experience in safeguarding" ICH (ODs 2018, para. 91.a), has no mandate to resolve possible mistranslations from a practice to its textual representation. Its task is to strictly and minutely assess information presented in the files in reference to inscription criteria. At the same time, the Committee members, generally speaking, have always endeavored to inscribe as many elements of ICH as possible. Although they, like the Evaluation Body, have to stick to the inscription criteria, as decision-makers they are freer in correcting possible misunderstandings or mistranslations, relying on the "spirit" of the Convention in addition to its "letter," as has been repeatedly underlined in the Committee's discussions. Procedurally speaking, one or more members of the Committee may invite the submitting state to clarify information that the Body did not find sufficient, and on that basis, if the clarification is satisfactory, the Committee is authorized to change an unfavorable recommendation into a positive decision. Although the tension between the recommendations of the Body and the decisions of the Committee—in terms of unfavorable recommendations turned ultimately into decisions to inscribe—has been present since the beginning of the program, it reached its dramatic peak at the session held in

---

[3] Since 2019, UNESCO's Secretariat on its website hosts an online database of research relating to the Convention—the 2003 Convention Research Bibliography (https://ich.unesco.org/en/2003-convention-and-research-00945), which started to be created in 2012. However, I cannot recall any instance where any of the participants at statutory meetings would refer to any of these publications.

2016. This turning point and the search for new solutions that followed deserve broader explanation.

On one hand, it is completely justified to concentrate exclusively on the information presented in the file. The rule was devised in order to prevent arbitrariness and possible biases, to treat all files in an equal manner, and thus to keep the credibility of the procedure leading to inscriptions (and more broadly speaking, the credibility of the Convention). At the same time, one also has to bear in mind that the Evaluation Body has to have the ability to read and translate the written text in relation to the actuality it stands for. Such an ability is what, after all, makes them experts in the field, and qualifies them to serve in the Body. On the other hand, the strict concentration on the information provided in the file created room for discrepancies between the state of affairs as described in the file and as lived on the ground. Elements, communities, and safeguarding practices that exist on the ground in compliance with inscription criteria may not be presented adequately in the nomination file. The opposite, unfortunately, can also happen. Up to 2015, it was believed that these two sides—actuality versus textuality—could be brought closer through further and further elaboration of the five inscription criteria, especially by insisting on *evidence* instead of mere assertions in the nomination files, including evidence of community participation and consent in the nomination process. The creation of Aide-mémoires represents a remarkable outcome in this direction. Since 11th Session of the Intergovernmental Committee for the Safeguarding of the Intangible Cultural Heritage (11. COM), held in Addis Ababa in 2016, however, coincided with the changes of key personnel in the Secretariat of the Convention, as well as changes in the composition of the Committee and the Body, the process has moved in the opposite direction, i.e., toward a more permissive approach regarding compliance to inscription criteria. At that session, the Committee overturned more than 80 percent of unfavorable draft decisions. After it had done so, being aware that such a high rate of overturning represented a threat to its credibility, it decided to "establish an informal ad hoc working group [ . . . ] to examine the issues related to the consultation and dialogue between the Evaluation Body and the submitting States," and requested the Secretariat to "propose a procedure [ . . . ] which would include an intermediary step in the evaluation of files, thus allowing submitting States to respond to preliminary recommendations that the Evaluation Body would have addressed beforehand to the Secretariat" (Decision 11.COM 10, para. 79–80).

It is hard to draw unambiguous and general conclusions about the nature of this shift. In some cases, it indeed seems to be a matter of strengthening "an appropriate dialogue mechanism," as interpreted by the Committee at its subsequent sessions (cf. document attached to agenda item 13.COM 16, Annex, para. 11; Decision 14.COM 14, para. 16); yet in other cases it might be closer to an "increased politicization in the Committee," as some States Parties have argued (cf. document 13.COM 16, Annex, para. 10). At the time of writing this chapter, a new procedure has been defined—the General Assembly in 2020 endorsed "an additional intermediary dialogue process in the nomination cycle," which is "initiated when the Evaluation Body considers that a short question and answer process with the submitting State(s), conducted in writing through the Secretariat, could influence the result of its evaluation" (Resolution 8.GA 10, para. 2, and Annex, para. 55 in the ODs 2020).

In parallel, the Evaluation Body, on its own, also has endorsed a more permissive approach, judging from the fact that in 2017 it recommended for inscription more than 80 percent of submissions (including cases where it proposed both favorable and unfavorable options, which were taken by the Committee, expectedly, as favorable), in contrast to around 50 percent in previous cycles. The atmosphere at the session in 2017 was very positive concerning such a development. Among a small chorus of dissenting voices was the ICH NGO Forum, which expressed a "concern for a development that weakens the credibility of the ICH Convention as well as the very relevance of the Evaluation Body," while also hoping that the advisory role of the Body "could eventually evolve from a judging role towards a more assisting one."[4]

In the context of this new direction, especially interesting were two music-related nominations presented at 13.COM, held in 2018. Once again, the greatest part of the session was dedicated to the examination of nominations, and within that to those which received unfavorable recommendations from the Evaluation Body. The peak in the debates around inscriptions happened in relation to the Argentinean nomination of *chamamé* and the Jamaican nomination of reggae music. The file on *chamamé* was, according to the Evaluation Body, insufficiently elaborated on three out of five inscription criteria. The recommendation was endorsed by the Committee, but some of its members insisted on devising a special decision that this referred nomination should be examined at the next session instead of in two years, as

---

[4] ICH NGO Forum Statement 12.COM—Jeju, item 7, available at http://www.ichngoforum.org/wp-content/uploads/2017/12/12-COM-NGO-Statement-Jeju-ENG.pdf

prescribed in the ODs. In the end, after a long first round of debate, which concluded with the request to the Secretariat to examine and propose a possible solution on an exceptional basis, followed by the second round two days later and the recommendation of a legal advisor, this did not happen.[5]

Another paradigmatic example was the nomination of Jamaican reggae which, according to the Body, did not satisfy two out or five inscription criteria—regarding the contribution of inscription to ensuring visibility and awareness of the significance of ICH in general, and to encouraging dialogue that respects cultural diversity (criterion R.2), and regarding the inclusion of the element in an inventory in conformity with Articles 11.b (participation of communities, groups, and relevant NGOs in the inventorying) and 12.1 of the Convention (regular updating of the inventory) (criterion R.5). Nevertheless, the file was eventually inscribed. Apart from clarifications by the Jamaican delegation, especially as regards R.2, arguments provided by a series of Committee members proved decisive.

It started with a representative of Cuba, who argued that reggae is itself a vehicle for dialogue toward peace, understanding, and tolerance, and a symbol of unity and diversity that contributes to social inclusion, which is today the essential path toward sustainable development. A Palestinian representative followed, expressing his surprise that such an element came so late, instead of being inscribed years ago. For him, there is no doubt that reggae will contribute to raising awareness and visibility of ICH in general, of the Convention, and of UNESCO itself, because reggae's visibility is—as he said—much greater than the visibility of UNESCO. This last point received applause from (a part of) the auditorium. A series of Committee members continued with similar and additional arguments, pertaining to the merits of reggae, and very rarely addressing the file itself (with Austria, Azerbaijan, and China being the most articulated exceptions). Some identified themselves personally as aficionados of reggae (e.g., Senegalese and Japanese representatives), and some stressed the importance of reggae as a catalyst in their own society (e.g., the Polish representative explained that reggae was a source of inspiration for the Solidarity movement, and the Senegalese representative

[5] The address of the Argentinean delegation immediately before and then after the decision to refer the file in a manner defined in the ODs is worth listening to, especially as regards its arguments against bureaucratic and unjust procedures. The recording is available at https://ich.unesco.org/en/13com, agenda item 10.b (afternoon session on November 30, 2018), while the summary records presented at the next session of the Committee are available at https://ich.unesco.org/en/14com (document attached to agenda item 14.COM 4, para. 1045, 1046, 1073).

pointed out links between reggae and Africans, referring also to Bob Marley's "One Love" and "Africa Unite").

As for the comments on the process of evaluation, several members complained that criterion R.2 is generally unclear (in the words of the Zambian representative, a number of submitting states still struggle to understand its meaning). Even though this criterion is extensively explained in the respective Aide-mémoire, this source was not mentioned at all, which implies that its time of meticulously elaborated criteria has obviously passed. Besides, several members reiterated the importance of dialogue between the State Party and the Evaluation Body before the Committee session, which, as the representative of Philippines said, would prevent a waste of precious time at the session. In the same vein, for her it was self-evident that the inscription of reggae would have a positive impact on the recognition of ICH as a whole, even though, in her words, this was not spelled out in black and white in the nomination dossier. Speaking of the evaluation process, Poland also raised an interesting point, similarly to Argentina regarding their nomination—that the Committee should not expect bearers to be experts on ICH terminology, thus referring indirectly to the use of so-called inappropriate vocabulary in the nomination file, and on the other side to community participation in all aspects ICH program, including the writing of nomination files.

This discussion was followed by clarifications that Jamaican representatives were asked to provide, and explanations by the chair of the Evaluation Body, requested in particular by the Netherlands. Then the chair of the session turned to the adoption of the amended draft decision that was proposed by Cuba and Palestine. A minute or so afterward, it was duly adopted (Decision 13.COM 10.b.18), as declared by the chair, while the debate had lasted for an hour.[6] At the end, after words of thanks on behalf of Jamaica, a number of people in the auditorium joined in dancing and singing Marley's "One Love," and an even greater number of attendees used their cameras to document the moment. Indeed, this was definitely the most memorable moment of the session, and the inscription gained great attention in the media worldwide, thus indeed helping the visibility of ICH in general, and fulfilling a part of criterion R.2.

The example of the inscription of reggae is highly illustrative for the discrepancy between the "letter of the Convention," integrated into the

---

[6] The discussion is available at https://ich.unesco.org/en/13com (item 10.b, morning session on November 29, 2018), and https://www.youtube.com/watch?time_continue=13&v=NI-dwx061cY. Its summary record is available at https://ich.unesco.org/en/14com, agenda item 4.

Convention itself and all ensuing directives, rules, criteria, reports, etc. (in this particular case, specifically the "letter" of inscription criteria), versus the "spirit of the Convention" that the Committee, as the governing organ of the Convention, is allowed to pursue even if it contradicts the letter. In other words, since the nomination file did not provide sufficient evidence of alignment of reggae music to inscription criteria, yet the file—that is, reggae—was nevertheless inscribed, the case is illustrative of the loss in translation from actualities into textualities, that is, of the tension between ICH as a complex living tradition versus ICH as an insufficiently elaborated written text.

But the example is illustrative in yet another way. Namely, if we ask ourselves who makes the reggae community, watching the process of its inscription on the Representative List, we may conclude that it is a community, even if a transient community, composed primarily of international diplomats, politicians, and decision-makers. We may also conclude that it is a community of aficionados of the late Bob Marley, an unquestionable star of the music industry on a global scale. This is not to say that it is a "fake" community that pushed a "fake" inscription; I would be more inclined to claim the opposite. But it is to say that the concept of community, not to mention community agency, is an ineffable concept, and that grassroots bearers of ICH and their immediate local communities are quite often overlooked in the system. In other words, the example of the inscription of reggae clearly demonstrates the problem of textualities versus actualities, and/or of paperwork versus on-site dynamics. If and how it can be overcome remain a big conundrum. A promising and attainable way out, to my mind, would be to open the Convention to so-called correspondence from the public.

## Potential of the Public and ICH NGOs

Ever since the 1999 Washington conference, various stakeholders, aside from bearing communities, have deliberated how to effectuate community agency, and concomitantly how to mitigate paperwork treatment of ICH, without losing credibility based on minutely defined criteria and procedures. In 2012, the Committee adopted guidelines for the treatment of correspondence from the public or other concerned parties with regard to nominations (Decision 7.COM 15). In that, the Secretariat of the Convention serves as a link between the entity that sent the correspondence, the submitting State Party that is expected to provide its response, and the Evaluation Body (that is, the Consultative Body and the Subsidiary Body at that time), ensuring also transparency as the entire correspondence is accessible to the public on the website of the Convention up until the examination of the nomination at the Committee's session. Nominations that are in the process of evaluation are also accessible. I remember a well-informed actor claiming at the time that the adoption of this mechanism may have far-reaching consequences. To my knowledge, the mechanism has not been much used so far; various interested parties are probably not even aware of its existence. But it has potential.

The subject of correspondence from the public reappeared at the session of the Committee in 2018, yet this time in reference to correspondence pertaining to the "issues concerning the follow-up of inscribed elements on the Lists of the Convention" (agenda item 13.COM 9). The Secretariat reported that "an increasing number of communities, institutions and individuals contact the Secretariat to report on the wide range of issues that arise after the inscription of an element and that might seriously affect its viability or could even call into question its inscription on one of the Lists of the Convention" (agenda item 13.COM 9, document ITH/18/13.COM/ 9, para. 2). There is no mechanism to bring such correspondence to the attention of the Committee; "the sole option for the Secretariat is to transmit it to the State Party" (agenda item 13.COM 9, document ITH/18/13.COM/ 9, para. 13).

In the discussion following the report of the Secretary, the prevailing tone was that this issue should be approached carefully, preventing possible abuses. Only a few states (mainly European) explicitly supported the development of a mechanism based on inclusiveness of all interested parties, dialogue, mediation, and mitigation. Belgium recalled that the Committee actually already decided, together with the adoption of Ethical Principles, "to develop an online platform with a toolkit based on the ethical principles [ ... ] and comprising practical guidance and examples of existing codes of ethics," as well as that the same decision incorporates invitation to "accredited non-governmental organizations to participate in enriching, sharing information, following-up, and contributing to update the online platform" (cf. Decision 10.COM 15.a, para. 9–10).

Further on, in the process of adoption of the draft decision prepared by the Secretariat, a discussion of over half an hour evolved around the paragraph that in the draft version reads: "the need to *strengthen* the follow-up of inscribed elements and to provide ways for *communities and civil society* to participate *more directly* in the monitoring of inscribed elements" (emphasis added; see also figure 1). The first to take the floor was a Committee member from the Philippines, arguing that up to now the Committee has no answers but only questions, and therefore suggested to replace "strengthen" with "reflect," "civil society" with "other stakeholders," and to omit "more directly." Other members of the Committee followed his reasoning, thus suggesting to keep only "communities," "concerned communities," "communities, groups and individuals," or "communities and all stakeholders," to add "practitioners and bearers," or to replace "communities" with "practitioners and bearers." In the end, informed also by the wording in the Convention, the adopted decision reads: "the need to reflect on the follow-up of inscribed elements and on ways for concerned communities, groups and, where applicable, individuals, and other stakeholders to participate in the monitoring of inscribed elements" (Decision 13.COM 9, para. 5). That is an illustrative example of the current, rather disapproving "spirit" of the Committee toward the idea of community agency.

The system implemented in the sister WH Convention relies on on-site monitoring conducted by expert agencies, organizations, and individuals independent from the States Parties concerned and from the WH Intergovernmental Committee. The main outcome of their work is the State of Conservation reports, which are inclusive of information received from NGOs, individuals, press articles, etc.[7] There are several important differences in relation to the ICH Convention. First, on-site monitoring in the ICH Convention does not exist; reasonably so, because living heritage cannot be adequately examined through short-term visits akin to those conducted by expert missions in the WH Convention. Monitoring is therefore limited to examination (always very benevolent examination, by the way) of written periodic reports submitted by States Parties. Second, as emphasized above, it is a matter of fact that the general principle of community agency has resulted in the downplaying of the role of experts and expertise in the 2003 Convention. Consequently, there is no room for analysis by independent scholars who have worked extensively and for a long time with the communities concerned, and thus could act as reliable reviewers,

---

[7] Cf. the document "Review—World Heritage Reactive Monitoring Process—Strengthening the Effectiveness of the World Heritage Reactive Monitoring Process—Final Report 31 August 2019" by UNESCO Reactive Monitoring Review Team (David Sheppard and Gamini Wijesuriya), pp. 40–42, 50–51. The document is available at https://www.google.com/url?sa=t&rct=j&q=&esrc=s&source=web&cd=&ved=2ahUKEwiKr8q4v6vtAhXo4IUKHba6BeoQFjAAegQIAhAC&url=https%3A%2F%2Fwhc.unesco.org%2Fdocument%2F174948&usg=AOvVaw2L-vZj2eHfNC3_rmxjXe4D.

as was the case long ago, in the time of the Masterpieces program (cf. Seeger, 2009). At the same time, the principle of community agency did not in any way endanger the role of States Parties as central actors. In contrast, in the WH Convention, the credibility of monitoring is effectuated primarily on the basis of *expertise* of the WH center and Advisory Bodies and their *independence* from governmental and intergovernmental entities. The same applies to all other conventions I have examined. Individual experts and NGOs involved in the ICH system (already due to their low status, as well as rather limited capacities in the case of majority of ICH NGOs) can in no way function similarly to expert bodies in the WH Convention. Third, the Secretariat of ICH Convention would say that WH and ICH Conventions are incomparable because of their opposing principle (of outstanding universal value vs. culturally/community-relative values). Yet, such a claim neglects the fact that the WH Convention has advanced its approaches in terms of attention paid to intangible aspects of WH, as well as, of special importance here, in terms of consultation with local experts, staff, and communities, followed by review of information by the relevant Advisory Bodies, and finally followed by integration of verified information in their highly influential, visible, and credible State-of-Conservation reports, which can hardly be overturned, in contrast to recommendations of the Evaluation Body in the ICH Convention.

Therefore, it seems it would be of great importance to establish an ICH NGO monitoring center that would integrate expertise in ICH and dedication to the principle of community agency. The main agenda of the center would develop around inputs (i.e., correspondence) from the public: to serve as a center that welcomes such inputs, directs the concerns raised by the correspondents to the States Parties in question, verifies all information received, compares the objectively verified information to that in the official periodic reports, prepares its own annual reports on the issues raised (and more broadly speaking on the state of safeguarding worldwide), and as a whole builds its power on its publicity and independence, combined with expertise and credibility.

It would be reasonable for the center to be established within the ICH NGO Forum, an association of NGOs accredited to the Convention. A favorable circumstance is that for the last couple of years, the Committee has paved a way for enhancing its partnership with NGOs by acknowledging their "important role and untapped potential" (cf. Decision 14.COM 15, para. 5) apart from their services in the Evaluation Body, and—more importantly—by deciding to include, for the first time in the history of the Convention, the "Report of the Non-Governmental Organizations Forum" as a separate agenda item at its 15.COM in December 2020 (Decision 14.COM 15, para. 9). Thus, for the first time, the Forum was given a chance to communicate with the Committee more directly and more comprehensively, presenting the scope of its activities, its organizational development, and its views on some ongoing topics and issues in the work of the Committee, along with a chance to respond to reactions of the Committee.

In such a context, however, the primary objective is to confirm and se-cure the importance of NGOs in the system—notably, as emphasized in the Forum's report for 15.COM, regarding their advising on specific thematic issues, the experience-sharing on good safeguarding practices, and par-ticipation in follow-up (reporting and monitoring) on inscribed elements, in addition to their current service in the Evaluation Body. A way to attain these functions is by enhancing partnership with States Parties, Category 2 Centers, and other official stakeholders, that is, by working "independently yet collaboratively" with them, as noted in the Forum's report for 15.COM. At the same time, the Forum constantly needs to reconcile or synchronize mul-tiple differences among its member organizations, the differences regarding their domains and modes of operation, their relationship with governments back home, their capacities, interests, and aims, the imbalance in the number of organizations representing different regions of the world, etc. This also requires the Forum to act carefully in this stage of its development,[8] and brings additional challenges to its possible monitoring center.

Such a center (maybe a humble mini-center for the beginning) would need to be both credible and relevant. Credibility means that it would wel-come and encourage inputs (correspondence) from the public, particularly from culture bearers and their communities, and find ways to bring them accurately and without impediments to the deliberations of the Committee. Relevance means that the center needs to operate within the Forum as the only non-governmental stakeholder on the international scale which—judging from the current, rather opportune moment—cannot be easily overlooked by the Committee. As much as I could think of paths out of the

---

[8] Forum's report for 15.COM addresses these last aspects only to a degree. More can be found in Chiara Bortolotto's and Jorijn Neyrinck's article about the role of accredited NGOs in the ICH Convention (Bortolotto & Neyrinck 2020). They also paid particular attention to the "tension be-tween the need to speak a diplomatic language, necessary to be heard within the UNESCO arena, and the need to straightforwardly voice actual issues," which "reflects the coexisting souls of accredited NGOs" (ibid., p. 160). I couldn't formulate this important point better.

conundrum of alleged community agency in the ICH Convention, no other path, to my mind, could be more appropriate or productive to take. If, in addition to its credibility and relevance, the center would nurture the culture of dialogue and problem-solving, it would be a worthy successor of the path designed in Washington in 1999.

# References

Bortolotto, C., & Neyrinck, J. (2020). Article 9: Accreditation of advisory organizations. In J. Blake & L. Lixinski (Eds.), *The 2003 UNESCO Intangible Heritage Convention: A commentary* (pp. 153–163). Oxford University Press.

Ceribašić, N. (2017). O participacijskom mehanizmu, ulozi zajednica i stručnjaka u programu nematerijalne kulturne baštine: Prilog analizi stranputica humanistike [On the participation mechanism, the role of communities and experts in the programme of intangible cultural heritage: A contribution to the analysis of bypaths of the humanities]. In P. Bagarić, O. Biti, & T. Škokić (Eds.), *Stranputice humanistike* (pp. 153–185). Institut za etnologiju i folkloristiku.

Seeger, A. (2009). Lessons learned from the ICTM (NGO) evaluation of nominations for the UNESCO Masterpieces of the Oral and Intangible Heritage of Humanity 2001–5. In L. Smith & N. Akagawa (Eds.), *Intangible heritage* (pp. 112–128). Routledge.

Seitel, P. (Ed.). (2001). *Safeguarding traditional cultures: A global assessment*. Smithsonian Center for Folklife and Cultural Heritage.

# PART II
# THE ICH CONVENTION
# IN ACTION

# 6

# The "ICH Movement" in China

## The Status of Traditional Musics after ICH Certification

*Xiao Mei and Yang Xiao*

Since the 1980s, Chinese scholars have been paying more attention to how culture bearers create sets of cultural sounds, symbols, and meanings within the ecosystem that nurtures them, akin to the concept of "the study of music in culture" in Western ethnomusicology (cf. Merriam, 1964). However, the traditional music we encounter in contemporary society has changed profoundly in its ecosystem from what we call "in the raw" or "Original Ecology" (原生态).[1] Therefore, the question arises: How and why should we preserve and protect traditional music, faced with the inevitable changes of social and natural ecosystems? It is a key question of this century, haunting our minds to ensure the sustainable development of traditional music. Strikingly, these issues strongly resonate with the promotion of the 2003 UNESCO policy on the safeguarding of human oral and intangible cultural heritage in China, which caused a veritable movement that continues to this day.

After Kunqu Art (昆曲艺术) and Guqin Art (古琴艺术) were inscribed during the first decade of the twenty-first century, over 10 kinds of Chinese traditional music genres have now been accepted into the Representative List of Oral and Intangible Heritage of Humanity by UNESCO. The central government was very excited about this success and considered "being on the list" as a national honor. Shortly after, the government established the "Preservation Project for Ethnic and Folk Cultures in China" (2004),[2] founded the China National Center for Safeguarding Intangible Cultural Heritage (2006), as well as the Bureau of Intangible Cultural Heritage under the Culture Ministry (2009). Next, all local governments from other cities

---

[1] See Rees (2016, pp. 53–88).
[2] This policy is marked by a notice issued by the Ministry of Culture and Finance in 2004 on the implementation of *the Preservation Project for Ethnic and Folk Cultures.*

Xiao Mei and Yang Xiao, *The "ICH Movement" in China* In: *Music, Communities, Sustainability.*
Edited by: Huib Schippers and Anthony Seeger, Oxford University Press. © Oxford University Press 2022.
DOI: 10.1093/oso/9780197609101.003.0006

and provinces started to support the policy, and the country institutionalized a China Intangible Cultural Heritage (hereafter referred to as ICH) system at the county, city, province, and state level. So far, we have included more than 500 kinds of traditional music, including folk songs, narrative singing, theatre, and instrumental music on the state list. The authoritative affirmation and public attention it raised made different powers and groups enthusiastic about the practice of ICH management. Government officials, academics and intellectuals, NGOs, mass media, commercial institutions, and culture bearers began to reconsider these musical traditions in terms of their complexity over the past decade, actively engaging in the safeguarding and promotion of ICH in different ways. We may call this the "ICH movement of traditional music in China."

How did the "ICH movement" influence the safeguarding of music traditions and the maintenance of cultural diversity? In 2014, we formed a research team with the Shanghai Conservatory of Music and Sichuan Conservatory of Music. Our research aims were to report the actual situation of musical traditions after they were selected as ICH. We focused on 11 kinds of music genres from different regions and different ethnic cultures to observe what role the government played in classifying the extreme abundance of Chinese traditional music forms and qualifying them as ICH at different grades. We investigated the actual effects of various safeguarding policies and acts that were carried out by different levels of government. We explored the dynamic relationship between the various forces that shaped the ICH movement, and how they contributed to the future of traditional music in China.

Based on our research data, we can now report on some very sensitive but core issues regarding how Chinese traditional music has been affected by the ICH movement, referring specifically to some of them, but focusing on sharing obvious and prominent commonalities, although in this movement the particularities or differences tend to be much greater than commonalities (Xiao & Yang, forthcoming).

## Overview of the "After ICH Certification" Project

As mentioned above, the project consists of 11 sub-projects. The selection of these 11 ICH items resulted from taking into consideration not only the types, forms, levels, and lifestyles, but also the balance between various ethnicities, regions, and lifestyles. Among the 11 projects selected, four occur mainly in urban areas, while seven flourish mainly in rural areas. The grand song (侗族大歌) of the Dong ethnic group, the Haicai tunes (海菜腔) of the Yi people, the female wedding lament (哭嫁歌) of the Tujia people, the Lmuhuw (Atayal oral tradition), the Shanghai Dock Worker's Song (码头号子), and the Zhuma show (bamboo pony, 竹马戏) of the Han people are singing folk ceremonies accompanying significant folkloric events; the Guqin（古琴）and the Jiangnan Sizhu (bamboo and silk, 江南丝竹) are typical music genres active in modern urban and rural lifestyles; Jonang Sanskrit Chanting (觉囊梵音) is the ritual sound of Tibetan Buddhism; Sichuan Yangqin (四川扬琴) and Dian Theatre (滇剧) are storytelling and theatre genres that have been handed down among the people for over two centuries. In addition to Han people, four ethnic groups from southwest China, mid-downstream Yangtze River, and Taiwan are involved in these 11 items: Dong (侗), Tibetan (藏), Yi (彝), and Atayal (泰雅) peoples. In addition, we made sure to take into account the varying perspectives of the culture bearers, the ICH institutions, the various ways re-contextualization takes place, the different forms of performances, and the relationships between all parties involved in the ICH movement in China.

The "After ICH" project, although it entailed theoretical considerations and interpretation, is essentially a practical project in applied ethnomusicology, aiming from the very beginning to meet two academic goals. First, through long-term fieldwork, we wanted to understand the trajectory of the traditional musics during the "ICH movement," and report on their survival situations as objectively as possible through data collection, interviews, recordings, questionnaires, and so on. Therefore, all investigators needed to have a clear understanding of each expression's traditional survival conditions, and the patterns of change from 1950 to 2000. It is also important to note that although the policy of the Chinese government on the preservation of ICH defines protection and rescue as the first and principal task, the premise of practical application and development plays an important role as well.

To these ends, the government has prescribed a series of protection measures in the form of legislation. These protection methods can be divided into two forms: "static state protection" and "living state protection." The so-called static state protection refers to the archival preservation of traditional music in the form of audiovisual recordings or material objects, while the living state protection aims to continue traditional music's vitality in the contemporary era, based on its original cultural ecosystem.

Among the 11 projects we surveyed, it is obvious that different projects represented different choices in the form of protection. Hence after joining the project, the investigators followed the case for two to three years of field-work. Based on the data of the report, this research also aims to elucidate some issues faced by traditional music in the ICH movement, such as the role of inheritors and culture bearers, the coexistence of traditional and modern performance formats, the role of scholars, and the overall dynamics of the ICH projects.

## The Institution of Inheritors (Culture Bearers)

Most traditional performing arts remain rooted in ritual or folkloric relationships to this day. They are based on certain social structures and communities; and their social and institutional functions are often realized by "communally collaborative performance." The Grand Song of the Dong people and Jiangnan Sizhu rely on troupes of singers and guilds of musicians, as do Sichuan Yangqin and the Dock Workers' Song. For each genre, one or a few representative individuals who demonstrate the highest level of practical ability must be identified and selected. Among certain performing communities, members who fail to receive the title of "inheritor" may be quite disappointed by feeling they are not being treated fairly, but those with the title do not necessarily feel relieved either. "Whoever are inheritors should teach and perform": for these inheritors, in addition to the above evaluation system, there is a corresponding protection system, including the payment of salaries. Therefore, the natural transmission, based on the idea that everyone can teach, has been changed, and the task of teaching the younger generation is considered to be the job of those individuals named as the inheritors. This has led to the decline of what was once an intimate relationship, leading to nostalgia for the past. At the same time, we find that these privileged individual inheritors must depend on communal collaboration in order to accomplish normalized performances and proper inheritance. By investigating the 11 performing genres, the conflict between the institution of individualized inheritors and the practice of communalized participation in most traditional arts in China clearly emerged. Originally passed on collectively, it has now become passed on individually.

This tension between individuality and communality within the institution of inheritors is not a new topic. It has in fact been actively discussed since the introduction of ICH to China. Contributions to the schemes for the institution of inheritors are constantly being made from within and outside of academia; yet as we try to systematize the "After-ICH" project, suggestions and plans that directly address the communal nature of traditional arts tend to be excluded from the institution of inheritors.

Another common problem that emerged from the 11 cases of the "After ICH" project is the criteria used for the recognition of inheritors. Before the recognition of the fifth batch of inheritors in early 2018, Yang Xiao received a phone call from a singer of the grand song of the Dong ethnic group who eagerly inquired about the specific requirements for the application of recognized inheritors. She said: "Those good at arranging and memorizing lots of songs are called 'Master of Songs' by the locals; however, it is us singers who can sing beautifully and teach songs that have made Dong songs influential out there, and we singers should be considered the genuine inheritors."

The concerns of this singer are common in the context of recognition of inheritors, according to the surveys in our project. In most traditional performing arts, the performers themselves are arrangers to some extent, and the performing process itself is an arranging process. With the development of and focus on staged performances, there is a rapid decline in contemporary society of such multiple abilities commonly found in traditional societies, which poses new challenges to the recognition of inheritors. In the case of the grand song of the Dong ethnic group, only by understanding that the essential goal of Dong multi-part singing is to strengthen traditional social structures by long-term rituals rich in singing can we realize the core of Dong singing, which revolves around the tradition of memorizing and arranging the lyrics by the "Master of Songs," rather than performances by individual singers. The nomination of the inheritors determines to a large extent the content and path of inheritance, and even to an extent the direction of contemporary development of certified ICH items, by recognizing who, with what ability, is the most suitable inheritor.

## Synergy and Tensions in a Compound Dynamic Field

Several scholars in our team have pointed out that the activity of intangible cultural heritage has created a complex social dynamic system in contemporary times. This dynamic system is composed of various forces impacting each other and thus forming an effective tension space, which we call the "compound dynamic field of ICH." Take guqin, included in the Representative List of Oral and Intangible Heritage of Humanity by UNESCO, as an example. There are at least seven important forces surrounding it, including inheritors, government, schools, scholars, artists, media, and merchants. The interplay among these seven forces forms extremely complicated conditions for guqin in contemporary China. In fact, as a typical Chinese traditional music culture with a traceable history of three thousand years, guqin plays historical, political, cultural, artistic, symbolic, educational, academic, and economic roles in contemporary China. That invites reflection regarding the different needs and the role of continuous revision as a form of expression and its place in cultural life.

In the investigation of the Sichuan school of guqin, the players mentioned several times that the flourishing of guqin in Chengdu, Sichuan province, is by no means only the achievement of intangible cultural heritage policies since 2000. They think guqin learning has deep roots; in recent years the government has consistently promoted its development. At the same time, the university enrollment expansion causes professionalization and popularizes an important foundation for the construction of guqin. For example, there was not a single student majoring in guqin before 2001 in the Sichuan Conservatory of Music, but from 2001 to 2020, current and graduated guqin-major students number around 40. Over the past decade, the rise of the consumer economy has also become an important factor through the commodification of guqin. All of these factors, and the ICH movement, have contributed to success of guqin in this area (Zeng & Liu, 2018).

An even more complex case illustrating this composite dynamic field comes from the Grand Song of Dong. The research team found that from the 1950s to the 2000s, the Grand Song of Dong was a genre of which the boundaries were constantly enlarged. After 2000, when one speaks about the Grand Song of Dong in Chinese, it may point to music forms of four different categories, depending on who is making the statement, the context in which it is made, and for whom. From "original meaning" to "narrow sense" to "broad sense" and then to "general meaning," this is a process in which the polyphonic aspect of Southern Dong folk songs prevails over other features. Among them, "original meaning of the Grand Song of Dong" and "narrow sense of the Grand Song of Dong" are the terms of the people, which directly correspond to *ga lao* in Dong language. The "broad sense of the Grand Song of Dong" is influenced by academics' focus on the multi-part Dong folk songs, and the folk knowledge system of the Dong folk songs has been influenced

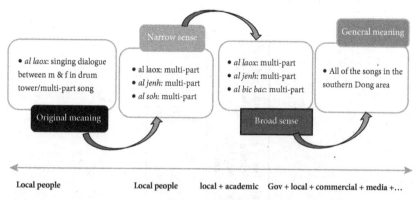

**Figure 6.1** Different ways of viewing the Grand Song of Dong.

and invaded by outsider researchers after it was recognized by the ICH list. The "generalized sense of the Grand Song of Dong" has become a means to develop the tourism market for Dong song, with the joint efforts of the government and business circles, after it was included in the UNESCO list. At present, these four approaches to Dong songs, with different connotations, are all used to different degrees, and constitute a fascinating challenge to the boundaries of so-called authenticity (see Figure 6.1).

## The Formation of Multiple Contexts for Performances

Most traditional performing genres in contemporary China exist across three types of contexts: traditional ritual and folklore; stage art; and commercial production. These three models for performances center on "ritual and folklore," on "works of art," and on "products," respectively.

For 9 of the 11 cases of the "After ICH" project, all three models for performances were identified, while only the Dock Worker's Song of wharf workers has completely lost its traditional singing occasion, and the Zhuma show only takes place in its ritual context. However, each case developed to a different extent in each of the three models. The S (Strong) and W (Weak) parts in Table 6.1 represent the strength of an item in a certain model for performances. Among them, the Grand Song of the Dong ethnic group and the Shu school (蜀派) guqin have strong developments in all three models. All items are producing works of art on stage nowadays, but not all of them have strongly become "products" (see Table 6.1).

Table 6.1 Assessment of Relative Strength of Certified ICH in Different Formats

| | Grand Song of the Dong People | Jiangnan Sizhu | Guqin | Jonang Sanskrit Chanting | Lmuhuw (Atayal oral tradition) | Dian Theatre | Sichuan Yangqin | Shanghai Dock Workers' Songs | The Female Wedding Lament | Zhuma Show | Haicai Tone |
|---|---|---|---|---|---|---|---|---|---|---|---|
| Customs | S | W | S | S | S | W | W | NO | S | S | S |
| Work | S | S | S | S | W | S | S | S | S | NO | W |
| Product | S | W | S | W | S | W | W | S | S | NO | S |

S = strong; W = weak.

The performances centered on "etiquette and custom" stand for performances based on certain folkloric rituals that have definite cultural purposes in the traditional social institutions. In such performances, both the participants and the observers are tradition bearers who arrange the characteristics of the genre to a certain extent during the performing process, following the ritual clues. The performances centered on "works of art" stand for performances based on fixed composed works on stage for aesthetic purposes, created by professional composers and played by professional performers; while those centered on "products" have clear commercial purposes, with programs generally evolving around the consumerist need of audiences.

The 11 cases of the "After ICH" project all include descriptions of these three models for performances to a different extent. Three of the case studies include in-depth comparative studies on the three models by means of ethnographies. In the case of Jiangnan Sizhu, amateur and professional musicians have distinctly different views toward its "authenticity": folk musicians often distinguish between music styles and nature of performances by the words "Minyue" (national music, 民乐) and "Sizhu" (silk and bamboo ensemble, 丝竹): They could say: "this technique on Erhu belongs to Sizhu, while that technique belongs to Minyue. We are not particular about skills, but instead about the special taste" and "Sizhu is not done by rehearsal, but instead by consort or dialogue in music; it would not be fun with notations and a conductor— that is the way of Minyue in which everyone rehearses according to the score in order to perform for others rather than to enjoy themselves."[3] Our study examined in detail the vast differences in choices of repertoire, structures of the music, uses of instruments, relationships among performers in amateurs' Sizhu and the Jiangnan Sizhu performed on stage as Minyue, which coexist simultaneously.

In addition to the above-mentioned points, we have learned about other phenomena in our work on intangible cultural heritage protection in recent years. As we just mentioned, the dynamic field is an intensive space which contains multiple forces. Even though the movement is led by the government in name, the actual process has always played among these forces.

---

[3] See Li (2020, pp. 12–32).

## Scholars: Between Government and Culture Bearers

As mentioned previously, music scholars have constantly been a major force in preserving traditional music. On one side, they discover and categorize as much traditional music as they can. On the other side, they move between culture bearers and officials, and are sometimes able to change policymakers' minds, as the following example about a Han Theatre (汉剧) exhibition of Hubei Provincial Museum illustrates.

Han Theatre, a kind of Chinese local theatre which has a 400-year history, was selected as one of the first national ICH art forms on the list, in 2006. What was the best way to preserve this art? In Wuhan, the capital of Hubei Province, there were two Han Theatre troupes. In 2010, the government had to eliminate one of them because of the financial and marketing burden, so they dissolved the provincial troupe, while the Wuhan troupe stayed. One of the reasons behind this decision was that the provincial troupe consisted of small troupes performing in villages and performing in small-scale theatres, while the Wuhan troupe had always been active in big cities and performs in large-scale theatres.

Meanwhile, the ethnomusicologists of Hubei Provincial Museum planned an exhibition about ancient theatre stage architectures, which involved a lot of research about the theatre itself. First of all, they began by investigating and collecting tangible things. Then, as the research went deeper, they discovered that traditions in both villages and cities are vital to the forming of Chinese theatres. The troupes which performed in villages in particular preserved the female impersonator tradition and many valuable performing skills, as well as the historical value of theatres in their tunes and performances.

Surprisingly, during the investigation, many Han Theatre fans, including professional actors, actresses, and amateurs, became seriously engaged and offered help in many ways. They collected manuscripts, costumes, facial makeup, and so on. The exhibition was originally planned to be held for three months, but due to high demand from visitors, it was extended to seven months. The exhibition was also invited to Beijing and Hong Kong, inciting great excitement in Chinese theatre circles. Moreover, it made the local government reconsider its decision about the Han Theatre troupes, and it re-evaluated that Han Theatre needs to be studied and promoted to ensure it survives.

In this case, the scholars played an important role in mediating between government decision-makers and Han Theatre troupes, with real engagement by the general public. Thanks to some scholars' efforts, some NGOs have started to flourish in Chinese society. They have special views about traditional cultures and their way of preserving them that are more in line with the times, including techniques and ways of promotion.[4]

## NGOs: Between Government and Culture Bearers

For the ethnographic film *Home Coming* by Qiaoqiao Cheng (Cheng, 2019),[5] a crew spent three years with the villagers in Xiaohuang, in Guizhou province. Meanwhile, they ran a parallel project cooperating with a Shanghai fashion/lifestyle brand. Together, they developed a residential plan for musicians, and released a new EP in 2019. The year before, SounDate also curated an exhibition called "The Manner of Giving" during the Spring Festival time in MoCA, a museum in Shanghai. The exhibition is a video and sound installation that begins exploring from a single Chinese character, 礼 (etiquette), to the concept of gift—the manner of giving as it is interpreted by festival traditions in the Dong minority culture.

Since 2013, SounDate has completed several ethnographic film projects cooperating with Shanghai Conservatory of Music and the Shanghai ICH Centre; a commercial documentary with Chevrolet; and a micro-film collaboration with an independent film studio. Their footage has involved traditional music and customs from more than 10 ethnic groups. In addition to recording and filming, SounDate also specializes in introducing diverse cultures to urban citizens across China. For instance, in 2016, they made a film trip to Tuva, Russia, for the international throat singing competition, and invited a Chinese web celebrity to come with them and upload daily vlogs during the whole trip on the Chinese social network Weibo. They introduced the nomads' culture and life and attracted more than 200,000 people watching on video, with 80% of the audiences under 25 years old. From 2017, SounDate cooperated with the ICH Centre in Shanghai and organized seven

---

[4] See Xiao (2017).
[5] Directed and produced by the cultural brand SounDate, this film won the first ever ICTM Prize for a music documentary.

concerts of different kinds of Chinese folk music from Tibet, Fujian, Anhui, Sichuan, and Inner Mongolia in different Shanghai community centers, high schools, and companies for the popularization of Chinese traditional music. Recently, they have focused increasingly on compositions with traditional and electronic music, as they think the music style can attract a younger generation, SounDate's primary target group.

While organizations like SounDate are taking responsibility to communicate with the general public and show the contemporary value of traditional culture to others, there is another type of organization that is based locally and directly interfaces with cultural bearers to support the preservation of their traditions. One example is Yunnan Ethnic Culture and Traditional Customs (云南民族文化传习馆, YECTC), founded by the famous Chinese composer Tian Feng in 1993, after an earlier organization failed after seven years of operation. That failure remains controversial and has left its impact in China. An intensive investigation and analysis by our team identified three reasons that led to the failure of this preservation project:

1. **Financial problems**: During the seven years of operation, they received US$50,000 from the Ford Foundation, as well as some support from individuals, companies, and even the Chinese army. However, most of the expenses relied on Tian Feng's personal income from his composition works; it was very hard to maintain dozens of folk musicians to stay and study with such limited resources.

2. **Conceptual problems**: Tian Feng's operating concept was to strictly preserve traditional music as the "original taste" without any influence from the outside world. He also refused any form of commercial performance. He had exacting rules for the students and the musicians in the institute, such as no love relationships, no TV watching, and no cell phones. He tried to prevent any effect from modernization. The intense pressure of this regime caused many musicians to leave, also given an unpredictable future.

3. **Contextual problems**: The institute was located in a factory building in Kunming, away from the cultural context where the music lives. That, in combination with the closed type of training method and the musicians living far away from home, made it impossible to continue.

The new "Yuansheng studio" (源声坊) was founded by a director Liu Xiaojin, who documented the YECTC and Tian Feng's career for eight years. Starting from her own interest in traditional music and bringing together people who were willing to continue the work, the reborn organization was dedicated to the transmission of the culture from the roots, inside the bearers' villages. The Yuansheng studio selected five villages as their working sites, and created several plans for educational programs and competitions with reward systems. They discovered different methods to encourage local people to learn their traditional music. For instance, they gave a financial reward to students, who could get 80 to 120 RMB per song they learn, depending on the difficulty levels (Wei, 2020).

In the village, much farm work is a group activity. Yuansheng studio takes this opportunity and makes them learn songs while working. In that way, the local people can earn money from both farm work and song learning at the same time. In this case, Yuansheng studio mainly focuses on the relationship with the local people and discovering an effective way to get on with the folk musicians. When we interviewed Liu Xiaojin, she told us the core work for the last 15 years is not about traditional music itself, but the experiences and methods they developed to deal with minorities, at a level of depth and detail that the work of officials or scholars can't match. As of last year, there was news that the teaching-learning system has already become autonomous behavior in one of the villages where they worked. Moreover, some local parents also support their children to learn local instruments after school, an education that may help them to become more familiar with part of their ethnic identity.

Such initiatives left us thinking that regardless of whether the involvement comes from the government, scholars, or NGOs, they are all trying to preserve or get involved with folk/traditional culture by their own experiences and knowledge systems. But who is the real insider? Who is the subject of folk cultural preservation? And who has the power to safeguard it? It would appear that the answer lies with the local people who carry the culture.

## The Power of the Cultural Bearers Themselves

In China, the policy description for safeguarding ICH is: "Led by the government, guided by the scholars, and participated in by the culture bearers."

The difference in authoritative status in this is clear. This section deals with the power of the cultural bearers themselves, taking Dong people and their "Grand Song of Dong" as an example.

The Grand Song of Dong was "discovered" and became known as the typical Chinese multi-part singing in musical and arts circles during the 1950s. However, its name didn't bring any advantage to or impact on the Dong people. During the last two decades of the twentieth century, a few members of the Dong elite realized that their own traditional education structure based on their Grand Song singing system was dying out. Their first move was to put Dong folk songs into the local contemporary school system. However, the effect was still very limited. With the emergence of the ICH movement in the country, the cultural identity of a singer who is selected for the ICH list could bring financial and political benefits to them. This is what led three counties, Liping, Congjiang, and Rongjiang, to fight for official titles relating to the Grand Song of Dong (see Table 6.2).

Xiaohuang, Sanlong, and Yandong are the top three villages on the list as most influential for the Grand Song of Dong, which represents a rich tourism resource. From Table 6.2, one can see those villages which own official or non-official titles, some of which were applied to the government by themselves, while others were given just by the local people. They know these titles increase the chance for them to host festivals, which can bring fame and secure investments from outside to help the village economically, for instance in road building or village reconstructing. In that way, the singing tradition is a direct resource to benefit their actual life. Put more simply, it is an important survival tool for them. Thus, the honors and official titles stimulate their own interest to continually sing and pass down the tradition.

The motivation for singing changed in this case. However, the time has changed as well: the cultural context and living environment are no longer that simple and isolated from globalization, and the Grand Song of Dong has transformed into a channel or symbol for local people to establish their social identity as well as their economic security. Now they can be proud to stand in front of an audience and sing, and self-determination is the real motive for preserving the traditional music.

Table 6.2  Location and Recognition of the Grand Song of Dong

| County Name | Village/Town Name | Natural Village Name | Honors or Titles | Authorization |
|---|---|---|---|---|
| Liping (黎平) | Yongcong | Sanlong | The origin of the GSD | Self-authorized/ Controversial |
| | Yandong | Yandong | The origin of the GSD: the first GSD village to be on the international stage (侗族大歌走出国门第一村) | Self-authorized/ Controversial |
| | Shuangjiang | Huanggang | The hometown for male GSD singing (男声侗族大歌之乡) The origin of male singing (男声侗族大歌发源地) | Self-authorized |
| | Zhaoxing | Tang'an | Museum of Ecological System in Tang'an Village (贵州黎平堂安侗族生态博物馆) | Provincial government |
| | Zhaoxing | Zhaoxing | One of six most beautiful ancient towns in China (中国最美的六大乡村古镇) | Selected by *China National Geographic* 2005 |
| | | | 33 most tempting global destinations (全球最具诱惑力的33个旅游目的地) | Selected by US *National Geographic & National Geographic Traveler, 2007* |
| | | | Best Dong village (侗乡第一寨) | Self-authorized |
| | Koujiang | Koujiang | The first GSD village to be on the international stage (侗族大歌第一次走出国门) | Self-authorized/ Controversial |

*Continued*

**Table 6.2** *Continued*

| County Name | Village/Town Name | Natural Village Name | Honors or Titles | Authorization |
|---|---|---|---|---|
| Congjiang（从江） | Gaozeng | Xiaohuang | The hometown of China folk arts (中国民间艺术之乡) | Provincial department of culture, National Ministry of Culture |
| | | | The origin of the GSD (侗族大歌发源地) | Self-Authorized/Controversial |
| | | Gaozeng | The village of Chinese vocal art (中国声乐文化村) | Provincial government |

## Conclusion

We have seen that the approaches through which people preserve traditional music are almost as diverse as the ethnic groups in China. Circumstances are always varied and changing in different places and regions due to various causes and reasons, including politics, the economy, or their own cultural characteristics. This makes the topic very complicated to describe in a limited space, as there are so many things that need to be realized, continued, discovered, communicated, and learned.

As early as the 1950s, Shanghai Dock Workers' Songs were only rarely used on the ships. This national ICH project was mainly preserved as audiovisual archives because of the complete loss of its living space. In contrast, until today, Jonang Buddhist chants of Tibetan and Bimo chanting of the Yi people are still popular and part of the daily life of Tibetan and Yi people, so their main form of protection is living protection in their own traditional ritual and folklore. However, for many ICH projects, such as Guqin, Jiangnan Sizhu Music, and Sichuan Yangqin, whose traditional folklore forms are almost detached from their roots in the contemporary era, the combination of static state and living state protection has become a logical choice. It is worth noting that integrating the living state protection of the 11 ICH projects has created five distinct living transmission trajectories in contemporary China for traditional music. These are: native transmission; stage transmission;

school transmission; new constructed folklore transmission; and new media transmission.

It is this multi-pronged approach to sustainability that shapes the various understandings of ICH preservation in China. Traditional music labeled as ICH has somewhat lost its everlasting "folksy character" and has become an item to be gazed upon and focused on by the synergy between efforts by the government, the population at large, the institutions, academia, and artistic and commercial circles. In this way, China constitutes a unique case study for the rich, complex, and sometimes problematic interaction between these various actors and the objects of their efforts.

# References

Cheng, Qiaoqiao. (2019). *Home coming: The ethnography of Dong People's New Year* (ethnographic film). SMPH & SLAV.

Li, Ya. (2020). Metropolitan "vintage sound": The contemporary interpretation of "Jiangnan Sizhu" in Shanghai. In J. Huang, Jing Li, et al. (Eds.), *Urban cultural spaces and exhibitory performances: New arrangements of vintage pieces and the appropriation of traditions* (pp. 12–32). China Social Publishing House.

Merriam, Alan Parkhurst. (1964). *The anthropology of music.* Northwestern University Press.

Rees, Helen. (2016). Environmental crisis, culture loss, and a new musical aesthetic: China's "original ecology folksongs" in theory and practice. *Ethnomusicology*, 60(1), 53–88.

Wei, Yukun. (2020). *Intervention in traditional music protection* [ 《传统音乐保护"介入"问题调查与研究》 ]. Postdoctoral dissertation, China Conservatory of Music.

Xiao, Mei. (2017). Practice engaged ethnomusicology in festival, museums and archives. Presented at the International Symposium "Negotiating Intangible Cultural Heritage," December 1, 2017, Osaka.

Xiao, Mei, & Yang, Xiao (Eds.). *After being recognized as ICH: Investigation Reports* [ 《非遗之后:非物质文化遗产(音乐、戏剧类)调查研究》 ]. Shanghai Music Publish House (SMPH). Forthcoming.

Zeng, He., & Liu, Panpan. (2018). Investigations on the current status of the Qin heritage in Chengdu: The musicians, transmissions and activities. Presented at the 20th National conference of Association for Traditional Music in China, July 17, 2018, Shenyang.

# 7

# UNESCO-Based and UNESCO-Free

## Governmental and Non-Governmental Efforts for Safeguarding Intangible Cultural Heritage in Turkey

*Olcay Muslu*

In Turkey, in addition to its traditional and aesthetic role, culture in the twenty-first century has acquired a new, strategically important place in politics and is now integrated into national and regional development plans, and in strategic alliances with other sectors (Council of Europe, 2013, p. 5). Societies which are in danger of losing their values due to the effects of globalization and industrialization, and the fear that cultural diversity is under threat, marked the starting point of the UNESCO Convention for the Safeguarding of the Intangible Cultural Heritage (ICH). However, this has raised important questions regarding how governments and their international commitments, such as UNESCO Conventions, safeguard intangible cultural heritage and re-energize interest in, or access to, culture. In particular, there is a question of where music stands in these governmental and non-governmental safeguarding efforts.

Legal responsibilities imposed on Contracting States to the ICH oblige them to play more active roles in its application. However, the "protectability" and "transferability" of intangible cultural heritage remain problematic in terms of the efforts to list and inventory elements, the form and performance of National Committees, and the structural organs of governments. In Turkey, new ways of working with cultural and political stakeholders were developed following major structural changes to the administration of the Republic of Turkey in 2018 and the adoption of the current presidential system.[1]

Drawing on seven years of fieldwork in urban and rural settings in Turkey, this chapter examines the successes and failures of two different approaches

[1] For details: https://www.cbiko.gov.tr/en

Olcay Muslu, *UNESCO-Based and UNESCO-Free* In: *Music, Communities, Sustainability.*
Edited by: Huib Schippers and Anthony Seeger, Oxford University Press. © Oxford University Press 2022.
DOI: 10.1093/oso/9780197609101.003.0007

to safeguarding intangible cultural heritage: a UNESCO-aligned approach, and an independent grassroots approach. The former is given through the example of traditional *sohbet* meetings (*sıra gecesi*) of the city of Şanlıurfa in southeastern Turkey in the period following its registration to the UNESCO Representative List. The latter is considered within the context of a "UNESCO-free" applied ethnomusicology project conducted in rural Anatolia.

## Actors and Determinants of Intangible Cultural Heritage in Turkey

To account for the changing cultural policy climate and its implications for intangible cultural heritage in Turkey, it is necessary to first understand the roles of state actors under the current presidential system.[2] Turkey's ruling Justice and Development Party (Adalet ve Kalkınma Partisi, AKP), and the country's first directly elected executive president, Recep Tayyip Erdoğan, won with 52.6% of the popular vote on June 24, 2018. Article 104 of the Constitution states that the president alone exercises executive power and can ensure coordination among ministries, control the administrative body, and appoint or dismiss high-ranking public personnel. In addition, structures such as "Presidencies and Departments" were established, the number of ministries was reduced while their functions were increased, and some ministries were merged to improve productivity. Overall, the number of ministries in the new government model (see Figure 7.1) was reduced to 16 from 24 (Sobacı, Köseoğlu & Mis, 2018, pp. 194–201).

The Ministry of Culture and Tourism (MoCT) is responsible for determining cultural policy targets and principles, with city culture tourism directorates and provincial units in 81 Turkish cities and control units in 44 external locations (MoCT, 2013a, p. 14). In addition, nine new executive councils were formed, including the Council on Culture and Art Policy.[3] Following new priorities at the government level, cultural sustainability

---

[2] For the duties and powers of the presidency of Turkey, see: https://www.tccb.gov.tr/en/preside ncy/power/.
[3] For further information: https://www.hurriyetdailynews.com/76-people-appointed-to-turkeys-presidential-policy-councils-137697.

**Figure 7.1** Organization of the presidency.
*Source*: Sobacı, Köseoğlu, & Mis et al. (2018, p. 195).

studies provoked the following question at the Third Cultural Council in Turkey:

> . . . how [are] nations with long cultural traditions to respond to the challenges of cultural impoverishment, alienation and globalization in the 21st century? (Kalın, 2017, para. 1)

On March 3, 2017, the president delivered a speech at the Third National Cultural Council in which he revealed the general framework for Turkey's new cultural policy, gave direction to the future intangible cultural heritage plans, and set out a new cultural course for the centennial of the Republic in 2023.

> We should rediscover and rebuild our national and cultural values, which reflect the native Turkish culture and arts, against cultural alienation and imperialism through a universal perspective. [ . . . ] In the final analysis, all cultures in fact emerge, develop and flourish within a certain community and specific geography. What renders it universal is the deepness and profundity of the message it gives. [ . . . ] What falls on us is to revive and carry into future our culture by interpreting it in the light of the needs of our day. In this regard, we should do our part to conserve and improve our national culture with an approach that is based on improvement not submission. (Presidency of the Republic of Turkey, 2017, para. 6)

President Erdoğan's speech was a distillation of the general discourses of governmental organs such as MoCT and the laws related to ICH, and aligned with the aims of the UNESCO 2003 Convention for the Safeguarding of the Intangible Cultural Heritage, to which Turkey became the 45th Contracting State on March 27, 2006. Turkey was also building on a legacy of over 100 years regarding state-led cultural pride and preservation, which began under Kemal Ataturk (Tekelioğlu, 2001, pp. 94–97). Whether these discourses translate into practices, however, is open to interpretation, with some commentators labeling cultural activities and products/elements as inauthentic and homogenous.

A stated aim of the 2015–2019 Term Second Strategic Plan was to contribute to global culture by ensuring the sustainable conservation of cultural heritage (MoCT, 2013b, p. 12). Turkish Law 4848 enshrines the MoCT's duty "to maintain, develop, spread, promote, evaluate and adopt the cultural values, prevent the damaging and destroying of cultural properties," to "lead public institutions and organizations related with culture and tourism," and to communicate and cooperate with "local authorities, non-governmental organizations and private sector" (MoCT, 2013a, p. 10).

Work relating to ICH within the framework of the UNESCO ICH Agreement is carried out by the General Directorate of Research and

Training Center of the MoCT. The Directorate is responsible for creating a broad legal and administrative context by inventorying, identifying, and defining ICH elements, raising awareness of the value of ICH,
implementing specific measures to safeguard ICH elements, and carrying out national/international promotional activities pertaining to ICH
(Aydoğdu Atasoy, 2018, p. 13). The Directorate also supervises the preparation of the nomination files for the Representative List of the Intangible
Cultural Heritage of Humanity.

In cooperation with provincial directorates of the MoCT and representatives from related institutions, bearers of ICH have formed local
ICH boards. These prepare and update forms for the inclusion of ICH
elements and reports on the provincial inventory to the ICH Commission
experts. As shown in Figure 7.2, the file of an element that fulfills ICH
criteria is sent to the ICH Commission for possible inclusion in the national inventory. The file must be approved by the General Directorate
of Research and Training of the MoCT before it can be evaluated by
the UNESCO Turkey National Committee, the Ministry of Foreign
Affairs, and the Permanent Representative of UNESCO-Paris and Other
Institutions and Operations. Finally, if the element is accepted, it is registered by UNESCO.

Turkey has undertaken many activities within the scope of the Convention
for the Safeguarding of the Intangible Cultural Heritage. It has also initiated

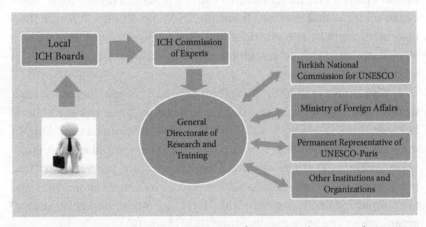

**Figure 7.2**  Administrative context diagram of UNESCO element evaluation.
*Source*: MoCT Research and Training Center (2016, p. 8).

the active participation of non-governmental organizations to increase support from the civil sphere. As a result, six Turkey-based NGOs have been accredited to the Convention: the Akşehir Nasreddin Hodja and Tourism Association (2010), the Buğday Association for Supporting Ecological Living (2010), the Folklore Researchers' Foundation (2010), the Turkish National Centre of the International Union of Puppet and Shadow Theatre (2010), the International Mevlana Foundation (2010), and the Cultural Research Foundation (2012) (Oğuz, 2013, p. 5).

The responsibility of the UNESCO National Commissions is vital for "fostering the recognition and protection of concerned practitioners, establishing more appropriate legislation and mechanisms of protection, and ensuring the dissemination, through education and awareness-raising, of the values and significance of the intangible cultural heritage" (Bouchenaki, 2003, Appendix 1, para. 2). The expertise of the commission members is paramount, but the selection process is controversial. Öcal Oğuz, president of the UNESCO Turkey National Committee, drew attention to possible divergences between decision-makers regarding additions or proposals to the list. In his criticism for the profiles of advisory bodies and World Heritage Committee, Oğuz stated:

> . . . it is possible to elect experts who aren't competent enough academically or scientifically or don't have the knowledge of the Convention due to the fact that 6 out of 12 members are elected on behalf of their governments and the remaining six members are representatives of NGOs. Therefore, this might cause some disputes over the accuracy of advice, and on the other hand, it might give way to frailty of authority as it may not be possible to hold the efforts of the committee members to include the elements with unfavourable opinion in the list. (Oğuz, 2018, p. 47)

Within the scope of this chapter, it is particularly important to question how many members come from a musical background, and how often the UNESCO Turkey National Committee includes ethnomusicologists on their Commission of Experts during the process of elimination.

The Turkish inventory system is based on a bottom-up perspective with the involvement of local communities, local governments, universities, and NGOs. As national committees can vary both in terms of their structure and the way in which they function, this adds to the difficulty in making accurate accounts and inventories of their areas of responsibility, namely the elements of intangible cultural heritage. Although the place of experts in the decision-making position is of crucial importance, another point that needs to be made is that there are many regions which face disadvantages due to the economic structure, geopolitical system, and physical geography of Turkey. These regions require assistance, support, and guidance to make their culture visible. This leads to inevitable questions regarding fairness from the UNESCO National Committee, and also signals the importance of alternative, "UNESCO-free" efforts to safeguard heritage.

## A City Action for Sustaining Music in Turkey: After the Registration of an Element with UNESCO

An "International Symposium of Music from Past to Present in Urfa" was held in Şanlıurfa,[4] a historic city in southeastern Turkey, from November 15th to 18th, 2018. The symposium was well attended and 68 delegates from both academic and non-academic fields presented papers. The impetus for the symposium was a desire to present the musical experience in Urfa to the scientific community and create an important archive in this field. This work was also expected to be an important contribution toward the registration of Şanlıurfa's candidacy to become a UNESCO creative city.

The Şanlıurfa Metropolitan Municipality initiated a number of local activities to promote local culture and re-energize social interest toward cultural heritage. Known as "a city of music," Şanlıurfa does not have a problem in this area due to the popular local tradition of *sıra gecesi*, or traditional *sohbet* meetings, which have been registered as an element on the UNESCO

---

[4] Şanlıurfa is inhabited mostly by people of Kurdish and Arabic descent, and is located 30 miles from the Syrian border. The city has a population of over two million, and has undergone very rapid growth and urbanization in the last two decades (Şanlıurfa nüfusu, n.d.). Since Şanlıurfa is located at a very important crossroads on the Silk Road and is a center for various religions, cultures and civilizations, its music has also been fed by a wide range of sources (Altıngöz et al, 2008, p. 25).

Representative List of the Intangible Cultural Heritage of Humanity since 2010.

While the inscription process of Representative Lists (RL) has been criticized with regard to its possible politicization (Aikawa, 2004, p. 81), what happens to intangible cultural (IC) elements after their acceptance has been a major focus of both researchers and local enthusiasts. On one hand, having an element registered on the UNESCO RL empowers communities, but as Kurin (2004) observes, it also commercializes the element (p. 73). Mountcastle (2010) sees the interpretation of the list as an intervention in culture (p. 344). For Grant (2013), the selection of ICH elements to the UNESCO list is not always about local people's concerns, but is instead driven by government interest (p. 12). Similarly, Seeger (2015) draws attention to the imbalance of benefits between various parties, noting that "the contrast between the honor of being elected to the RL and the tangible rewards to local tradition-bearers has often been quite large" (p. 274).

This raises important questions. For example, what does it mean to be inscribed, or not inscribed, on the UNESCO RL for the local community? (Foster, 2015, p. 151). And who takes on the role of following the elements after their acceptance? Şükrü Üzümcü, the General Secretary of Şanlıurfa City Culture and Education Foundation, was positive about the addition of *sıra gecesi* to the UNESCO RL. He stated that "after its registration to UNESCO, there are 40 or 60 music groups travelling around the country. Now everybody knows it thanks to UNESCO's approval, and the musicians are making money" (Üzümcü, personal communication, September 12, 2019).

Having strong local administrations surrounded by folklorists, tradition bearers, and a large number of culture volunteers has a strong impact on actions toward attempts aimed at cultural safeguarding. The realization of the commercialized version of *sıra gecesi* energized all cultural stakeholders in the region. The Şanlıurfa Metropolitan Municipality started to implement action plans which formed the infrastructure for a "city of music" to be achieved through several projects. One of these was the establishment of the Şanlıurfa Conservatory Branch Directorate in 2018. Made in accordance with the stated aim of the UNESCO 2003 Convention Article 1, "to raise awareness at the local, national and international levels of the importance of the intangible cultural heritage, and of ensuring mutual appreciation thereof . . . ," this step was encouraged and supported by many ethnomusicologists, local artists, governmental entities, and local authorities. The project was an important step for the city's UNESCO candidacy. The Metropolitan Municipality also initiated the forming of local music groups such as "Urfa Ahengi" for the *sıra gecesi* and organizing theatre plays based on this concept.

Although the Şanlıurfa symposium presentations regarding *sıra gecesi* were mostly concerned with variations in practice, the associated debates were dominated by the rapid changes the tradition has undergone. Over three days of panel discussions, a broad consensus emerged that the custom of *sıra gecesi*[5] had quickly become commercialized and touristic, especially following the international attention generated by its inclusion on the list. The well-known folk music singer, Turkish Radio and Television Cooperation (TRT) artist Mehmet Özbek stated:

> A different perception of the *sıra gecesi* was created, as if they consist of only musical performances. In these nightly gathering[s], Turkish folk literature, folk dances and music are transmitted, as well as societal values. We seemed to forget that. In these kinds of academic platforms, the nuances and the essence of it should be transmitted to younger generations. (Özbek, personal communication, November 16, 2018)

Since its ratification by UNESCO, there is a broad perception that the practice has diverged from its real meaning. The following news agency article, which depicts a touristic rendering of *sıra gecesi*, exemplifies the concerns of local folklorists and some traditional bearers:

> The name of the entertainment on your trip to Sanlıurfa, "*sıra gecesi.*" One of Turkey's most important belief and cultural tourism centers is Sanlıurfa, and one of the indispensable parts of the music culture of the city, organized in historical guest houses and some hotels, the *sıra geceleri* attract the attention of local and foreign tourists. (Egtü, 2018, para. 1, 3)

---

[5] Because it is a frequently used terminology in Şanlıurfa, *sıra gecesi* will be used throughout the paper instead of "traditional *sohbet* meetings." Literally, *sıra* can mean "line," "queue," or "sequence," and *gece* means "night." Local folklorist Kürkçüoğlu points out that the *sıra gecesi* is the most important factor in the development and survival of music in Şanlıurfa and the emergence of new compositions and artists. For centuries, the local music culture has played a great role in the recognition of Urfa (Kürkçüoğlu, 2017, p. 9).

In today's Şanlıurfa, it is arguably difficult to witness an (authentic) version of the ceremonial and traditional *sıra gecesi*. It has become a regular source of income for many musicians, and in a city that is famous for its male singers and instrumentalists, those who have knowledge of local and traditional "classical *maqam*" and/or folk songs, get together and perform as groups. According to Abdullah Balak, a well-respected local folklorist and composer, this transformation started when *sıra gecesi* events were broadcast on television in the 1990s (personal communication, April 15, 2015). These 90-minute TV programs were hosted by İbrahim Tatlıses, arguably the most famous folk singer from Şanlıurfa, and included musicians, vocalists, and a traditional *sıra gecesi*[6] repertoire.

While the UNESCO RL is intended to represent better visibility for elements of intangible cultural heritage and to heighten awareness of their significance, the Urfa case reveals that this can be a double-edged sword. *Sıra gecesi* certainly became more visible after its registration to UNESCO, both nationally and internationally. However, they became standardized and turned into stage performances and material for tourism. Similarly, the *Mevlevi Sema* ceremonies, renowned for their "Whirling Dervishes," have been facing the same reality for much longer. The "Derwish Experience— Live Show and Exhibition" at the Hodja Pasha Culture Center in Istanbul is just one of many examples.

Government-sponsored cultural elements can often become homogenous and generic, as observed in the case of the *sıra gecesi* and *Mevlevi Sema* (inscribed in 2008). As Ölçer Özünel (2019) pointed out, the Convention emphasizes sustainability in line with the 2030 United Nations Sustainable Development Goals, and on promoting the revitalization of the element in a way that does not result in excessive commercialization and excessive tourism (p. 43). Taking the necessary measures to keep the element from commercialization and preserving its core essence should begin at the local level, with support from ministries, independent reviewers, and civil society. As Seeger (2015) observed, "UNESCO can make recommendations, offer training or technical assistance, and sometimes provide funding, but it cannot interfere with the internal operations of its member nations" (p. 274).

---

[6] Şanlıurfa *Sıra Gecesi* and Elazığ *Kürsübaşı* meetings function as a master-apprentice type of conservatoire to produce traditionally trained performers (UNESCO, 2010, p. 5).

128 OLCAY MUSLU

## Domaniç: What Happens in Rural Areas without Power Structures?

Case studies into the sustainability of music have drawn different conclusions concerning the safeguaring of endangered cultures, revealing the multi-disciplinary structure of ethnomusicology (e.g., Hawkes, 2001, pp. 52–53; Hemetek, 2006, pp. 35–57; Hofman, 2010, p. 30; Howard, 2012, pp. 113–141; Seeger, 2006, p. 222; Schippers & Grant, 2016; Sheehy, 1992, pp. 324–331; Titon, 2009, p. 119; Pettan, 2010, p. 123). What follows is an account of my own work as a researcher and a woman to support the safeguarding of the traditional dance and music practices in the Domaniç region of Anatolia. Due to the effect of gender discrimination on dances, female practices became the focus of this study. The bulk of fieldwork was undertaken between 2013 and 2016, and the findings reflect the political and cultural environment of that time. In contrast to the UNESCO-driven response in Urfa, this example can be considered as an independent ethnomusicologist's efforts toward sustaining traditional practices. It highlights some key challenges and opportunities for sustaining ICH in Turkey, and shows that without the support of local, national, and international authorities, the safeguarding capacity of independent actors remains limited.

## Local Community: The Dimensions of the Model

Domaniç is a district of Kütahya in western Anatolia, in the north Aegean side of Turkey, and has a history that goes back to 5500–3500 BCE. Domaniç is an important region not only because of its cultural richness, but also because it was the founding place of the Ottoman state (İnalcık, 2009, pp. 11–14). As the Domaniç region has no specific cultural element (especially within the criteria of UNESCO ICH RL), and because its cultural elements are in danger of vanishing, it is almost impossible to present them to international organizations such as UNESCO or to governmental entities. Instead, grassroots efforts are more appropriate.

As Common argued, emphasizing current and prospective threats to sustainability is more important than preparing the blueprint for a sustainable system (1995, p. 6). In seeking to identify obstacles to cultural sustainability, and reasons for sustainability being at risk, one must first understand the roles of arbiters of power within the culture's systems of government and

SUGGESTED MODEL FOR THE DOMANIÇ CASE

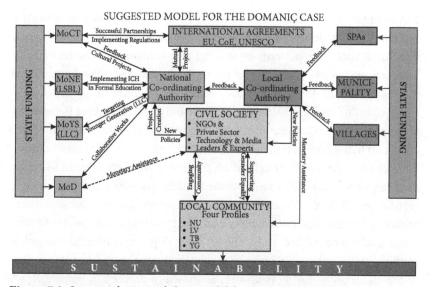

Figure 7.3  Suggested sustainability. model for the Domaniç case.

Abbreviations used in the model: CoE: Council of Europe; EU: European Union; LCA(s): Local Coordination Authorities; LV(s): local villagers; MoCT: Ministry of Culture and Tourism; MoNE: Ministry of National Education; MoYS: Ministry of Youth and Sport; MoD: Ministry of Development; NCA(s): National Coordination Authorities; ND(s): nomadic dances; NGO(s): non-governmental organizations; NU(s): nostalgic urbanites; SD(s): settlers' dances; SPA(s): Special Provincial Administrations; TB(s): tradition bearers; UN: United Nations; UNESCO: United Nations Educational Scientific and Cultural Organizationl; YG: Young Generation (Muslu Gardner, 2015b, p. 137).

community. The first task therefore was to identify all of the stakeholders that have an effect, however small, on sustaining the intangible cultural heritage of the region. This resulted in a model[7] (Figure 7.3) to identify the various stakeholders who may play a role in the development of practical approaches to cultural sustainability in Turkey.

Kurin (2004) observed that "revitalizing communities to participate in cultural projects and working with the isolated community is logistically and sociologically challenging" (p. 72). Providing access to culture is the most problematic issue for Domaniç since its remoteness from central government restricts opportunities. This rang true particularly for the younger generation, who increasingly leave Domaniç for other parts of the country. Domaniç's gradually decreasing population (which dropped from 19,560 to

[7] The model was conducted under the supervision of Prof. Songül Karahasanoğlu at Istanbul Technical University.

15,901 in two years, according to the 2014 data from the Turkish Statistical Institute), its associated economic and industrial decline, the separately structured social life patterns of its men and women, and the restrictions imposed on women through the legitimized gendered roles have all put the region's traditional female dance and music culture in danger of vanishing (Muslu Gardner, 2015a, p. 64). Since only a few members of the older generation—the custodians of the traditional heritage—were still alive, focusing on living human treasures was a top priority.

Since the values of ICH cannot be preserved and kept alive in libraries, archives, or museums, but rather come to life in people's minds and actions (Proschan, 2008, p. 17), developing participatory projects became paramount following the compilation and documentation of the traditional music and dance culture of the region. Four different community member profiles were developed in order to follow and trace the traditional practices in the community during fieldwork, as shown in Figure 7.3, namely NUs[8], LVs, TBs, and YGs.

Several collaborative projects, including the filming of two regional television programs, establishing the *Domaniç Kayı Boyu Kültür Derneği* (Domaniç Kayı Clan Culture Association), organizing dance and music workshops and a stage show with local villagers, arranging weekend folk dance courses for children, and recording local folk songs, were conducted in 2015 according to the guidelines set out in the 2003 UNESCO Convention. These projects were made possible due to the efforts of local administrators (for transportation and financial support), local folklorists and villagers, a folk dance teacher, local musicians such as the brothers Osman and Mehmet Demiröz (both *bağlama* players), institutions, local-regional media organs, and myself (as the only music scholar). The success of the projects increased the general community's interest in its own cultural inheritance and facilitated the revival of some dances and musical practices.

## Traditional Practices, Gender, and Power Structures

Gender is a central concept in contemporary culture and draws attention to both real and perceived differences between men and women. In Domaniç,

---

[8] Educated, socially and geographically mobile people, whose reason for performing the folk repertoire often stems from a sense of nostalgia for their vanishing culture.

the separately structured social life patterns and the restrictions imposed on many women through legitimized gendered roles have contributed to putting the region's traditional female dance culture in danger. One of the most striking findings from my fieldwork was that the only female dance and music form which has a potential to survive, as it proved to be the favorite dance style among the local women, was in fact a men's dance called *Domaniç Havası* (Domaniç style).

This male dance style is inclusive, energetic, and, thanks to the social mores of the area, regularly and publicly demonstrated (by men!) at most festivals and celebrations. As Nettl observed, in many cultures, men live a more or less public life and are thus responsible for dealing with the outside world. As a result, fieldworkers often encounter difficulty in attracting female participants (2005, p. 410). As Domaniç is a place where I have family ties, it was possible for me as an independent researcher to gain access to local people and their traditions that would normally be closed to "outsiders." In addition, being female also allowed me to interview and interact with the women of the region. The women of Domaniç are therefore subject to two different sets of restrictions: those imposed by the wider society and also those imposed by their own group. The roles commonly imposed on women restrict their status in many areas, including artistic productions such as music and dance, and the availability of time and space (Ergur, 2009, p. 68). This can also be seen in some of the elements of Turkey's UNESCO Representative List, where no women are given the status of "female artist."

Awareness raising requires "scientific and educational support, together with modern training processes" and partnerships among the institutions, cultural organizations, and local groups (Kutlu, 2013, p. 52; Herrick, 2015, p. 553). There is a "natural" connection between cultural participation and lifelong learning, and both are well targeted by structural funding and programming, and take a central place in EU long-term strategies (Sacco, 2011, p. 14). As a non-formal education system of the Ministry of National Education, Life-long Learning Centres and Let Schools Be Live were used in this project as venues for participatory activities and as a way to promote them to the community through weekend dance and music courses.

Having the opportunity to access these existing educational platforms was crucial to ensuring participation, but my capacity to do so is undeniably limited in comparison with that of an organizational response. Another crucial parameter of the ICH is the local administrative systems of culture.

The sub-national government level in Turkey includes 81 provinces, 3,225 municipalities and 35,000 villages. These local administrative units were defined in the 1982 Constitution as "public entities and decision-making bodies constituted by electorates in order to address the common needs of the city, municipality and village communities" and were recognized as indispensable components of administration, together with central administration (Ministry of the Interior, 2013, n.p.). Thus, the local administrative structure in Turkey can be characterized by the coexistence of two institutional frameworks: the central government and the local government. All ministries specialize in a field, such as education, health, or culture, and have provincial field branches.

In addition, the MoCT is represented in the provinces by Provincial Directorates of Culture and Tourism (Aksoy & Enlil, 2011, pp. 35–38). According to the MoCT's own reports, "nearly 2,634,900 Turkish Lira (TL; approximately US$323,000) has been given to a total of 540 local, national, and international organizations, charities and local municipalities during 2012" (MoCT, 2013a, p.78). The monetary support of the MoCT for local municipalities, Special Provincial Administrations, and villages creates opportunities for future projects and plans. However, when examining the municipal budget for the Kütahya governorship, it is worth noting that the share for Domaniç municipality is only 2% (Governorship of Kütahya, 2013, pp. 73–76). The former mayor of Domaniç, Sahvet Ertürk, regretted that while "our main aim is to develop regional and rural tourism to create revenue for the region [and to] support culture and art with a greater level [ ... ], we can only act within our limits" (personal communication, May 12, 2014).

Maintaining relationships with the related power structures is important in the development of local projects, even when these structures are considered harmful (Seeger, 2015, p. 40). However, managing relationships between stakeholders outside of formal structures is a colossal task. A lack of cooperation between the local municipality and the Kütahya city Governorship (Valilik) due to differing political affiliations prevented many participatory projects in Domaniç. A few local festivals organized by the Domaniç municipality have provided platforms for local folkloric practices. Traditionally, such festivals include demonstrations from various folk-dance groups, the General Staff Janissary marching band, and a unit of cavalry, all of which are favorably viewed by both participants and spectators.

In addition, relationships between stakeholders such as the local community, the media, and the Municipality of Domaniç require management. My attempts to reach out to the SPA, and thereby provide coherence between the Governorship and the Local Municipality, failed. This illustrates how both authorities and stakeholders must be encouraged to interact with elements found within civil society through policies and investments, but also that formal administration is required.

## After the Fieldwork

Follow-up visits (after 2016) to the region have helped to reveal both successes and failures, as well as the current needs of the region. Today, *the Kayı Boyu Domaniç Kültür Derneği* [Kayı Boyu Domaniç Culture Association] is still active, but it is struggling to survive due to the local villagers' lack of interest and financial limitations. In village weddings, male dances are still more visible. Thanks to the encouragement of folk-dance groups offering weekend courses for both primary and secondary schools, participation remains quite strong.

This example illustrates the point that without support from local, national, and international authorities, the safeguarding capacity of researchers remains limited. This often stems from the economic, infrastructural, and sociological structure of the society at large. In this case, the attempt to propose a model for the sustainability of traditional music of the region remained solely local. The collaborative obligations of the SPAs, municipalities, and villages could not be fulfilled due to the political differences between the groups in Domaniç. This ultimately made it almost impossible to reach any consensus in identifying the local cultural elements for any future attempts for their candidacy for UNESCO list. On the other hand, the region's administrative center, Kütahya, has become one of the world's 180 "creative cities" as designated by UNESCO in 2017, and is registered as one of the 37 craft and folk-art cities.[9] However, isolated regions like Domaniç are still in need of more attention from the local boards and their dependent units of the UNESCO Turkey National Committee.

Based on the statements of the representatives of the cultural departments and organizations in UNESCO, there is no acceptance or support for individual projects regarding the safeguarding of ICH unless they are completely

---

[9] For details: http://www.kutahya.gov.tr/unesco-yaratici-sehirler-aginda-kadim-birsehir-kutahya.

directed by the Committee's fieldwork team. Partnerships between the local governments and cultural NGOs or independent cultural organizations are very minimal, and often nonexistent.

## Conclusion

Since the entry into force of the 2003 UNESCO Convention on the Safeguarding of the Intangible Cultural Heritage, the intangible cultural heritage platform has witnessed dramatic changes in the perception of heritage. The text of the Convention primarily refers to the group, community, and individuals as carriers, transmitters, and protectors of heritage. However, the implementation of the Convention is largely left to state actors. This becomes a basis for the dominance of diplomacy and bureaucracy in the functioning of the convention. While the Convention itself explicitly encourages intermediaries and mediators who will build bridges between these points to ensure meaningful communication, the landscape is in fact extremely political, diplomatic, and bureaucratic, as other contributions to this volume also illustrate.

There have been strong critiques of the commodification of registered elements on the UNESCO RL over the past 15 years or so. However, the registered elements of intangible cultural heritage such as Mevlana and *sıra gecesi* have always been used as promotional materials, regardless of whether or not they have been registered by UNESCO. Even though the commodification of ICH elements and their usage as material for tourism are seen as destructive by some communities, there is also a counter argument that states that in fact such usage allows the elements in question to be better safeguarded. In Turkey, whirling dervishes, *sıra gecesi*, and *âşıklık* (minstrelsy) traditions have always been used as entertainment and cultural promotional materials, although the extent to which the performing groups accurately reflect traditional practices remains a matter of some debate.

UNESCO Turkey National Committee member Ekici (2011) emphasizes that active participation by heritage bearers must be encouraged and that heritage must be assured a continued place in daily life in accordance with the aims of the UNESCO Convention. However, it should be remembered that the goals of safeguarding projects are almost impossible to achieve in economically and socially challenged places. Detecting the obstacles within such regions and the problems arising from their power structures is a matter of paramount importance, and the Local Boards of UNESCO should become more aware of this issue. There is a need to organize and revise the steps to be taken at the national level in order to implement the Convention by ensuring visibility for both the local and public actors.

Finally, if practices are gender specific, I would argue that they should not be accepted without accompanying proposals or explanations. If UNESCO lists are to generate genuinely positive action and contribute to equity, they cannot contain elements from one half of a culture with no representation of the other. Without this, there is a danger in creating a permanent imbalance, and the Convention requires more inclusive criteria to assure gender equality, and practical instruments to implement it. If only the most visible or exploitable cultural heritage elements are selected for inclusion on the UNESCO RL lists, it risks tainting a process that can and should have positive outcomes for all.

## References

Aikawa, N. (2004). What have been the effects of the UNESCO ICH lists? *Museum International, 56*(1–2), 75–85. https://www.unesco-ichcap.org/eng/ek/sub8/pdf_file/06/06.Chapter%203_What%20Have%20Been%20the%20Effects%20of%20the%20UNESCO%20ICH%20Lists.pdf.

Aksoy, A., & Enlil, Z. (2011). *Cultural economy compendium Istanbul 2010.* Istanbul Bilgi University Press.

Altıngöz, İ. H., Karadağlı, B., & Yüzgen, F. (2008). *Urfalı bestekarlar.* Şanlıurfa: Şanlıurfa Valiliği İl Kültür ve Turizm Müdürlüğü Yayınları.

Aydoğdu Atasoy, Ö. (2018). *Somut olmayan kültürel mirasın korunmasında icracı kurum T.C. Kültür ve Turizm Bakanlığı'nın çalışmaları üzerine bir değerlendirme (2006–2016)* [An evaluation on the works of the executive institution, the Republic of Turkey Ministry of Culture and Tourism regarding safeguarding the intangible cultural heritage (2006–2016)]. Unpublished master's thesis, Ankara University Social Sciences Institution, Ankara, Turkey.

Bouchenaki, M. (2003). *The interdependency of the tangible and intangible cultural heritage.* Paper presented at the 14th ICOMOS General Assembly and International Symposium: "Place, memory, meaning: Preserving intangible values in monuments and sites," Victoria Falls, Zimbabwe. http://openarchive.icomos.org/468/1/2_-_Allocution_Bouchenaki.pdf.

Common, M. (1995). *Sustainability and policy limits to economics.* Cambridge University Press.

Council of Europe. (2013). *Review of cultural policy in Turkey: Expert's report.* http://www.coe.int/t/dg4/cultureheritage/culture/Reviews/ CDCPP-Bu-2013-19-Turkeynational_en.pdf.

Egtü, M. (2018). Şanlıurfa'da eğlencenin adı "sıra gecesi" [The name of your entertainment in Şanlıurfa is "*sıra gecesi*"]. *Anadolu Ajansı.* https://www.aa.com.tr/tr/turkiye/sanliurfada-eglencenin-adi-sira-gecesi/1315195.

Ekici, M. (2011). Âşıklık geleneğinin güncel sorunları [Current problems of the tradition of minstrelsy]. In Ö. Oğuz & S. Gürçayır (Eds.), *Somut olmayan kültürel miras yaşayan âşık sanatı uluslararası sempozyum bildiri kitabı* (pp. 7–15). Gazi Üniversitesi THBMER Yayınları.

Ergur, A. (2009). *Müzikli aklın defteri* [The notebook of the musical mind]. Pan Yayıncılık.

Foster, M. D. (2015). UNESCO on the ground: Local perspectives on global policy for intangible cultural heritage. *Indiana University Press Journal of Folklore Research, 52*(2–3), 143–156. https://www.jstor.org/stable/10.2979/jfolkrese.52.2-3.143.

Governorship of Kütahya. (2013). *Provincial local government union briefing file.* http://www.kutahya.gov.tr/kitap_mahalli.pdf.

Grant, C. (2013). Developing a triage system for sustaining intangible cultural heritage. *International Journal of Social Sustainability in Economic, Social and Cultural Context, 9*(1), 11–22. doi: 10.18848/2325-1115/CGP/v09i01/55208.

Hawkes, J. (2001). *The fourth pillar of sustainability: Culture's essential role in public planning.* (Original work published in 1946). Cultural Development Network.

Hemetek, U. (2006). Applied ethnomusicology in the process of the political recognition of a minority: A case study of the Austrian Roma. In *Yearbook for traditional music* (Vol 38, pp. 35–57). Cambridge University Press. http://www.jstor.org/stable/20464971

Herrick, S. E. O. (2015). Strategies and opportunities in the education sector for applied ethnomusicology. In S. Pettan & J. T. Titon (Eds.), *The Oxford handbook of applied ethnomusicology* (pp. 553–600). Oxford University Press.

Hofman, A. (2010). Maintaining the distance, othering the subaltern: Rethinking ethnomusicologists' engagement in advocacy and social justice. In K. Harrison, E. Mackinlay, & S. Pettan. (Eds.), *Applied ethnomusicology historical and contemporary approaches* (pp. 21–35). Cambridge Scholars.

Howard, K. (2012). Authenticity and authority: Conflicting agendas in the preservation of music and dance at Korea's state sacrificial rituals. In K. Howard. (Ed.), *Music as intangible cultural heritage: Policy, ideology, and practice in the preservation of East Asian traditions* (pp. 113–141). Ashgate.

İnalcık, H. (2009). *Devlet-i 'Aliyye Osmanlı İmparatorluğu üzerine araştırmalar-I* [Research into the Ottoman Empire-I: Devlet-i 'Aliyye]. İş Bankası Kültür Yayınları.

Kalın, İ. (2017, March 7). Third Culture Council discusses culture, change, globalization. *Daily Sabah.* https://www.dailysabah.com/columns/ibrahim-kalin/2017/03/07/third-culture-council-discusses-culture-change-globalization.

Kurin, R. (2004). Safeguarding intangible cultural heritage in the 2003 UNESCO Convention: A critical appraisal. *Museum International, 56*(1–2), 66–77. doi: 10.1111/j.1350-0775.2004.00459.x.

Kutlu, M. M. (2013). ICH and formal education: Folk culture course experience. In M. Ö. Oğuz, E. Ö. Özünel, & S. G. Teke (Eds.), *The future of intangible cultural heritage: Turkey experience* (pp. 49–52). UNESCO Turkey National Commission. https://www.unesco.org.tr/Content_Files/Content/Yayinlar/sokum_deneyimioptimize.pdf.

Kürkçüoğlu, S. (2017). *Şanlıurfa sıra gecesi geleneği ve türküleri* [Sıra gecesi tradition and folksongs in Şanlıurfa]. Şanlıurfa: Şanlıurfa Kültür Eğitim Sanat ve Araştırma Vakfı Yayınları.

Ministry of Culture and Tourism. (2013a). *European programme of national cultural reviews: Cultural policy in Turkey.* http://www.coe.int/t/dg4/cultureheritage/culture/Reviews/CDCPP-Bu-2013-19-Turkeynational_en.pdf

Ministry of Culture and Tourism. (2013b). *Turkey's 2015–2019 term second strategic plan.* http://www.kultur.gov.tr/Eklenti/ 36784,stratejik-plan-2015-2019pdf.pdf?0.

Ministry of Culture and Tourism General Directorate of Research and Education. (2016). *Administrative context diagram.* https://www.slideshare.net/UNESCOVENICE/turkey-intangible-culture-heritage-in-turkey

Ministry of Interior Republic of Turkey. (2013). *General directorate of local authorities.* https://www.icisleri.gov.tr/illeridaresi/.

Mountcastle, A. (2010). Safeguarding intangible cultural heritage and the inevitability of loss: A Tibetan example. *Studia ethnologica Croatica, 22*(1), 339–359. https://hrcak.srce.hr/62257?lang=en.

Muslu Gardner, O. (2015a). Sustaining endangered music and dance culture: A case study from rural Turkey. *Müzik Bilim Dergisi, 1*(6), 60–95.

Muslu Gardner, O. (2015b). *Sustainability of traditional dances and music: A model for Domaniç, Turkey.* Unpublished PhD thesis, Istanbul Technical University Social Sciencies Institute, Istanbul, Turkey.

Oğuz, M. Ö. (2013). Preface. In M. Ö. Oğuz, E. Ö. Özünel, & S. G. Teke (Eds.), *The future of intangible cultural heritage: Turkey experience* (pp. 5–6). UNESCO Turkey National Commission. https://www.unesco.org.tr/Content_Files/Content/Yayinlar/sokum_deneyimioptimize.pdf

Oğuz, Ö. (2018). Advisory bodies of UNESCO's 1972 and 2003 Conventions: Experiences and problems. *Millî Folklor, 30*(120), 46–58.

Ölçer Özünel, E. (2019). *Geleneğin geleceği: Somut olmayan kültürel miras unsuru olarak âşıklık* [The future of tradition: Minstrelsy as an element of intangible cultural heritage]. *AHBV Edebiyat Fakültesi Dergisi,* (1), 39–45. https://dergipark.org.tr/tr/download/article-file/910709.

Pettan, S. (2010). Applied ethnomusicology: Bridging research and action. *Music and Arts in Action, 2*(2). https://ore.exeter.ac.uk/repository/bitstream/handle/10036/3950/pettan_2010.pdf?sequence=1

Presidency of Republic of Turkey. (2017, March 3). *We should set new cultural goals for ourselves in accordance with the 2023 vision.* https://www.tccb.gov.tr/en/news/542/72201/we-should-set-new-cultural-goals-for-ourselves-in-accordance-with-the-2023-vision

Proschan, F. (2008). Basic challenges of sustaining intangible heritage. *Meeting report UNESCO-EIIHCAP regional meeting safeguarding intangible heritage and sustainable cultural tourism: Opportunities and challenges* (pp. 17–22). https://ich.unesco.org/doc/src/00349-EN.pdf

Sacco, P. L. (2011). *Culture 3.0: A new perspective for the EU 2014–2020 structural funds programming.* http://www.interarts.net/descargas/interarts2577.pdf.

Schippers, H., & Grant, C. (Eds.) (2016). *Sustainable futures for music cultures: An ecological perspective.* Oxford University Press.

Seeger, A. (2006). Lost lineages and neglected peers: Ethnomusicologists outside academia. *Ethnomusicology. 50*(2), 214–235. http://www.jstor.org/stable/20174450.

Seeger, A. (2015). Understanding UNESCO: A complex organization with many parts and many actors. *Journal of Folklore Research, 52*(2–3), 269–280. https://www.jstor.org/stable/10.2979/jfolkrese.52.23.269?seq=1#page_scan_tab_contents.

Sheehy, D. (1992). A few notions about philosophy and strategy in applied ethnomusicology. *Ethnomusicology, 36*(3), 323–336. http://www.jstor.org/stable/851866.

Sobacı, M. Z., Köseoğlu, Ö., & Mis, N. (2018). Reforming the policymaking process in Turkey's new presidential system. *Insight Turkey, 20*(4), 183–210. https://www.jstor.org/stable/pdf/26542179.pdf.

Tekelioğlu. (2001). Modernizing reforms and Turkish music in the 1930s. *Turkish Studies, 2*(1), 93–108. doi: 10.1080/14683849.2001.11009175.

Titon, J. T. (2009). Music and sustainability: An ecological viewpoint. *The World of Music*, *51*(1), 119–137. http://www.jstor.org/discover/ 10.2307/41699866?sid= 21105219936091&uid=2&uid=4577404757&uid=60&uid=70&uid=3&uid= 4577404767&uid=2134.

United Nations Educational, Scientific and Cultural Organization. (2003). Convention for the safeguarding of the intangible cultural heritage. http://unesdoc.unesco.org/images/0013/001325/132540e.pdf.

United Nations Educational, Scientific and Cultural Organization. (2010). Nomination file no. 00385 for inscription on the representative list of the intangible cultural heritage in 2010. Presented at the Intergovernmental Committee for the Safeguarding of the Intangible Cultural Heritage, Fifth Session, Nairobi, Kenya. https://ich.unesco.org/doc/src/07483-EN.pdf.

# 8

# Community Engagement as a Site of Struggle

## UNESCO Conventions, Intangible Cultural Heritage, and State Agendas in Malaysia

*Tan Sooi Beng*

Over the past three to four decades, the concept of community engagement has changed how international organizations create and implement policies regarding development. Following the Brundtland Report that introduced the idea of "sustainable development" (WCED, 1987, p. 43), agencies of the United Nations, such as the World Bank, the Food and Agriculture Organization (FAO), and the United Nations Children's Fund (UNICEF), began to endorse the "participatory approach" where development becomes the collective responsibility of all the stakeholders, including the government, corporate sector, civil society, and communities in urban, environmental, agricultural, and medical planning.

Similarly, the UNESCO Convention for the Safeguarding of the Intangible Cultural Heritage (ICH) has called for the involvement of communities and bottom-up approaches to sustain their own cultures (Blake, 2008; Kurin 2004). Article 15 of the 2003 Convention for the Safeguarding of ICH states that "each State Party shall endeavor to ensure the widest possible participation of communities, groups and, where appropriate, individuals that create, maintain and transmit such heritage, and to involve them actively in its management." In 2015, the Intergovernmental Committee for the Safeguarding of ICH adopted the point that "Communities, groups, and where applicable individuals should have the primary role in safeguarding their own ICH" as one of the 12 "Ethical Principles for Safeguarding ICH" (Windhoek, Namibia, November 30–December 4, 2015). Heritage bearers and communities should also play a key role in identifying what is their heritage and how

Tan Sooi Beng, *Community Engagement as a Site of Struggle* In: *Music, Communities, Sustainability.*
Edited by: Huib Schippers and Anthony Seeger, Oxford University Press. © Oxford University Press 2022.
DOI: 10.1093/oso/9780197609101.003.0008

it is to be safeguarded and transmitted. Their participation is required in the nomination to the UNESCO ICH lists and in the follow-up plans (https://ich.unesco.org/en/ethics-and-ich-00866).

Despite the drive toward community engagement in the safeguarding and transmission of ICH at the global level, heritage bearers in many countries of the Global South face challenges that are beyond their control. Cultural conservation remains state-centric in these nations. Through appointed cultural experts and the introduction of cultural policies, these national governments determine the content and aesthetic values of art forms, make conservation plans, and control funding for the safeguarding of ICH. The top-down initiatives can be problematic, as they lack the understanding, knowledge, and engagement of the grassroots communities who own the ICH. As a consequence, certain forms of ICH continue to decline, and cultural custodians are increasingly being sidelined. As the 2003 Convention for the Safeguarding of ICH commits the relevant States Parties to seek nomination and manage activities, genres of the majority are often selected for nomination; community participation and bottom-up approaches frequently become tools for the nomination process (Seeger, 2009; Lixinsky, 2011; Bertorelli, 2018).

Malaysia, the country where I was born and live, is a case in point. The national government has been implementing top-down cultural policies and censorship laws since 1970 in an effort to unify all the ethnic groups in the country. The top-down policies illustrate the political paradox of a modern postcolonial nation that projects multicultural images of diversity globally for the purposes of tourism, but attempts to create a distinct national identity based on the majority and sidelines indigenous, minority, and mixed cultures within its boundaries. For this reason, Malaysia did not endorse the UNESCO Convention on the Protection and Promotion of Diversity of Cultural Expressions (2005), and the Universal Declaration of Cultural Diversity (2001). It also did not ratify the Declaration on the Rights of Indigenous Peoples (2007), and the Convention on the Elimination of All Forms of Racial Discrimination (1969) that were introduced by the United Nations High Commission for Human Rights. Malaysia ratified the 2003 Convention for the Safeguarding of ICH in 2013, as the latter did not specifically refer to the human and cultural rights of minorities and indigenous peoples.

Notwithstanding, this chapter shows that ICH and community engagement are contested spaces. Even though ICH is constantly being appropriated by hegemonic structures of power such as nation-states, universities, and local cultural agencies that intervene in heritage-making following their own agendas, challenges occur among different communities and stakeholders over the ownership of ICH, as well as how art forms are to be represented and conserved (Logan et al., 2016). Diverse groups are continually reconstructing ICH and using UNESCO conventions and the ethical principles for their own purposes in specific states of Malaysia (Tan, 1990, 2003).[1]

This chapter adds to the few academic works on policies and regulations that have affected the safeguarding and sustainability of ICH in Asia (Schippers & Grant, 2016; Foley, 2014; Park, 2013; Howard, 2012; Smith & Akagawa, 2009). Although the focus is on Malaysia, the discussion feeds into the global debate of how postcolonial countries employ ICH to create a sense of national identity among their multiethnic citizens, while top-down cultural engineering has marginalized the communities who practice the ICH and has mired the transmission processes. UNESCO designations might not facilitate the empowerment of communities to sustain their traditions if state cultural agencies continue to use top-down approaches and are not open to or understand the idea of community engagement in ICH conservation. Here I am offering two different examples of how sociopolitical and religious issues can affect the community engagement paradigm that the 2003 Convention passes over.

The first section of this chapter examines how the Malaysian national cultural policy and centralization by the federal government in the past 60 years have resulted in the standardization of selected national forms of culture. National heritage agencies have also incorporated the top-down national culture narratives into the international UNESCO discourse in the country. Following this, I discuss the complex intersections between the international UNESCO designations, national agendas, strategies of local state governments, and attempts of local cultural custodians to keep their traditions alive. Specifically, I look at the fates of (1) the Mak Yong dance theatre of Kelantan that was inscribed as a "Masterpiece of the Oral and Intangible Heritage of Humanity" in 2005, and three years later was placed on the Representative List of the Intangible Cultural Heritage of

---

[1] Different ethnic groups and individuals negotiate with the nation-state and among themselves to create their own national identities. See Tan (1990, 2003) for an account of the Malaysian government's attempts at social control through the national culture policy and other laws created in the 1970s and 1980s, and the responses of various ethnic and social groups involved in the performing arts.

Humanity; and (2) the multicultural ICH of George Town, inscribed as a World UNESCO Site, together with Malacca, in 2008.

## National Top-Down Policies: "Malaysia Truly Asia" versus One National Culture

Those who have visited Malaysia are familiar with the slogan "Malaysia Truly Asia," a marketing strategy to attract tourists to the country. Tourism brochures, posters, and television advertisements showcase neatly packaged stereotypical excerpts of dances from the various ethnic groups and Indigenous communities, staged by national performers wearing colorful traditional costumes and carrying scarves, fans, or hats. These spectacles convey the image of a nation rich in ethnic diversity where people live harmoniously. They are also iconic of a nation that is technologically advanced; yet rooted in its own cultural identity.[2] However, these displays make cultural particularities and conflicts insignificant.

Within its boundaries, Malaysia has attempted to promote one national culture and one national identity so as to unify the many ethnic groups living in Malaysia. Malaysia is typical of many independent nations with a multiethnic and multireligious population whose boundaries were demarcated by the British colonialists. The formation of Malaysia and the inclusion of Sabah and Sarawak in 1963 further enriched the country with many other indigenous ethnic communities.[3] From the last population census (Department of Statistics, 2020), Malaysia's 32.7 million citizens consist of 69.6% Bumiputera (translated as "sons of the soil," which comprise Malays and other Indigenous groups such as the Orang Asli, Kadazan, Bajau, Bidayuh, Melanau, Penan, etc.), 22.6% Chinese (of different dialect groups from South China), 6.8% Indians (originating mainly from South India), and 1% others (including Arabs, Eurasians, Indonesians, Thais, Burmese, etc.).

[2] The creation of spectacles of multiethnic traditions is in keeping with *Wawasan 2020* [Vision 2020], Malaysia's narrative of Asian modernity. *Wawasan 2020* envisions Malaysia as an "industrialized" country by the year 2020; a nation which is "fully developed along all the dimensions: economically, politically, socially, spiritually, psychologically, and culturally" (Mahathir Mohamad, 1991). See Tan (2003) for detailed analysis.

[3] Malaysia consists of 14 states with their own state assemblies; 12 of the states form Peninsular or West Malaysia, while Sabah and Sarawak are situated on the northern coast of Borneo.

Following the 1969 riots when ethnic relations broke down in the country,[4] the national government prioritized the task of creating a national and common culture through policies that could promote national unity. In 1971, it was decided at a national congress that the national culture of Malaysia should be "based on the cultures of the people indigenous to the region," that "elements from other cultures which are suitable and reasonable may be incorporated," and that "Islam will be an important element" (KKBS 1973, p. vii). National styles of the performing arts based on selected Malay folk and popular arts were created and presented as the traditional arts. In particular, Malay folk social dances such as the Joget, Inang, and Zapin were adapted and went through a process of standardization. These folk dances, which were once popular entertainment at Malay weddings and other social functions, were highly charged, as the male and female dancers executed flirtatious movements, teasing without touching one another. National versions of these dances that were created in the early 1970s had the rowdy nature eliminated, while teasing and flirtatious dance movements were stylized (Mohd Anis, 1993, p. 84). As I have analyzed in an earlier study, Bangsawan (Malay commercial theatre that combines Malay, Western, Indian, Chinese, Javanese, and Middle Eastern elements) was another selected genre that underwent nationalization. The eclectic Bangsawan was gradually Malayized in the 1970s and 1980s (Tan, 1993). National dancers and musicians were trained to showcase the selected forms of national culture locally and overseas (Ismail Zain, 1977; Tan, 1990).

What are the consequences of these top-down policies and cultural engineering in Malaysia? It cannot be denied that state intervention in the arts has provided new contexts and opportunities for learning and performing the Malay traditional arts. It is also possible for the younger generation to learn the Malay traditional arts in institutions of higher learning and colleges. Nevertheless, the creation of specific national forms in line with state policies has facilitated the homogenization and sanitization of selected traditional performing arts. Cultural administrators, who act in the state's interests, and control resources and funding for the arts, have the

---

[4] Policies for restructuring society and the inculcation of loyalty to the nation were also introduced. The New Economic Policy (NEP) was implemented in 1970 to ensure economic growth, eliminate poverty among the rural Malays, and to create a commercial-industrial *bumiputera* community.

prerogative to interpret traditions. Certain Malay forms are chosen as representative of the Malays and are decontextualized so that they become part of national culture. While some multicultural elements are inserted, they are often decorative. Standardization has also occurred through certain criteria set by cultural officers for school, state, and national competitions and festivals. These recreated traditions are now recognized as the norm by the younger generation.

After five decades of cultural centralization, a single national culture that is accepted by all the different ethnic groups has not emerged. Instead, cultural policies and the top-down approaches for cultural conservation have posed threats to Malay veteran artists and the performing art traditions of the country. The nationalized forms of spectacles are performed by professionals from the government agencies rather than by the traditional practitioners themselves. Once folk forms of culture are taken out of their context, standardized, packaged, or recreated grandiosely, they can also lose their spirit.

At the same time, the national culture and top-down policies created controversy among the minority and Indigenous groups whose cultures were not considered as part of national culture. In response, the respective ethnic communities that were usually divided by class, language, and religion came together to rejuvenate their cultures. For instance, the different Chinese communities have promoted selected forms of Chinese music, dance, and theatre through various cultural clubs, despite the lack of government support; street processions for religious festivals in honor of the birthdays of Chinese deities have drawn large numbers of devotees and have become symbols of ethnic identity in various parts of the country (see Tan, 2000). Likewise, the Orang Asli (Indigenous People) from different parts of Peninsular Malaysia and other Indigenous groups from Sabah and Sarawak converge annually to celebrate the annual International Day of the World's Indigenous Peoples (Hari Antarabangsa Orang Asal Sedunia); they showcase their dance and music as a way to assert their identities and to bring attention to their concerns and rights (Nicholas, 2000, pp. 193–194). This event was started by the United Nations in 1982 to raise awareness about the cultures and rights of Indigenous peoples of the world (https://www.un.org/en/obse rvances/indigenous-day/background; https://www.facebook.com/joasm alaysia/posts/4329936237047352).

## The National Agenda of the Department of National Heritage

It is not surprising that the National Heritage Act of 2005 (passed in 2006), which is aimed at promoting the conservation, preservation, and safeguarding of "natural heritage, tangible and intangible cultural heritage (including the traditional arts and food), underwater cultural heritage, and living human treasure," emphasizes that all legislations, directives, and policies regarding intangible and tangible heritage come under the control of the minister of Tourism, Arts and Culture, who is appointed by the federal government (http://extwprlegs1.fao.org/docs/pdf/mal130377.pdf). A Department of National Heritage, headed by a commissioner, has been established to gazette the objects or persons of cultural significance in the heritage lists of the country and to manage heritage programs with the aim of "formulating national identity" (https://www.heritage.gov.my/).

Since its inception, the Department has focused on top-down activities with minimal community engagement; they include the organization of big nationwide events together with the Ministry of Tourism, Arts and Culture (MOTAC), such as the annual cultural and religious festivals of the major ethnic groups. These festivals are in line with the national strategy to create spectacles of multiculturalism for attracting local and foreign tourists. The Department has also created an inventory listing of national heritage and the identification of Living Human Treasures. As of October 2017, over 700 heritage items, including sites, monuments, performing arts, crafts, and food of different ethnic groups, have been listed. Since 2019, 21 people (3 of them were deceased) have been recognized as Living Human Treasures and have been given a one-off incentive of RM 30,000 to help them practice their arts (http://www.heritage.gov.my/index.php/ms/daftar-warisan/senarai-warisan-kebangsaan/seni-warisan-kebangsaan-orang-hidup).

Although the Department of National Heritage has good intentions to conserve ICH, it has limited staff and lacks expertise to run safeguarding programs that involve the communities in the different local states. Due to these constraints, operational directives for transmission such as training programs, funding for new apprentices to learn art forms with the Living Treasures, and plans for capacity building among young people have not seen the light of day. Even though the public is allowed to nominate heritage items on the website, the Department does not provide the support system for community artists listed in the heritage register to sustain and transmit the forms at the local state level.

Additionally, the Department of National Heritage does not intervene in the ICH safeguarding plans of local states that have UNESCO inscriptions. In fact, the 2005 National Heritage Act articulates that "the appointed Minister at the national level should not interfere with matters that fall under the power of any particular State unless the relevant State Authority has been consulted." In the following section, I show that this particular clause has worked both to the advantage and disadvantage of performing communities in their attempts to sustain their ICH. To what extent have the UNESCO inscriptions that call for community involvement enabled tradition bearers to safeguard and transmit their ICH in the states of Kelantan and Penang, two states that are governed by opposition parties?

## Counterpoints in the Local States in Response to UNESCO Inscriptions

### The Banning and Decline of Mak Yong in Kelantan

In 1990, the Parti Islam Se-Malaysia (PAS; Pan Malaysian Islamic Party) took over the predominantly Malay state of Kelantan. Kelantan is situated on the northeast coast of Peninsular Malaysia and is known for its Malay performing arts traditions that straddle the borders of Kelantan and Thailand. In an effort to Islamize the state, certain forms of theatre, such as Mak Yong, Wayang Kulit (shadow puppet theatre), and Maïn Puteri (healing ritual), were considered *haram* (forbidden) and were banned in 1998 on grounds that spirits were invoked during the performances.[5] Cultural activist Eddin Khoo, the founder of Pusaka (Heritage), a non-profit organization researching and archiving traditional arts, adds that the ban was also because of women performing on stage; female performers used to play the major roles and even male characters in Mak Yong. According to the conservative Islam promoted in Kelantan, the costumes in Mak Yong did not adequately cover the *aurat* (intimate parts) of the women that should not be displayed publicly.

---

[5] In September 2002, the PAS government banned public performances of all rock and pop bands except *pop nasyid* (pop with Islamic content). The PAS state executive committee announced to the press that "the move was aimed at checking moral decadence among the youth in Kelantan" (*Star*, September 19, 2002).

Cross-dressing has also not been tolerated by the Islamic officials in Kelantan (https://www.todayonline.com/world/asia/despite-ban-mak-yong-has-not-breathed-its-last).

The ban on Mak Yong was not lifted, even when UNESCO declared Mak Yong as a Masterpiece of the Oral and Intangible Heritage of Humanity in 2005, and three years later inscribed it on the Representative List of the Intangible Cultural Heritage of Humanity. When Karima Bennoune, the special rapporteur for cultural rights of the United Nations, attended the Eighth World Summit on Arts and Culture in Kuala Lumpur in March 2019, she made a public statement that "it will be a shame if these art forms were left to die, for with its death, Malaysians especially the Kelantanese would lose a part of their culture." She said "the ban was in violation of cultural rights of the Malaysians in enjoying their own rich cultural heritage, thus it's very essential for Malaysia to respond effectively" (*New Straits Times*, March 13, 2019).

The Kelantan state government responded to say that it had set up a "special committee" to check if the Mak Yong shows complied with *syariah* (Muslim code of religious law) requirements before they were allowed to be performed (*New Straits Times*, March 13, 2019). The state-sanctioned versions can and have been performed in closed venues for tourists, such as the Gelanggang Seni (Cultural Centre) in Kota Bahru, the capital city of Kelantan. Mohd Raizuli, the director of the Kelantan office of the National Department for Culture and Arts (Jabatan Kebudayaan dan Kesenian Negara, JKKN) in 2019 added that among the conditions set by the Islamic government were "no involvement of any female in the show and no *mantra* [spells] recitation prior to the show." The Kelantan JKKN, a branch office of the national MOTAC, then experimented with the Kumpulan Makyong Kijang Emas, directed by Ruhani Mohdzin (one of the veteran performers of Kelantan) (*Star*, April 14, 2019) to stage a "*syariah*-compliant" Mak Yong dance performance on April 25, 2019, in conjunction with the Seni@Kelantan (Art@Kelantan) program.

The Kelantan state government finally lifted the ban on Mak Yong in September 2019, with the reason that Mak Yong and other traditional performances can help to promote tourism in the state. The Deputy Chief Minister of Kelantan, Datuk Mohd Amar Nik Abdullah, however, stressed that the performances must first be screened and approved by the religious committee: "Those who wish to stage the dance can only do so after they comply with *syariah* requirements and guidelines, that include making it compulsory for Mak Yong performers to cover their *aurat*." The organizers also need to "ensure separation between men and women on stage and in the audience" and "there must also be no element of worship in the performances," he reiterated (*New Straits Times*, September 25, 2019). These rules for the state-sanctioned *syariah*-compliant versions are similar to those imposed on the Mak Yong shows for tourists during the ban. What is disconcerting is that the recreated forms have to be cleansed of their animistic and spiritual elements. Moreover, the separation of men and women on and off stage and the regulation of covering of one's *aurat* might lead to women performers (who used to play the main roles) giving way to male performers on stage.

The ban of Mak Yong has almost eradicated the folk entertainment form in Kelantan. The number of troupes is on the decline in Kelantan; the cultural bearers also find it difficult to make a living from Mak Yong and have to rely on part-time jobs in coffee shops, tapping rubber, or building houses. Correspondingly, transmission processes that are crucial for conservation have been hindered. In an article on the demise of Mak Yong in Kelantan, Eddin Khoo said the impact of the 1998 ban can be seen three decades later: "There is an entire generation of young people (now) who have no link to their local traditions. . . . There are currently at most four traditional troupes left in the country" (*New Straits Times*, March 12, 2019). However, village performers in Kelantan have continued to hold ritual performances known as Mak Yong-Main'teri for purposes of healing in the compounds of their houses as the state government does not have enough enforcement officers outside of the capital city to check on ritual performances. Or they perform with the Thai Menora (dance drama) groups that have not been banned. In this way, cultural custodians have attempted to hold on to their tradition and survive the ban.

Outside of Kelantan, the national government has attempted to bring Mak Yong to the urban public. Performances are concentrated in Kuala Lumpur at the government-funded National Theatre (Istana Budaya) and the National Art, Culture and Heritage Academy (ASWARA). At the urban national institutions and theatres, the form went through a process of standardization following the national agenda. As Mohamad Kamarulzaman, who developed the Mak Yong curriculum at ASWARA, emphasizes, the students learn the basic structure, dance, and music of Mak Yong and memorize scripted plays; this type of performance lacks the spirit and improvisation found in traditional performance (Hardwick, 2020).[6] Moreover, national

---

[6] See Hardwick (2020) for a discussion of how practitioners of Mak Yong inside and outside of Kelantan have tried to change and transmit the form to the younger generation.

funding is for big shows for the urban middle-class audience, rather than the owners of the genre in Kelantan. The Kuala Lumpur urban form is based on the creations of a few Mak Yong artists who moved from Kelantan to Kuala Lumpur, such as Khadijah Awang (1941–2000); she was one of the 1999 Seniman Negara (National Artists) who taught at ASWARA. Her sister-in-law Fatimah Abdullah staged a production in 2011 in Istana Budaya, which was performed by the professional performers of the National Theatre. For instance, Rosnan Rahman played the leading role of Pak Yong in Dewa Indra (Foley, 2014; Zulkifli, 2012).

Nevertheless, some activists who are not part of the government agencies are challenging the national and *syariah*-compliant models of Mak Yong. Through community-based projects, they promote the village performers and forms, and maintain the dominant role played by women and the ritual elements in Mak Yong. Pusaka has documented the village Mak Yong genres and has worked with the Kumpulan Mak Yong Cahaya Matahari, one of the famous Mak Yong groups in the nearby state of Trengganu (https://www.pus aka.org/communities).

The federal government and the local Islamic state of Kelantan are often at odds and perceive the Malay performing arts as risks, as the arts can offer alternative ways of being Malay and Muslim. However, the Mak Yong tradition bearers are not involved in and yet suffer the consequences of this struggle. As Hardy Shafii, a Mak Yong researcher from Universiti Sains Malaysia emphasizes, "There is an entire generation of Kelantanese who do not know what it [Mak Yong] is, but you can't blame the people because it's banned." He added that "the tussle between those who are against the cultural tradition and those seeking to preserve it had been going on for the past 28 years. In the end, traditions such as Mak Yong and Wayang Kulit may lose out" (*New Straits Times*, March 12, 2019). One can only hope that with the recent lifting of the ban, transmission efforts by the tradition bearers and ritual performances can be held openly in Kelantan.

Accordingly, UNESCO inscription and the ban in Kelantan have fortified the power of the nation-state and its administrators in the reconstruction of Mak Yong as a national form. Be that as it may, the institutionalization of Mak Yong has contradicted the principle of community engagement in heritage safeguarding, which in turn has led to the further decline of the village traditions in Kelantan.

## Revitalization of ICH in the World Heritage Site of George Town, Penang

On the island of Penang, situated off the northwest coast of Malaysia, a brighter situation exists. Concerted efforts have been made to revitalize the diverse ICH in Penang after its capital city, George Town, was inscribed a UNESCO World Heritage Site (together with Malacca) on July 7, 2008, under the category of Cultural Heritage. This is mainly because the opposition Democratic Action Party (DAP) that took over the state of Penang in March 2008 has been more open to dialogue and collaboration with local non-governmental organizations (NGOs), academics, community stakeholders, and tradition bearers in its efforts toward creating a sustainable society. I relate some of my experiences as a researcher, performer, and stakeholder involved in the community-based performing arts initiatives in the city.

Unlike Kelantan, Penang is a cosmopolitan state with a non-Malay majority.[7] The trading of spices and the export of tin and rubber attracted settlers from the Malay Archipelago, Thailand, Burma, Hadhramaut, India, China, and Europe in the eighteenth century. The meeting of different peoples in Penang is expressed in the multiple places of worship, eclectic food and architecture, blending of languages spoken, and multiethnic performances in the heritage enclave. These are George Town's Outstanding Universal Values (OUVs) as a World Heritage Site.

On the sunny side, the World Heritage Site inscription has seen many local and foreign tourists visiting the island to experience the diverse cuisine and the tangible and intangible heritage. Tourism has boosted the economy but has also resulted in the gentrification of the heritage enclave. Since the UNESCO inscription, cafes, boutique hotels, hostels, mini-museums, and entertainment businesses catering to tourists have taken over the shophouses from which historical communities used to practice their ICH. Many traditional craftsmen and artists have moved out of the heritage zone as they cannot afford the rentals that have escalated by virtue of the Repeal of the Rent Control Act by the federal government in 1998. After the UNESCO

---

[7] According to Penang Institute's Quarter 2, 2020 Statistics, Penang's current population of 1.77 million people remains multiethnic: Chinese of various dialect groups make up 39%, Malays originating from different parts of the Malay Archipelago 44%, Indians from various parts of India 9%, others (including Arabs, Eurasians, Indonesians, Thais, Burmese, and non-Malaysian citizens 8%. Cultural mixing has occurred as the diverse communities interact with one another (https://penanginstitute.org/wp-content/uploads/jml/files/quarterly_penang_statistics/2020/PQS-Q22020.pdf).

listing, the rentals have further spiked as investors convert the heritage houses into business outlets. As gentrification takes place and historical communities take their ICH with them as they leave, there is fear that the soul of the city might be lost.

In 2010, the local government set up the George Town World Heritage Incorporated (GTWHI) to manage and promote the heritage city's eclectic architectural and cultural assets, and to keep over-development and commodification of ICH at bay. In keeping with George Town's OUVs and the need for community engagement for sustaining ICH, GTWHI worked with NGOs, international and federal agencies, academics, and community stakeholders in the implementation of multiple projects for safeguarding the diverse ICH, including those of the minorities in George Town (see http:// gtwhi.com.my/ for activities). In collaboration with the Penang Heritage Trust (PHT), an NGO that is actively promoting the conservation of Penang's heritage, an ICH inventory was launched in 2012 to locate, identify, and create a database on the traditional trades, crafts, and cultural practitioners in George Town. According to the GTWHI website, surveys of over 5,000 premises in the heritage site were made; 20 case studies were documented and published. Further, in 2019, in collaboration with UNESCO, a pilot project to document the community rituals and festivals of George Town was carried out with community participation. GTWHI has also produced video documentaries about the lives and working methods of 15 practicing artisans, including Chinese joss stick makers and Muslim *songkok* (headgear) makers in Penang (http://gtwhi.com.my/wp-content/uploads/2019/ 05/Intangible-Cultural-Heritage-Twenty-Practitioners-Eng.pdf).

Concurrently, GTWHI aligned with the urban regeneration agency, ThinkCity, to provide funds for the documentation, transmission, and performances of the multicultural musical theatre of Penang that I facilitated. These projects included data collection on the endangered Chinese Potehi (glove puppet theatre) that was carried out collaboratively with researchers, artists, designers, young community members, tradition bearers, and students (see Tan et al., 2017; Tan, 2019). Additionally, schoolchildren of different ethnic backgrounds have been encouraged to learn and perform the multiethnic performing arts from the tradition bearers and to interview residents about their histories and problems. Having contributed to the research, making of the script, music, and performance itself, the young people developed a sense of empathy for the concerns of the various communities in the city (see Tan, 2018).

Over and above, GTWHI has collaborated with community stakeholders and heritage practitioners in the organization of the Heritage Celebrations, an annual festival held on July 7 to celebrate the inscription of George Town as a UNESCO World Heritage Site. This is a significant community engagement event that has rejuvenated the ICH of Penang.[8] Based on the concept of street celebrations that Penang has been famous for, the festival takes place in the historic lanes of George Town. The community-oriented festivities feature performances, food and crafts, exhibitions, interactive games, open houses, architecture, heritage trails, public talks, and workshops with the participation of all the ethnic communities of George Town.

The local communities are at the heart of the celebrations as co-organizers, stakeholders, presenters, participants, and carriers of tradition. They work closely with a core organizing team comprising visual and performing artists and educators; I was one of the curators from 2013 to 2015. In order to ensure that this community festival is sustainable and that capacity development takes place, the organizing team employs participatory approaches and action research methods. Planning, training, and organization are done together with all stakeholders, including the community groups (see Tan, 2015). In 2013, free outdoor multicultural performances by local artists of all ethnic backgrounds were staged at open-air sites at the heritage enclave, where the communities and residents of the city as well as outsiders could watch, participate, and socialize. The 2014 and 2015 festivals focused on handcrafted heritage and festival foods, respectively.

Through the participatory processes involving research, members of the communities are engaged in the heritage celebrations and are empowered to identify, represent, transmit, and revitalize their own ICH. They showcase their own cultures, which offer variations to the stereotypical cultural representations for tourists. The communities acquire ownership of the festival as they take part actively in its planning, research, and implementation, and are inspired to continue to organize and participate dynamically in it annually. As part of the process, they train younger volunteers throughout the year, who are then involved in the running of workshops for the public at the celebrations. Capacity building and skills development also take place through cultural documentation, mapping, and presentation. A measure of

[8] The community-oriented Heritage Celebrations is one of the core events of the George Town Festival that was started in 2010 to celebrate the inscription of George Town as a World Heritage Site (together with Melaka).

success is that the communities have now taken over the running of their own programs in the annual Heritage Celebrations.

World Heritage listing in Penang has also created new opportunities for the Muslim and non-Muslim religious communities to safeguard their temples and religious festivals. Following the World Heritage Site inscription, the Muslim, Thai, Chinese, and Indian communities have opened their religious sites and carried out their rites for local and foreign tourists of different ethnicities; they have allowed researchers to document the rituals. By so doing, the communities have gained recognition for their rituals and have received funding for the restoration of their temples and mosques (http://gtwhi.com.my/activities).

In George Town, local government support and cooperation with NGOs and agencies that engage communities have rejuvenated the multicultural ICH of the heritage site. What remains important is the transmission of ICH to the younger generation so that they can take ownership of their heritage and make use of them in their own manner.

## Challenges and Prospects

This chapter exemplifies how global UNESCO narratives about community engagement in the safeguarding and transmission of ICH have to cope with the politics and top-down policies of the nation-state. In Malaysia, the national cultural policy has resulted in the standardization of specific Malay traditions and the marginalization of their owners. Nevertheless, local state authorities, heritage activists, and cultural bearers have responded to both the global UNESCO principles and national agendas in diverse and disparate ways. In Kelantan, political controversies over what is Malaysian national culture, what is Malay, and what is Islamic have impacted the safeguarding of Mak Yong by the tradition bearers themselves. The banning of Mak Yong for three decades by the Islamic state of Kelantan has resulted in the diminishing of village performance groups and young people learning the genre, as well as the gradual demise of the entertainment form in Kelantan. At the same time, concertized Mak Yong, staged in auditoriums by the national theatre and institutions of learning in the capital city of Kuala Lumpur, has been recreated as spectacle, as in other national forms of theatre, and has been cleansed of its ritualistic and spiritual aspects. To survive, local performers in Kelantan have turned to ritual healing performances or other theatre forms belonging to the Thai community that have not been banned. In this case, the UNESCO listing did not help community village performers to negotiate with state officials over interpretations, performance, and transmission of the form.

Conversely, at the multicultural UNESCO World Heritage Site of George Town, Penang, specific forms of ICH belonging to minorities such as the Chinese, Indian, Eurasian, Thai, and other ethnic groups in Penang that are not recognized as national culture, and thus do not receive funding from the national government, seem to be reinvigorated after the UNESCO designation. The Penang state government authorities have been relatively open to collaborating with NGOs, academics, urban renewal agencies, and heritage activists in their conservation efforts. By using the OUVs of the UNESCO World Heritage Site and the ethical principle of community engagement as devices for negotiation, heritage activists have been able to raise awareness that, as the "living heritage embodied in people," ICH can only be sustained if there is active involvement of the cultural practitioners themselves in the safeguarding initiatives. As a result, the communities who own the ICH have more opportunities to delineate, interpret, and transmit them in their own way.

I have also demonstrated that a rigid top-down system within UNESCO that gives power to the State Party to nominate and manage ICH, and distribute funding at the national level, may be an obstacle to the quest for community engagement in ICH safeguarding. In countries where power is centralized at the national level and the top-down conservation approach persists, as in the case of Mak Yong, the local communities may lose control over defining the form and how to transmit it, and the right to choose who should or should not perform. UNESCO's dependence on the nation-state to allocate funding has further enhanced glitzy sanitized versions of the form. These shows may attract urban audiences and tourists, but they also promote homogeneity, following globalized forms in many parts of the world.

Further, the Convention does not offer protection against the misappropriation and cleansing of cultural forms to suit the requirements of political and religious elites, the suppression or exclusion of women in performance, and the dispossession of the tradition bearers, particularly in conservative Islamic states. A possible way to deal with this problem is to make explicit in the 2003 Convention the inclusion of cultural, gender, and human rights. These rights can empower all communities to define their own heritage and influence decision-making regarding the interpretation and transmission of ICH. With the present Convention, action cannot be taken if governments choose not to follow the Operational Directives and Ethical Principles regarding community engagement. The addition of human rights and introduction of a more flexible nomination system could open doors for the community stakeholders and tradition bearers to decide their future for themselves.

Needless to say, solutions to problems are case specific. While the 2003 Convention provides a reference point, detailed implementation can only be carried out at the local level. As such, the local government can play an essential role in identifying the types of living heritage and their functions in the state, the threats faced by the practicing communities, and solutions to these difficulties. The local government of George Town, for instance, has carried out an inventory of ICH that involves the multi-ethnic communities and cultural researchers; this has in turn activated bottom-up self-organization and collaboration among the different ethnic communities in the running of their own transmission programs and the annual Heritage Celebrations. The local government can then use the success stories as examples to lobby at the national level for legislations and policies that can unlock doors for community engagement initiatives in safeguarding ICH.

Finally, partnerships among international groups and the formation of hubs can help members share resources about ICH conservation. As Duong Bich Hanh, the program specialist and chief of the Culture Unit, UNESCO Bangkok, said at the Southeast Asian Collaborative Meeting in Penang, there is a "need to pool resources rather than working in silos" (Duong, 2017, p. 37). Local government agencies can also learn from other countries regarding safeguarding strategies and best practices through the establishment of cultural hubs. The local governments can then act as "laboratories of ideas" (implemented at the national level by UNESCO), as it is often easier to implement new approaches at the local level (https://www.youtube.com/watch?v=zt7l1Ky4-gQ). Besides disseminating alternative ways of engaging, safeguarding, and transmitting ICH, the international hubs and local "laboratories of ideas" can also collectively deal with emergent issues such as the gentrification of World Heritage Sites and the development of alternative community-based tourism models. They can create new approaches using culture toward achieving the Goals of the 2030 Agenda for Sustainable Development.

# References

Blake J. (2008). UNESCO's 2003 Convention on Intangible Cultural Heritage: The implications of community involvement in "safeguarding." In L. Smith & N. Akagawa (Eds.), *Intangible heritage* (pp. 45–73). Routledge.

Bertorelli, C. (2018). The challenges of UNESCO Intangible Cultural Heritage. *Journal of Tourism Studies, 3,* 91–117. http://id.nii.ac.jp/1060/00009834/.

Department of Statistics. (2020). Current Population Estimates, 2020, Kuala Lumpur. https://www.dosm.gov.my/v1/index.php?r=column/cthemeByCat&cat=155&bul_id= OVByWjg5YkQ3MWFZRTN5bDJiaEVhZz09&menu_id=L0pheU43NWJwRWVSZ klWdzQ4TlhUUT09 (accessed February 28, 2022).

Duong Bich Hanh. (2017). UNESCO efforts towards integrated approaches in Safeguarding Tangible and Intangible Cultural Heritage, Southeast Asian Collaborative Meeting on Safeguarding Intangible Cultural Heritage, September 18–19, 2017, Penang, Malaysia; co-organized by the George Town World Heritage Incorporated and the International Information and Networking Centre for Intangible Cultural Heritage in the Asia-Pacific Region (UNESCO Category 2 Centre). https://www.ichlinks.com/ archive/materials/publicationsV.do?nation=TH&page=1&ichDataUid=138584091 47907202614& (accessed February 28, 2022).

Foley, K. (2014). No more masterpieces: Tangible impacts and intangible cultural heritage in bordered worlds. *Asian Theatre Journal, 31*(2), 369–398.

Hardwick, Patricia Anne. (2020). Makyong, a UNESCO "Masterpiece," negotiating the intangibles of cultural heritage and politicized Islam. *Asian Ethnology, 79*(1), 67–90.

Howard, Keith (Ed.) (2012). *Music as intangible cultural heritage: Policy, ideology, and practice in the preservation of East Asian traditions.* Ashgate.

Ismail, Zain. (1977). *Cultural planning and general development in Malaysia.* Kuala Lumpur: The Ministry of Culture, Youth and Sports, Malaysia.

KKBS (Kementerian Kebudayaan, Belia dan Sukan Malaysia or Ministry of Culture, Youth and Sports Malaysia). (1973). *Asas Kebudayaan Kebangsaan* [Basis of National Culture]. Kuala Lumpur.

Kurin, R. (2004). Safeguarding intangible cultural heritage in the 2003 UNESCO Convention: A critical appraisal. *Museum International, 56,* 66–77.

Lixinsky, Lucas. (2011). Selecting heritage: The interplay of art, politics and identity. *The European Journal of International Law (EJIL), 22*(1), 81–100.

Logan, William, Craith, Máiread Nic, & Kockel, Ullrich (Eds.). (2016). *A companion to heritage studies.* Wiley-Blackwell.

Mahathir, Mohamad. (1991). *Malaysia: The way forward. Vision 2020.* Centre for Economic Research and Services, Malaysian Business Council.

Mohd, Anis Md. Nor. (1993). *Zapin: Folk dance of the Malay world.* Oxford University Press.

Nicholas, Colin. (2000). *The Orang Asli and the contest for resources, indigenous politics, development and identity in Peninsular Malaysia.* IWGIA Document No. 95.

Park, S-Y. (2013). *On intangible heritage safeguarding governance: An Asia-Pacific context.* Cambridge Scholars.

Seeger, A. (2009). Lessons learned from the ICTM (NGO) evaluation of nominations for the UNESCO, Masterpieces of the Oral and Intangible Heritage of Humanity, 2001–5. In L. Smith & N. Akagawa (Eds.), *Intangible heritage* (pp. 112–128). Routledge.

Schippers, Huib, & Grant, Catherine (Eds.). (2016). *Sustainable futures for music cultures: An ecological perspective*. Oxford University Press.

Smith, L., & N. Akagawa, N. (Eds). (2009). *Intangible heritage*. Routledge.

Tan Sooi Beng. (1990). The performing arts in Malaysia: State and society. *Asian Music, VXXI*(1), 137–171.

Tan Sooi Beng. (1993). *Bangsawan: A social and stylistic history of popular Malay opera.* Oxford University Press.

Tan Sooi Beng. (2000). The Chinese performing arts and cultural activities in Malaysia. In Lee Kam Hing & Tan Chee-Beng (Eds.), *The Chinese in Malaysia* (pp. 316–341). Oxford University Press.

Tan Sooi Beng. (2003). Multi-culturalism or one national culture: Cultural centralization and the recreation of the traditional performing arts in Malaysia. *Journal of Chinese Ritual, Theatre and Folklore, 141*, 237–260.

Tan Sooi Beng. (2015). Cultural engagement and ownership through participatory approaches in applied ethnomusicology. In S. Pettan & J. T. Titon (Eds.), *The Oxford handbook of applied ethnomusicology* (pp. 109–133). Oxford University Press.

Tan Sooi Beng. (2018). Community musical theatre and interethnic peace-building in Malaysia. In B-L. Bartleet & L. Higgins (Eds.), *The Oxford handbook of community music* (pp. 243–264). Oxford University Press.

Tan Sooi Beng. (2019). Breathing new life into *Potehi* glove puppets in Penang, Malaysia: Advocating a community-engaged approach. *Journal of the Oriental Society of Australia (JOSA), 51*, 84–102.

Tan Sooi Beng, Liew Kungyu, Ong Ke Shin, & Foo Wei Meng. (2017). *Potehi of Penang: An evolving heritage*. George Town World Heritage Incorporation.

World Commission on Environment and Development (WCED). (1987). *Our common future*. Oxford University Press.

Zulkifli, Mohamad. (2012). Report: The Mak Yóng Spiritual Dance Heritage Conference, performances and workshops. *Asian Theatre Journal, 29*(2), 444–460.

# 9

# There Is No Price for That

## UNESCO as Translator Between Conflicting Value Systems in Guatemala

*Logan Elizabeth Clark*

The mixing of money and religion has a widespread and long-standing history of causing moral anxiety. From biblical admonitions about commerce in the temple to the many historical cases in which funding from religious sources has enabled the destruction of entire populations in the "name of God," the conflation of moral *values* and economic *value* has been problematic at best and has led to horrific outcomes at worst. It is no wonder, then, that there is a certain amount of moral anxiety surrounding economic support for elements of intangible cultural heritage, especially those elements that are sacred in nature. While inscription on the UNESCO Representative List of Intangible Cultural Heritage does not automatically come with economic support, it often elicits external donations, funding commitments from local government agencies, and in many cases results in increased tourism and the consequential exploitation of the practice for economic gain. How does the increase in economic investment affect the social values tied to the recognized cultural practice? In the case of the *Danza del Rabinal Achi*, a Mayan dance-drama from the town of Rabinal, Guatemala, concerns arose after its designation as a UNESCO Masterpiece of the Oral and Intangible Heritage of Humanity that the increase in economic activity surrounding the dance risked desecrating its spiritual essence; as one community historian commented, "the dances are for spiritual fortification. There is no price for that."

The goal of this chapter is to examine the meaning of "value" in both its economic and social contexts, in an effort to look critically at how the designation of a practice as Intangible Cultural Heritage (ICH) affects value systems imbued within that practice. UNESCO's World Heritage Convention (1972) lists "outstanding universal value" as one of its criteria for declaring a location

Logan Elizabeth Clark, *There Is No Price for That* In: *Music, Communities, Sustainability*.
Edited by: Huib Schippers and Anthony Seeger, Oxford University Press. © Oxford University Press 2022.
DOI: 10.1093/oso/9780197609101.003.0009

as a World Heritage Site. Likewise, "outstanding value" is mentioned in UNESCO's (1998) Proclamation of Masterpieces of the Oral and Intangible Heritage of Humanity (Masterpieces Proclamation), but no similar criterion appears in the 2003 Convention for the Safeguarding of the Intangible Cultural Heritage (UNESCO, 2003) (ICH Convention). This is likely due to the involvement of anthropologists and cultural scholars, who questioned the "universality" of value and strove to challenge assumptions about what was deserving of safeguarding. While the resulting ICH Convention is devoid of terms such as "value" and "masterpiece," assessments of value persist in the implementation of the Convention. After all, the process of nominating and accepting an element requires evaluations, and, as Valdimar Hafstein reminds us, the very act of creating a Representative List is in itself a declaration of universal value, even if words like "masterpiece," and "excellence" have been eliminated (Hafstein, 2009). While value has been discussed in analyses of the World Heritage Sites and other tangible elements of cultural heritage safeguarding (Golinelli, 2015; Fredheim & Khalaf, 2016; Labadi, 2013), there are very few in-depth critiques of value in terms of the intangible, save Meissner's (2017) theorization of ICH as a form of cultural capital. Yet even Meissner, using Bourdieu's types of capital, considers cultural capital only for its ultimate conversion to economic capital. The practitioners of the *Danza del Rabinal Achi*, however, center forms of value that are not reducible to, or dominated by, economic capital.

Inspired by Terrence Turner's treatise on the effects of colonization on Indigenous communities, I am interested in exploring these effects from the point of view of the Indigenous community itself. Turner proposes a deconstruction of value, stemming from his observation that anthropological critiques of colonialism often "fail to give the people who are the objects of their concern the attention and respect that their own demonstrated tenacity and capacity for struggle command" (1979, p. 4). He proceeds to propose a complex theoretical framework that brings economic (material) value and social (moral) values into the same rubric. In so doing, he proposes a model that allows for translation between differing Indigenous and colonialist value systems. As (well deserved) critiques regarding neocolonial flaws intrinsic to the UNESCO ICH Convention abound, I want to echo Richard Kurin's exhortation, in Chapter 2 of this volume, that we see the Convention not as an imposed value system, but more as a tool. In the particular case of the *Danza del Rabinal Achi*'s inscription as a UNESCO Masterpiece, the Masterpieces Proclamation, and later the ICH Convention, serves as a tool through which

Maya-Achí spiritual values can be translated to the economic values of the postcolonial Guatemalan government.

## UNESCO: Cultural Savior or Cultural Imperialist?

The majority of scholars who write about the music and dance performances inscribed in the ICH Convention acknowledge the need for some sort of government promotion of folklife, while also being critical of the effects of government intervention on local folk practices. UNESCO efforts in ICH safeguarding have been criticized for their "institutional machinery" (Kurin, 2004), which can be incompatible with local power structures (Beardslee, 2015) and can exacerbate local economic tensions (Yun, 2015). At their worst, safeguarding institutions risk "standing in for colonial relations of power" (Weintraub & Yung, 2009, p. 9), and thus perpetuating the conditions that have led to the decline of the cultural practice in the first place. On the other hand, the ICH Convention has empowered communities (León, 2009) and has promoted the diversity of human expression around the world (Kurin, 2004, 2007; Smith & Akagawa, 2009; Weintraub & Yung, 2009).

Critics of the ICH Convention identify an array of problems for critique. Of course, the disparity between policy and praxis is evident in many case studies, which unveil a variety of issues ranging from failure of national governments to follow through with the commitments outlaid in their applications' action plans, to altering local power struggles within the community. Apart from the myriad on-the-ground analyses of ICH Convention implementation, a more theoretical critique has arisen over the concern that UNESCO, as an organization mostly funded by Western nation-states, risks replicating colonialist social values, the cultural sheen of which can be scratched off to reveal the neoliberal basis for many of the ICH Convention's basic goals. Jason Beardslee (2015), for example, observes that while the ICH model contains promises of community empowerment, its actual execution can in fact disempower many, in the end merely replicating existing inequalities in the new context of ICH management. Kathy Foley (2014) adds that UNESCO itself is based on the hegemony of the nation-state, which is fundamentally incongruous with the characteristics of cultural practices and risks nationalizing what are in many cases transnational practices. Foley and Timothy D. Taylor (2014) both make arguments that the values espoused in ICH documents—such as identity, creativity, and the concept of culture itself—are products of late capitalism, based on the commodification of cultural production and the subsuming of "creativity" into the concept of genius. And Sophia Labadi (2013) has pointed out that even judging something based on social or artistic value is often related to neoliberal pursuits, such as employment for those who make a living from evaluating the world's various traditions.

At the national level, many case studies have shown that the neoliberal foundations of national governments can also undermine the good intentions of cultural safeguarding, promoting traditions that bolster the bottom line. Javier León observes that when consulting "local-level" leadership in cultural preservation programs in Peru, government programs tend to support those community leaders whose cultural production might economically benefit the government through tourist opportunities, sale of musical recordings, and so forth (2009, p. 132). Joshua Tucker (2011) sees this becoming a government prescription for Indigenous identity and utilizes the term "permitted Indian" to analyze the ways in which government programs promote certain atavistic expressions of Indigeneity above others. Charles Hale characterizes all of these government safeguarding trends (especially throughout Latin America) as "neoliberal multiculturalism" (2002, 2006, 2007) which is akin to one of Ana María Ochoa's terms: "cultural politics" (Ochoa Gautier, 2003). According to Ochoa and Hale, the bureaucratic structure of cultural agencies in government programs manipulates the resulting formation of culture into an irreversible trajectory toward the sellable rather than the salvable. In her evaluation of the Colombian Ministry of Culture, Ochoa notes that political practices like clientelism have become compulsory to be considered for grants, and on the other hand (as Hale also observes in Guatemala), the cultural practices that are supported are those that benefit the national government financially in the first place.

Historians of the Convention, however, point out that UNESCO took many precautions to make sure national government involvement didn't threaten to commoditize, marginalize, or nationalize the traditions nominated. In Anthony Seeger's report on the nomination process, he noted that the evaluators felt that it was "very important not to reify the link between a tradition and a nation-state" (Seeger, 2009, p. 189). He continues to explain that the evaluators prioritized local community involvement in the application, local individuals contributing to the management of the plan, and especially the involvement of the artists who were leaders in the practice nominated (2009, p. 189). Furthermore, its original goal was to not only "protect the rights of custodians as individuals but also to encourage a system whereby *the State recognizes the importance of a particular cultural expression in a broader sense*" (Aikawa-Faure, 2009, p. 26; emphasis in original), and that the Convention (and the Masterpieces Proclamation as a stop-gap measure before it) could at least provide more leverage for cultural rights struggles among minoritized groups.

## The "Masterpiece": A Cultural Commodity or a Gift from God?

The recognition of the *Danza del Rabinal Achí* (the *Danza*), an Achí-Mayan dance-drama proclaimed a Masterpiece of the Oral and Intangible Heritage of Humanity in 2005 (in the third round of lists resulting from the Masterpieces Proclamation), elicited an influx of economic capital into the mostly Indigenous, rural town of Rabinal, Guatemala. After initial celebration, however, concerns arose from both the dancers and the community at large that the resulting increase in economic activity surrounding the dance risked desecrating its spiritual essence. As several of the associated dancers and musicians stated, "*No queremos que se 'folclorice'*"--We don't want the dance to "folklorize"--drawing to my mind Durkheim's assessment that folklore is nothing more than the "debris of vanished religions" ([1912] 2001, p. 36).

After the *Danza* was declared a Masterpiece in 2005, a donation of $70,000 from Sheikh Zayed Bin Sultan Al Nahyan was distributed through the Guatemalan Ministry of Culture and Sports (but overseen by UNESCO throughout the active funding period of 2006–2009) (García Escobar, 2012). Besides the donation facilitated by UNESCO, cultural tourism began to take off in Rabinal, with domestic and international tourists traveling to the town to see its annual performances. Several businesses distinguished themselves to tourists and locals alike by naming themselves after the dance (the Rabinal Achí Hotel and the Rabinal Achí bookstore patronized by the author being only two salient examples). Not only was the recognition bringing in money to support the dance, the dance was bringing in money to support the town.

While some local businesses associated with the tourism market benefited from this change, community members and even participants in the *Danza* were understandably unsettled by some people's economic profit from this spiritual, community-based practice. Furthermore, though local entrepreneurs benefited, the dancers themselves didn't benefit noticeably from this influx in tourism. Likewise, though the national Ministry of Culture and Sports did disburse the $70,000 donation during the period of UNESCO oversight, it has not upheld its duty to continue to support the dance annually. Furthermore, those funds that *did* come during 2006–2009 were largely spent on administrative salaries and obsolete office appliances for an office provided to the dancers at the local Academy of Mayan Languages. As a result, the dancers turned to the local municipal government to ask for support to offset the annual expenses in putting on the dance. Even municipal support has waned, however; sometimes they receive nothing at all, depending on the administration.

Despite the fluctuating support from the Rabinal municipality, the transfer of patronage to the municipal government did help counterbalance the decreasing ability of Rabinal's community *cofradías* (religious fraternities) to provide the resources needed to carry out the dance. However, separating the funding from the *cofradías* meant that the spiritual rituals associated with the dance (including over a month of performances, ceremonies, and pilgrimages by the dancers, musicians, and spiritual leaders) might eventually become disconnected from the public performance of the dance itself.

But community members could not deny the cultural benefits of outside funding for the dance: lost instruments had been replaced, dance regalia repaired, and several publications commissioned to inform the world about the importance of their *Danza*. More importantly, what had been an intermittent practice, due to lack of funding, was now back to a regular, annual cycle—thus fortifying the benedictions that the dance bestows on the town through honoring the Ancestors. For hundreds of years, UNESCO application manager Carlos René García Escobar explained, the leaders of the *cofradías* would gather money and donations of food to support the dancers. However, the investment in religious celebrations had been significantly reduced due to the increasing costs of commodities, the introduction of chemical agriculture, an increasing dependency on wage labor, and the civil war that lasted from roughly 1960 to 1996. The recognition, then, precipitated stabilizing measures through funding at the local level, the national level, and the international level. Though the funding dropped precipitously after the first five years, the dance cycle has been more regular.

Yet, to realize this increased regularity in performance, the organizational structure of the *Danza* had to undergo some drastic realignments in order to be eligible to receive payments from the Guatemalan government. In order to legally receive monetary support, the dancers and musicians had to form a legal entity. They formed the Rabinal Achí Cultural Association (La Asociación), appointing the "owner" (at the time, José León Coloch, who had inherited the dance from his wife María Xolop's father) as the president, and three other practitioners as secretary, treasurer, and speaker of the association. This seemingly innocuous act resulted in redistributing the hereditary power of the leader, who, as the owner of the libretto and main instrument (*tun*), had traditionally maintained creative and political control of the dance. Despite this radical organizational shift resulting from the UNESCO application process, however, the practitioners of the *Danza* have maintained control over its spiritual nature, deciding when and where they perform the dance and, so far, preventing its appropriation and folklorization by the local and national governments. For example, after UNESCO recognition, the dancers had increasingly been offered payment to perform the dance outside of Rabinal—in the tourist city of Antigua, Guatemala, and even outside of the country. They had refused, however, holding that the dance cannot exist in 15-minute "snippets" as requested by cultural organizations, and that it should not even be performed outside of Rabinal, since it is specifically performed for (and with) the Ancestors in *those* hills and nowhere else. It cannot be broken up into pieces and performed in exchange for money—in other words, it is not commodifiable.

The fear that UNESCO Masterpiece declaration might commodify the *Danza* may be subsumed by its larger purpose: the very act of performing the dance is what reinforces Achí connection to the land, and thus its inhabitants' autonomy. The land comprising Rabinal and the surrounding Achí settlements is a gift from *Ajaw* (roughly, "God"), Rabinal's founder, King Job Toj, and the rest of the Ancestors who fought for it.

## The Value of Social Action

In spite of the anxiety around economizing spiritual practice, several economic anthropologists argue that economic and social values are not always mutually exclusive. Terence Turner, David Graeber, and Michael Lambek all posit that economic value and other kinds of social values are linked to a common denominator: the value of social action. Terence Turner first called for the creation of a theory of action in a 1979 article in order to analyze, in a more nuanced way, "the values that orient action and the organization of the processes through which it is socially channeled and coordinated" (1979, p. 6). Social action, he continues, is organized into producing material products (commodities) or social products (relationships) based on the goals of the overarching social structure. Translating this into Marxian terms, Timothy D. Taylor clarifies, "if productive labor in Marx's thinking is productive because it produces surplus value for capitalists, surely labor of other sorts of action considered to be unproductive can nonetheless produce sorts of values other than those theorized by Marx" (Taylor, 2017, p. 175). Lambek concurs that "certain acts are a different kind of activity from labor, *not* reducible to economics, but to the contrary, constitutive of ethics" (Lambek, 2013, p. 145). Using action as a measure of value, then, these theorists argue that economic value and other sorts of value are in fact subsets of an all-encompassing value of social action.

Graeber's take on the action theory of value illuminates how we might assess a community's priorities. First, he posits, value is how actors represent the *importance* of their own actions to themselves as part of some larger whole; second, this action is determined as important only *in comparison* to another possible action; and third, its importance can only be realized in some sort of *public recognition* (e.g., as represented by money, or public performance) (Graeber, 2001, 2005). Reframing social and economic value this way means that even if they are incommensurable, they are at least comparable based on the amount of action that individuals in organized societies spend accumulating one or another form of public recognition.

If, as Arjun Appadurai emphasizes, an object's monetary value is determined only at the moment of commensurable exchange (1986), Taylor postulates that the value of social products, such as performances, is determined through the exchange of meaning between the performer and the audience (2020, p. 33). Because social meaning has a more localized regime of value than monetary currency, it is not as easily commodifiable. In the case of the Achí people, the form of public recognition of value for hundreds of years has been performance—not only for the public of Rabinal, but also (and primarily) for the Ancestors and Ajaw. Thus, the more the *Danza* is performed (with the accompanying rituals), the more valuable the original act it commemorates. If Achí self-realization is the desired social product of this dance (the plot of which is a re-enactment of the Achí secession from the K'iche' empire in the fifteenth century), the frequency of the *Danza's* performance proportionately increases or decreases that self-realization.

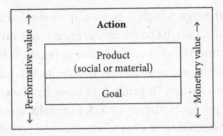

**Figure 9.1**  Action-based model of value.

## Representing Value Systems

I employ these theories of value because they allow the evaluative spheres in Rabinal, Guatemala City, and UNESCO meeting rooms to be considered and compared on equal terms by measuring economic gain and social values alike in terms of action. In this way, the asymmetry of the Guatemalan state's social value system (driven by neoliberal economic development) and the Maya-Achí social value system (driven by spiritual development) becomes apparent. The diagram I present in Figure 9.1 is a tool that combines all of the above definitions of value into one conceptual space, allowing the analyst to come to a new understanding of a society's value system from a reference point different from her own. Thus, I do not propose this model in order to tell Indigenous people what their values are, but rather as a heuristic tool allowing me to approach understanding a value system different from my own through observing actions. It may also be useful for the reader to employ in her own analyses.

In order to clarify the model, I must first define a few terms from Turner's 1979 article. In his conceptualization of the action theory of value, actors organize their "Actions" in order to achieve "Goals," or "(socially-determined) needs and symbolic social values" (1979, 21). These "Goals" are achieved through "Actions" that result in "Products," be they material products ("material goods, services and the social relations through which these productive activities are accomplished") or social products ("the production of human beings as social actors and of the social groupings through which this is accomplished") (1979, 23). Turner's model, represented graphically in Figure 9.1, forms the kernel of my analysis: social Actions are guided by social "Goals" in creating material or social "Products."

It is essential moving forward to clarify that if I am to consider economic and other social values as refractions of the overall value of social action, I must find a way to measure both economic value *and* social values. Throughout literature on the theory of value, the word is presented both as an ethical ideal (a social value) and as a rating scale (something is more or less valuable). In order to standardize its use, I will use Turner's term, "Goals," to refer to social/ethical values, focusing almost entirely on using "value" as a form of measurement (for comparison purposes only). Further, I will use Graeber's reference to public recognition of value, focusing on "performative value" as a subset of the polysemous "social value" and "monetary value" as a specific subset of "economic value," thereby employing terms that, while not commensurable, are at least comparable. As argued above, performative value increases through repetition and incorporation of meaningful rituals, just as monetary value of an object increases based on the amount of money offered in exchange for it. As a summary of what I propose moving forward:

> Social Actions are guided by social Goals in creating material or social Products. The more valuable Goals are made evident through the amount of socially organized Action taken to create Products (goods or meanings) that further that Goal. Socially organized Actions can produce more or less monetary value, just as they can also produce more or less performative value. Importantly, these forms of value are not mutually exclusive, but exist in parallel as measures of the consequence of a certain action.

While monetary value rises or lowers depending on global markets, performative value is contained to more local regimes of value, as indicated by ideologies such as religious scriptures, constitutional documents establishing laws, and ritual knowledge. Furthermore, if monetary value is measured in currency (which inherently incorporates the productive labor of others), performative value can be measured in time and effort put into non-productive labor. To clarify this model, I apply it below to value systems in both Rabinal and the Guatemalan nation, as represented through its government's actions.

## Translating Performative Value to Monetary Value in Rabinal

To determine the Goals of the Achí community in Rabinal, I have observed the actions of the dance community (dancers, musicians, spiritual guides, supporting *cofradías*, spectators) as shown through performance of the actual dance and the music, the things that the dancers and community members have told me about past performances, and textual analysis of the *parlamento* (the script recited by the characters portrayed in the dance).[1]

For the *Rabinal Achi* dancers, the most important action is the ritual cycle that accompanies the dance performances. Starting two weeks before the actual festival for Saint Paul (January 25), when the dance is publicly presented in the Rabinal town square, the dance troupe, including musicians and spiritual guides, begins a cycle of daily ceremonies. These are held in the house of the dance owner (*dueño*), in the neighborhood associated with Saint Paul, and in pilgrimages to the hills surrounding the town, where the Ancestors reside. The series of pilgrimages and performances requires a great amount of physical and temporal sacrifice. These rituals memorialize and re-create the social product of relationships with the Ancestors by commemorating their founding of Rabinal, and also through direct dialogue and embodiment of the Ancestors in the masks and instruments, which are brought to life ("animated") by the rituals. The actions taken to continue the rituals create the social relationships with the Ancestors and Ajaw in the spiritual realm. This illuminates the underlying goal, which is to prevent the *Danza*'s detachment from its spiritual function—to prevent it from becoming folklore.

For hundreds of years, these pilgrimages were associated with high performative value and low monetary value: the donations to the dancers and musicians often took the form of food, ritual materials, and sometimes small monetary donations, but only to sustain the ritual activities. However, since the civil war hit Rabinal particularly hard, the funds and food materials needed to conduct the rituals were increasingly difficult for the *cofradías* to collect, and thus the *Danza* was not performed annually. Because performative value is not simply the accumulation of performances, but rather the efficacy of meaningful exchange (Taylor, 2020), the rituals must accompany the *Danza* to give it performative value. The Rabinal Achi value system represented in Figure 9.2 shows that, before UNESCO intervention, it was economically costly (low monetary value) to perform the *Danza* with the ritual cycle, which is where performative value was accrued. The alternative, performing the *Danza* only (or not performing at all) was more economically viable (high monetary value), but involved low performative value.

---

[1] Detailed ethnographic analysis and commentary by the dancers exceeds the length limit allowed here, but will be published in a forthcoming coauthored article.

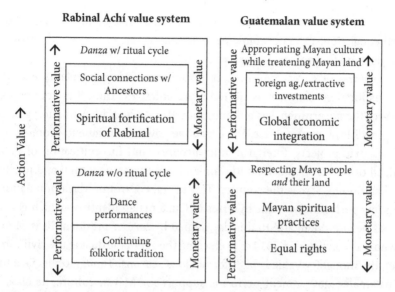

**Figure 9.2**  Rabinal versus Guatemalan value systems pre-UNESCO.

Though Indigenous peoples' rights have improved since the end of the civil war, there are many examples in which the militarized executive power in each successive government administration has taken actions which indicate that monetary gain is more important than the political and cultural autonomy of Indigenous communities. Throughout the twentieth century, the Guatemalan government and dominant *ladino* (mixed-race) culture have gone from disparaging Mayan practices to appreciating them as a unique contribution to Guatemalan culture. In the mid-twentieth century, Mayan dress and iconography were appropriated to create a national identity and bolster political cohesion within the nation; later, cultural diplomacy through marimba performances created new economic and political connections between the Guatemalan government and the US government (Amado, 2011; Arrivillaga Cortés, 2010). However, its respect for Maya populations and their autonomy only goes as deep as the bottom line (cf. Hale, 2002 & 2007; Hale & Millamán, 2006). Many cultural policies were therefore guided by a desire to integrate economically, with only cursory gestures toward respect for Mayan culture and history. Any real actions protecting or promoting Mayan autonomy would compromise economic gain, as Indigenous communities stand in the way of development. Performing pride in Mayan culture helped Guatemala advertise itself as a friendly and culturally rich place for foreign investors, but when it came to actually supporting Mayan culture and equal rights, the economic benefits did not match those of destroying Mayan land for profit.[2]

Since the 1996 Peace Accords, more and more Maya people have joined the national government as elected representatives. Thus, it is not possible to see "the government" as a monolithic strong arm with a singular goal to oppress Maya communities. Yet, executive powers continue to promote hydroelectric projects, foreign mining licenses, and the cultivation of palm oil, all of which encroach on Mayan land and threaten cultural and territorial autonomy across the country. This brutal control of Maya populations has low performative value in terms of Guatemalan identity—which is why it has been hidden, and to this day denied by former president Ríos Montt (who was convicted in 2014 of overseeing the genocide during the civil war). Yet, the monetary value is high for obvious reasons. Though on its face the Guatemalan government performs support for Mayan culture, its chosen actions betray the actual goal of the Guatemalan government: economic integration into the global marketplace, often at the expense of Mayan equality.

Figure 9.2 demonstrates the incongruous nature of Achí and Guatemalan value systems: the Achí main goal of spiritual fortification of Rabinal's territory is in direct conflict with Guatemala's top goal: global economic integration. The practice of Mayan spiritual rituals strengthens the Achí belonging to the land, which in turn threatens Guatemalan agro-industrial development. The Guatemalan government's actions show that Mayan culture is valued only insofar as it does not threaten their development and potential for foreign investment—this aligns with folkloric dance devoid of spiritual practice. UNESCO's involvement redirects these trends in a way that translates, but does not transform, performative value into monetary value.

## UNESCO's Role in Translation and Recontextualization of Value

In a recent critique of the effects of the UNESCO Masterpieces declaration on the *Danza de Rabinal Achi*, ethnomusicologist Sergio Navarette

---

[2] Rabinal was especially hard hit during the last decade of the 30-plus-year civil war. The Río Negro community in northern Rabinal was completely displaced to build a hydroelectric dam. Their protest was met with the brutal retaliation characteristic of the ongoing genocide by the Lucas García and Ríos Montt government militaries (Comisión para el Esclarecimiento Histórico (CEH), 1999).

Pellicer argues that UNESCO's process of declaring a cultural practice a "masterpiece," or even "cultural heritage of humanity" considers it as a fixed object. Having lived in Rabinal for years and written his dissertation on the marimba and other musical practices there, he was asked to evaluate the *Danza*'s application to be accepted to the list. He has a better understanding than anybody, then, when he writes about the way in which UNESCO evaluates "heritage" as something resting mostly on the past, an "object capable of being 'fixed' in order to be classified, safeguarded and manipulated as a 'good' that has legitimate owners and can be packaged and sold" (Navarrete Pellicer, 2019, p. 96). He is certainly not wrong in his assessment, the most salient example in Rabinal perhaps being the creation of La Asociación in order to be legally recognized by the government. But this does not fundamentally change its spiritual purpose and its effectiveness in reproducing Achí autonomy. Fred Myers argues that just because something has monetary value within one regime does not affect its qualitative (or performative) value in another. "The effect is not a replacement of regimes of value," he states. "The attempts to make qualitative value commensurate with monetary value represent an effort to mediate these value regimes, one in which some participants can imagine that monetary value will reinforce (rather than destroy) indigenous distinctions" (Myers, 2001, p. 19). In the case of the *Danza*, for each value system, or "context," as Myers calls it, to meet on equivalent terms, the potential declaration as a UNESCO Masterpiece was the catalyst that presented the dance as something more valuable to the Guatemalan government, by translating performative value to monetary value.

Anthropologist Anna Tsing writes about translation of value as it happens from gifts to commodities and vice versa (Tsing, 2015). Her overarching observation describes the way in which capitalist systems and assemblages intermingle in messy, destructive, yet collaborative ways, contradicting the assumption that these regimes of value are independent and exclusive. The concept of salvage accumulation—the creation of capital from non-capitalist regimes of value—is used to prove that there is almost always a bit of gift in the commodity and vice versa. Just as the sorting camps in Tsing's account of the matsutake mushroom translate the spoils of a "free" lifestyle into commodities to be sold at high prices in Japan, the UNESCO declaration translates the *Danza*, originally intended as a gift (to the Ancestors, to the town) into something economically valuable to the national government. But in this translation of the performative value of gifts to monetary value, neither the quality of the mushroom nor the spiritual essence of the dance is lost.

UNESCO operates within the same system of neoliberal capitalism as the Guatemalan government, but its actions, especially in the ratification of the ICH Convention, serve a different goal: to promote cultural sustainability over the effects of economic globalization. It also plays an important role as mediator in the transfer of economic capital to the dancers. In the case of the *Danza del Rabinal Achi*, UNESCO's actions to consult local leadership and oversee the initial implementation of the monetary awards ensured that practitioners would be able to use the money as they saw fit, thus enabling them to continue making the pilgrimages and performing the ceremonies to awaken the masks and the instruments for communion with the Ancestors. If we were to look at the Rabinal Achi value system in Figure 9.2 *after* UNESCO's Masterpieces program, the arrow representing the monetary value of the action of performing the "*Danza* with the ritual cycle" would change directions due to supplemental monetary support for the full performance. Funding from the municipal government, though still insufficient to cover the costs, leaves more community money to support the accompanying rituals. As a result, meaningful performance can take place more regularly. In this way, UNESCO's neoliberal underpinnings do not threaten their spiritual goals. Instead, they translate spiritual practice into a language the Guatemalan government can understand: cultural tourism.

The monetary value of "Respecting Maya people and their land" (lower righthand box in Figure 9.2) will also go up as a result. Once UNESCO declared the *Danza* a masterpiece, it put Guatemala on the international map as a destination for cultural tourism, and the Guatemalan government recognized that respecting Mayan culture and political autonomy was a performatively valuable goal, *as well as* a monetarily valuable one. Tourism revenue in Guatemala more than doubled between 2004 and 2009, going from $630 million to $1.36 billion per year, or from 2.6% to 3.6% of the country's GDP, the fastest in Guatemala's recent history (World Tourism Organization, 2020). As more foreigners came to see the riches of Mayan culture, the Guatemalan government could not afford *not* being seen to respect Mayan culture and land internally. In other words, a post-UNESCO version of the model in Figure 9.2 might show the arrow representing monetary value going up, thus elevating the valence of "Respecting Maya people *and* their land" slightly. Though the government's reason for this action may not be equal rights for Maya citizens, and while for now there may still be

more monetary value in foreign investment in agriculture and mineral ex-
traction than in tourism, the increased monetary value in respecting Mayan
autonomy may have started to change the balance in action value.

As long as UNESCO remains a party in the relationship, the Guatemalan
government cannot restrict the ritual aspect of the dance that it funds.
I should end with a caveat that the value system models are not meant to represent an entire society, but rather the actions of a group of people—in this
case, the Rabinal Achi dancers. From the perspective of other Guatemalans,
or even other residents of Rabinal, the increase in frequency of the rituals
might not have the same performative value, or there might be entirely different Goals and corresponding Actions that make up a separate value
system. Huib Schippers and Catherine Grant's model for factors affecting
cultural sustainability might be useful in comparing those different factors
on a broader level.

## Conclusion

In considering the value system of the Maya practitioners of this pre-
colonial dance drama, compared to that exemplified by the Guatemalan
government, I have explored to what extent UNESCO safeguarding efforts
have shifted existing value systems in the Achí-Maya town of Rabinal, evaluating those shifts as much as possible using the value system of the dance
practitioners. In consulting with them, we conclude that UNESCO recognition resulted *not* in the replacement of local values, but rather in the translation of one type of value to another, and, consequentially, greater agency
for the dance practitioners. In this case, the *Rabinal Achi* practitioners
used UNESCO's very ties to global capitalism as a tool to translate performance value into monetary value in order to garner more respect from the
Guatemalan government.

The goals of the 2003 UNESCO ICH Convention are to counteract the
destructive outcomes of overemphasizing economic value. It does so not by
superimposing its own values on nation-states or local communities, but
rather through the creation of opportunities for creative manipulation; of
a political platform on which to dance, a space for Indigenous expression
through which to teach and subvert, and a flow of symbolic and economic
capital coming from the government to be used ultimately for resisting the
government. But in order for this to be the case, UNESCO has to use its

relative political power to continue to advocate for local involvement in planning, proposal, and evaluation of the ICH declaration.

## Acknowledgments

This project is only possible because of the kindness, camaraderie, and trust bestowed upon me by José León Coloch (QEPD), María Xolop, and their son, José Manuel Coloch Xolop, in addition to José Manuel Román (QEPD), Manuel Solomán, Pedro de Corazón, Hendry, Wuilfredo Iboy, Esedonio Iboy, and members of La Asociación. I thank Francisco Mendoza and Sergio Navarrete Pellicer for introducing me to Rabinal, and Alex Cal Jom for accompanying me on my first visit to José León's house in July 2012; Carlos René García Escobar (QEPD) for our many chats over coffee and for his dedication to safeguarding the dances of Guatemala. Travel for this research was funded by the UCLA Center for Ethnic Studies, the UCLA Office of Graduate Research, and the UCLA Herb Alpert School of Music's Department of Ethnomusicology. Tara Browner, Sergio Navarrete Pellicer, Tony Seeger, Huib Schippers, and Tim Taylor, José Manuel Coloch, and Manuel Solomán provided invaluable advice and guidance in conceptualization, development, and revision of this chapter.

## References

Aikawa-Faure, N. (2009). From the Proclamation of Masterpieces to the Convention for the Safeguarding of Intangible Cultural Heritage. In L. Smith & N. Akagawa, *Intangible heritage* (pp. 13–44). Routledge.

Amado, A. (2011). The fox trot in Guatemala: Cosmopolitan nationalism among ladinos. *Ethnomusicology Review, 16,* ethnomusicologyreview.ucla.edu/journal/volume/16/piece/457.

Appadurai, A. (1986). *The social life of things.* Cambridge.

Arrivillaga Cortés, A. (2010). *La marimba Maderas de Mi Tierra: Embajadora musical de Guatemala.* SAAS.

Beardslee, T. (2015). Whom does heritage empower, and whom does it silence? Intangible cultural heritage at the Jemaa el Fnaa, Marrakech. *International Journal of Heritage Studies, 22*(1), 1–13.

*Guatemala: memoria del silencio.* Oficina de Servicios para Proyectos de las Naciones Unidas (UNOPS).

Durkheim, É. ([1912] 2001). *The elementary forms of religious life.* Oxford University Press.

Foley, K. (2014). No more masterpieces: Tangible impacts and intangible cultural heritage in bordered worlds. *Asian Theatre Journal, 31*(2), 369–398.

Fredheim, L. H., & Khalaf, M. (2016). The significance of values: Heritage value typologies re-examined. *International Journal of Heritage Studies, 22*(6), 466–481. www.tandfonline.com/doi/full/10.1080/13527258.2016.1171247.

García Escobar, C. R. (2012, July 27). Interview in Aldea lo de Bran, Mixco, Guatemala (L. E. Clark, interviewer and translator).

Golinelli, G. M. (2015). *Cultural heritage and value creation.* Springer.

Graeber, D. (2001). *Toward an anthropological theory of value: The false coin of our own dreams.* Palgrave.

Graeber, D. (2005). Anthropological theories of value. In J. G. Carrier (Ed.), *A handbook of economic anthropology* (pp. 430–454). Edward Elgar.

Hafstein, V. T. (2009). Intangible heritage as a list: From masterpieces to representation. In L. Smith & N. Akagawa, *Intangible heritage* (pp. 93–111). Routledge.

Hale, C. (2002). Does multiculturalism menace? Governance, cultural rights and the politics of identity in Guatemala. *Journal of Latin American Studies, 24*, 485–524.

Hale, C. (2007). *More than an Indian: Racial ambivalence and neoliberal multiculturalism in Guatemala* (1st ed.). Asociación para el Avance de las Ciencias Sociales en Guatemala.

Hale, C., & Millamán, R. (2006). Cultural agency and political struggle in the era of the Indio Permitido. In D. Sommer (Ed.), *Cultural agency in the Americas* (pp. 281–304). Duke University Press.

Kurin, R. (2004). Safeguarding intangible cultural heritage in the 2003 UNESCO Convention: A critical appraisal. *Museum International, 56*(1–2), 66–77.

Kurin, R. (2007). Safeguarding intangible cultural heritage: Key factors in implementing the 2003 Convention. *International Journal of Intangible Heritage, 2*(1), 10–20.

Labadi, S. (2013). *UNESCO, cultural heritage, and outstanding universal value: Value-based analyses of the World Heritage and Intangible Cultural Heritage Conventions.* AltaMira Press.

Lambek, M. (2013). The value of (performative) acts. *HAU: Journal of Ethnographic Theory, 3*(2), 141–160.

León, J. F. (2009). National patrimony and cultural policy: The case of the Afroperuvian Cajón. In A. N. Weintraub & B. Yung (Eds.), *Music and cultural rights* (pp. 110–139). University of Illinois Press.

Meissner, M. (2017). The valorisation of intangible cultural heritage: Intangible cultural heritage as cultural capital in sustainable development. In S. Lira, R. Amoêda, & C. Pinheiro (Ed.), *Sharing cultures cultures 2017: Proceedings of the 5th International Conference on Intangible Heritage* (pp. 295–303). Green Lines Institute for Sustainable Development.

Myers, F. R. (2001). *The empire of things: Regimes of value and material culture.* School of American Research Press.

Navarette Pellicer, S. (2019). El baile drama del Rabinal Achi: Notas críticas a la proclama. *DIGI: Revista de Ciencias Socialies y Humanidades, 6*(1), 93–99.

Ochoa Gautier, A. M. (2003). *Entre los deseos y los derechos: Un ensayo crítico sobre políticas culturales, Colección Ensayo Crítico.* ICANH—Instituto Colombiano de Antropología e Historia.

Seeger, A. (2009). Lessons learned from the ICTM (NGO) evaluation of nominations for the UNESCO Masterpieces of the Oral and Intangible Heritage of Humanity, 2001–2005. In L. Smith & N. Akagawa (Eds.), *Intangible heritage* (pp. 176–192). Routledge.

Smith, L., & Akagawa, N. (2009). *Intangible heritage: Key issues in cultural heritage.* Routledge.

Taylor, T. D. (2014). New capitalism, UNESCO and the re-enchantment of culture. In M. Herren (Ed.), *Networking the international system: Global histories of international organizations* (pp. 163–173). Switzerland: Springer.

Taylor, T. D. (2017). *Music in the world: Selected essays.* University of Chicago Press.

Taylor, T. D. (2020). Musical performance as a medium of value. In G. Borio, G. Giuriati, A. Cecchi, & M. Lutzu, *Investigating musical performance: Theoretical models and intersections* (pp. 25–38). Routledge.

Tsing, A. L. (2015). *The mushroom at the end of the world: On the possibility of life in capitalist ruins.* Princeton University Press.

Tucker, J. (2011). Permitted Indians and popular music in contemporary Peru: The poetics and politics of indigenous performativity. *Ethnomusicology, 55*(3), 387–413.

Turner, T. S. (1979). Anthropology and the politics of Indigenous peoples' struggles. *Cambridge Anthropology, 5*(1), 1–43.

UNESCO. (1972). Convention concerning the protection of the world cultural and natural heritage. United Nations, 17th General Conference. Paris: UNESCO.

UNESCO. (1998). Regulations relating to the proclamation by UNESCO of masterpieces of the oral and intangible heritage of humanity. United Nations, 155th Executive Board. Paris: UNESCO.

UNESCO. (2003). Convention for the safeguarding of the intangible cultural heritage. United Nations, 32nd General Conference. Paris: UNESCO.

Weintraub, A. N., & Yung, B. (2009). *Music and cultural rights.* University of Illinois Press.

World Tourism Organization. (2020, October 08). *Tourism in Guatemala.* Retrieved from WorldData.info: worlddata.info/america/guatemala/tourism.php.

Yun, K. (2015). The economic imperative of UNESCO recognition: A South Korean shamanic ritual. *Journal of Folklore Research, 52*(2–3), 181–198.

# 10

# Sustainability, Agency, and the Ecologies of Music Heritage in Alentejo, Portugal

*Salwa El-Shawan Castelo-Branco*

On April 23, 2017, following a few years of absence, I revisited Cuba, a town in southern Alentejo (a region in the south of Portugal) where I have conducted field research, intermittently since the mid-1980s, focusing on a local practice of two-part singing known as *cante*, enacted by formally structured men's or women's choirs with no instrumental accompaniment, and informally in private gatherings, fiestas, and taverns. I am struck by several changes in the town: a new office of tourism, filled with brochures advertising local and regional attractions, a hotel, several new restaurants, a cultural center, and a statue of Christopher Columbus presumed by some of his biographers to have been a native of the town after which he supposedly named the Caribbean Island of Cuba. On the road to town through rural Alentejo, signboards advertise the "wine route" and the recently invented Bread Fiesta. I later learned about other "routes" that tourists could follow, such as forts and fortifications, megalithic and Baroque monuments, and an itinerary of Intangible Cultural Heritage, including *cante*.[1] Cuba is acknowledged as a vital center for the practice of *cante* mainly due to the recognition of the town's oldest men's choir, the Grupo Coral os Ceifeiros de Cuba (founded in 1933), as a custodian of *cante*. Five other groups have also been active: the Grupo Coral os Amigos do Cante (a men's choir founded in 1986 and disbanded in 2018); the Grupo Coral Feminino as Flores do Alentejo;

---

[1] The "Routes of Alentejo" are the regional component of the "Routes of Portugal," a strategy for marketing territories for tourists by offering organized itineraries of historical monuments, natural landscape, gastronomy, wine, local "traditions," among other attractions (http://rotasdeportugal.pt/index.htm). The Routes of Alentejo include sites and cultural practices classified on UNESCO's lists of World Cultural Heritage, Biosphere Reserves and Intangible Cultural Heritage, including *cante* (https://www.visitalentejo.pt/pt/o-alentejo/cultura/rotas-culturais/roteiro-do-pci/). The *cante* route offers tourists the possibility of attending choir rehearsals, visiting taverns where *cante* is traditionally enacted, and participating in organized activities that feature *cante* in local museums and restaurants.

Salwa El-Shawan Castelo-Branco, *Sustainability, Agency, and the Ecologies of Music Heritage in Alentejo, Portugal*
In: *Music, Communities, Sustainability.* Edited by: Huib Schippers and Anthony Seeger, Oxford University Press.
© Oxford University Press 2022. DOI: 10.1093/oso/9780197609101.003.0010

the Grupo Coral Feminino as Ceifeiras do Alentejo (women's choirs founded in 1986 and 1997, respectively; the Grupo Coral Raízes do Cante (founded in 2015); and the Grupo Coral Bafos do Baco (founded in 2014).

The turn toward tourism by Cuba's Municipality (Balbino 2021) is part of a strategy by the Entity for Regional Tourism (ERT) for converting Alentejo into a tourist destination, constituting tourism as a major resource for the region's economic sustainability. Designed and implemented by the ERT and supported by funds from the European Union, one of the strategies for the tourist promotion of Alentejo is to "requalify" existing products for tourist consumption (ERT 2014–2020; see recent work by Simões 2021). In particular, (In)tangible Cultural Heritage of Humanity should be offered to tourists as an "exceptional and singular product that can structure tourists' emotional relationship to the Alentejo" (ERT 2015; see also Balbino 2021). The "heritage of humanity" is converted into a brand that adds value to other products (ERT, 2015). In fact, ERT supported the inscription of four regional cultural practices of Alentejo on UNESCO's Representative List of Intangible Cultural Heritage (ICH): *Cante Alentejano* (2014), Manufacture of Cowbells (2015), Falconry (jointly with sixteen other countries) (2016), and Craftsmanship of Estremoz Clay Figures (2017). In Alentejo, as elsewhere in Portugal, the legitimation and prestige conferred by inscription on one of UNESCO's ICH lists and the potential of an international certification to draw visitors to depopulated and economically debilitated areas have galvanized municipalities to promote the inscription of local practices on Portugal's national list (Matriz PCI) as a first step toward the much-desired UNESCO certification.

This chapter aims to contribute to the debate on music sustainability, taking into account the impact of state and international heritage regimes (Bendix, 2012, pp. 12–13) and the practices, powers, processes, agents, and interests at play. Focusing on the heritagization of *cante* and the revival of the local guitar (*viola campaniça*) in Alentejo and its articulation with the practice of *cante*, I address central issues in the study of contemporary heritage practices and music revival, and their impact on sustainability. I examine the processes and legacies of the heritagization of *cante* institutionalized by Portugal's authoritarian regime (1933–1974), their resignification in democracy, the impact of UNESCO's ICH paradigm, and the agency of individuals and associations. I adopt the ecological perspective on music sustainability proposed by Titon (2009, 2015, 2021), Schippers and Bendrups (2015), Schippers and Grant (2016), and Cooley (2019).

## Alentejo Resounding

Narratives about *cante* are intertwined with those of Alentejo, the region where it is rooted. Located south of the Tagus river (as its name indicates, Alem-Tejo, literally beyond the Tagus), it is the largest yet the most sparsely populated region, with the oldest resident population in Portugal (www. ine.pt). This demographic imbalance has been at the heart of debates on the region's economic, social, and cultural sustainability and is considered a major threat to the continuity of *cante* by its custodians. A historical region that was delimited since the fifteenth century, Alentejo is currently divided into three administrative districts, each with a capital city. The practice of *cante* predominates in southern and central Alentejo, corresponding to the districts of Beja and Évora,[2] as well as among the region's migrants to the Lisbon metropolitan area (which I will refer to heretofore as Lisbon). Beyond being a geographically defined location, Alentejo is a discursively and performatively constructed "imagined community" that signals particular social, political, and cultural modalities (Anderson, 1983; Appadurai, 1988; Feld and Basso, 1996, p. 5). As I argue, *cante* has been central in the construction of Alentejo.

Alentejo's economy was traditionally based on agriculture. Wheat has been the predominant crop, and the region has often been referred to as the nation's granary. Up to the 1974 revolution that ended Salazar's authoritarian regime that had ruled Portugal since 1933, agriculture was structured by the latifundiary system of landownership, and the population was divided into three major groups: landowners, sharecroppers, and a majority (over 80% at the end of the 1960s) of salaried agricultural workers who labored under harshly exploitative conditions (Aguiar, 2012; Cutileiro, 1971). Alentejo also saw workers' resistance movements supported by the Portuguese Communist Party and subsequent repression by the authoritarian regime. Following the national trend, between the 1960s and 1970s, social injustice, lack of employment, and poverty led to mass migration, most of which, in the case of Alentejo, was to the Lisbon area, where tens of *cante* choirs were formed and still thrive. As a result of this massive exodus, by 1970 Alentejo had lost one-third of its agricultural workers (Baptista, 2017, pp. 14, 17).

Between 1975 and 1980, agrarian reform was mobilized by workers who occupied the land and fought for its redistribution among them. In the 1980s,

---

[2] I will use the designation "Alentejo" as a shorthand to refer to central and southern Alentejo.

through state intervention, the land was returned to its original owners. Following Portugal's integration into the European Economic Community (presently the European Union) in 1986, the agricultural sector in Alentejo was reorganized according to the European Agricultural Policy. Since the 1980s, there has been a tendency toward the abandonment of farming. A new dynamic of intensive agricultural capitalism was implemented that is dependent on investments in crops such as vineyards, and olive and oak cork forests (*montado*). However, agricultural activity only occupies part of the land. Politicians and investors gave the remaining "environmental property" (Baptista 2017, pp. 14–15) a "second life" (Kirshenblatt-Gimblet 1995, p. 369) by transforming it into a tourist destination, offering value-added products and "certified commodities," including landscape, ecological reserves, monuments, gastronomy, festivities, and expressive cultural practices like *cante*.

Alentejo as a lived experience of place, a memory, or an imagined community is central to the heritage discourses and the expressive practices that are the focus of this chapter. Whether practiced in the region, among its migrants in the Lisbon area, or elsewhere, *cante*, performed by choirs in local costumes, on stages, in street parades, or fiestas, constitutes an "iconic embodied referent" (Hellier-Tinoco, 2011) of a bucolic "authentic" Alentejo in regional, national, and, since its inscription on UNESCO's Representative List of ICH, global contexts. Through the practice of *cante*, in choirs or informally, Alentejo is "actively sensed" and "rendered meaningful" (Feld and Basso, 1996, p. 7). Many Alentejans bond through their memory of a mythicized Alentejo, resounded through the collective singing of poetry that embodies multiple dimensions and emotions associated with their life in the region: rural landscapes, flora and fauna; villages, towns, and cities; agricultural professions and activities; religious devotion; reverence toward the mother figure, romantic love, and the hardship of agricultural labor, poverty, and forced migration. For Alentejans, sounding and moving together create a feeling of oneness and social intimacy (Turino 2008, pp. 2–3) and reinforce identification with Alentejo.

Stories of past lives in Alentejo by research partners emphasize the centrality of collective singing that accompanied arduous agricultural work, permeated moments of conviviality among coworkers, families, and friends, and marked religious and secular festivities. Many also evoke a rural Alentejo under authoritarian rule where the joy of group singing and dancing was imbricated with the pain and hardship of exploitative agricultural labor, police repression, the deprivation of freedom and other basic human rights (food, education, healthcare), and migration.

## From Field, Yard, and Tavern to Stage: A Provisional Genealogy of *Cante*

A historically and politically situated critical study of the trajectory of *cante* and other vernacular expressive practices in Alentejo is yet to be undertaken. I propose a provisional genealogy, drawing on the memory of interlocutors, other primary sources, and extant research, in an attempt to contextualize and delineate the dynamics of sustainability and the transformation and resignification of expressive practices under different political regimes.

The earliest descriptions of music and dance practices, and their social and ritual contexts in rural Alentejo, go back to the late nineteenth and early twentieth centuries. This was a period that saw the rise of nationalist discourse in Portugal, as elsewhere in Europe. Ethnographic research was centrally concerned with the definition of "national culture" (Sobral, 2003, p. 1106) and "national identity" (Leal, 2000) on the basis of what was often referred to as *cultura popular* (literally, popular culture),[3] especially in rural areas. It was within this context that the monthly ethnographic journal *A Tradição* (Piçarra and Nunes 1899–1904) was published in the town of Serpa in southern Alentejo, between 1899 and 1904, including articles on rural practices throughout the country by prominent Portuguese ethnographers and folklorists, and music transcriptions of dance-songs and solo songs. During the same period, an ethnography of rural life in Alentejo was published by Picão (1903). Both publications emphasize the centrality of "participatory performances" (Turino, 2008) of music and dance for providing moments of "heightened social interaction" (Turino, 2008) and communal bonding in homes, yards, and other public spaces, celebrating weddings, dance parties (*balhos*), and religious and secular fiestas. We also learn that on these occasions the participants sang to the accompaniment of the *viola campaniça*, harmonica, square frame drum (*pandeiro* or *adufe*), and diatonic accordion (*harmónio*). A diversity of genres and styles were

---

[3] Widely used in scholarly and everyday discourse since the nineteenth century, and resignified by different heritage regimes and agents, the notion of *cultura popular* has been central in the "authorized heritage discourse" (Smith, 2006) since the late nineteenth century (Castelo-Branco, 2013; Castelo-Branco & Cidra, 2010).

documented. Strophic songs and dance-songs performed solo, or in parallel thirds (*descante*), predominated, with some of the lyrics created in the course of performance. Reference is also made to sung poetic competitions (*desgarradas*) in which improvised poetry on a simple melody provided commentary on current events and individuals (Picão, 1903, pp. 186–189, 201–208).

Accounts by folklorists and ethnographers (Leça, 1947; Roque, 1940; Marvão, 1955), as well as interlocutors in the field, attest to the centrality of participatory music and dance performances in the social life of rural Alentejo up to the mid-twentieth century, even as the authoritarian regime exercised control over when, where, and how music and dance performance could take place. However, by the end of the twentieth century, most participatory performances were largely replaced by the presentational model of choirs with no instrumental accompaniment or dance, albeit the continuity of informal two-part singing by men in some taverns (see Balbino 2021), and by both genders in private gatherings and some fiestas .

*What accounts for the transformation of Alentejo's sound ecology? How and why did the shift from participatory to presentational performance take place? How did the changes in the sound ecology of Alentejo affect the sustainability of local expressive practices, including* cante?

A heritage regime was institutionalized by Portugal's authoritarian state as part of its vast program for inculcating its nationalist ideology and exercising power. The Estado Novo was characterized by traditionalist and corporatist nationalism (Monteiro and Pinto, 2011, p. 65), state economic interventionism, and colonial imperialism. The state's cultural policy aimed at constructing a national identity grounded in the regime's ideological cornerstones (nationalism, Catholicism, ruralism, and traditionalism) and promoting its image in the country and abroad. Intellectuals, artists, and other elites were mobilized to fabricate, aestheticize, modernize, and stage rural music and dance practices and artifacts to embody the regime's ideology. All cultural activities were tightly regulated, monitored, and censored; and professional musicians were required to hold a license (*carteira profissional*) to exercise their activity. A state heritage regime was configured, implemented, and regulated by a network of government institutions operating on the national and local levels in collaboration with local mediators (priests, folklorists, ethnographers, musicians, tradition custodians, among others). In the 1930s, a performance model that assured the "disciplining of bodies" (Foucault, 1977) and an authenticated repertoire were selected for the visual and sonic representation of each region of Portugal. Folklore groups (*ranchos folclóricos*), constituted by dancers, singers, and instrumentalists performing in local costumes presumably used in the early twentieth century, were the predominant model. An authenticated dance-song genre was selected as the iconic representation for each region, for example, the *vira* for the Minho and the *corridinho* for the Algarve.

It was within this political context that the transformation of Alentejo's sound ecology began in the 1930s. Men's amateur choirs, clad in rural costumes, performing without instrumental accompaniment or dance, were institutionalized as the performance model for southern Alentejo. An authenticated core repertoire of *modas* and *cantigas* was selected and adapted for singing in parallel thirds by choirs.[4] By the 1950s, both the performance model and authenticated repertoire were established. In addition, a choir movement was in evidence in Alentejo and was regulated by state institutions, notably, the National Foundation for Joy at Work, and, starting in 1946, through annual competitions organized by the governor of Beja, in collaboration with local folklorists and prominent musicians (Castelo-Branco and Lima, 2018, vol. 2, pp. 27–30).

Initially, the performance model and associated repertoire selected to "represent" Alentejo were referred to by folklorists and ethnographers by the generic designations *cantos* (songs), *cantos populares* (popular songs), or *canto a vozes* (multi-part singing). During the last quarter of the twentieth century, both performance and repertoire were branded as *canto Alentejano* (Alentejo's song), or *cante* (the regional pronunciation of *canto*), or *cantar à Alentejana* (singing in Alentejo's style) (Castelo-Branco and Lima, 2018, vol. 2, p. 32).

*Why was two-part polyphonic singing by men's choirs selected as the sonic representation of southern Alentejo?*

It is likely that the choice of men's choirs to represent the region was a process that involved the adaptation of the orpheonic model of choral singing to the local practice of two-part singing (Castelo-Branco, 2008),[5] an option that was in tune with the totalitarian regime's policy of promoting choral singing as a vehicle for "disciplining bodies," creating a sense of community and inculcating nationalist ideology. The first orpheons were founded at

---

[4] For more on the repertoire, performance format and aesthetics of *cante*, see Castelo-Branco (2008) and Castelo-Branco & Moreno Fernández (2019).

[5] Orpheon designates a cappella choirs and the voluntary associations they formed, initially introduced to the north of Portugal in the 1880s (Pestana, 2015).

Coimbra's University in 1880 (Orfeão Académico de Coimbra—OAC) and in Porto in 1881 (Orpheon Portuense). Subsequently, similar groups were constituted in other parts of the country. In 1907, a former law student of Coimbra's university founded an orpheon in Serpa, composed of 100 men who performed "art music" and arrangements of local vernacular repertoires for four voices (Pestana, 2014, pp. 4–6). Two other orpheons were formed in the same town in 1916 and 1940 (Pestana, 2014).

The choir movement in Alentejo was also curated through the agency of three seminary-trained Catholic priests and folklorists who resided and worked in the region: António Marvão (1903–1993), Joaquim Roque (1913–1995), and José Alcobia (1914–2003). All three collected, documented, and published local repertoire, founded and directed men's choirs, selected and adapted an authenticated repertoire that became canonical, and helped shape performance styles and aesthetics. Marvão's claim that cante had originated in the fifteenth-century religious practice of fauxbourdon (Marvão, 1966), was influential in legitimizing the authenticity and value of the local two-part singing tradition, a perspective that was in tandem with the ideology of the conservative, Catholic-oriented authoritarian regime.

As in countless cases of heritage production, the state heritage regime, designed and implemented by the authoritarian government, entailed the following processes:

Governmentality: An "ensemble formed by institutions, procedures, analyses and reflections, the calculations and tactics that allow the exercise of . . . power" (Foucault, 1979, p. 20) served as the "common ground for . . . political thought and action" (Rose et. al., 2006, p. 86).

Institutionalization and regulation: Selected expressive cultural practices were institutionalized and regulated through performance groups, associations, and competitions. These processes were mediated by social actors such as musicians, folklorists, and ethnographers. In Alentejo, men's choirs were institutionalized and regulated by governmental institutions and local agents.

Selection and reconceptualization: Musical genres, styles, repertoires, and performance formats that fulfill social and political agendas and aesthetic criteria were selected for production as heritage to the exclusion of others, a process that led to diminishing the diversity of local expressive practices. The authenticated repertoire and performance format were reconceptualized as "representations" of Alentejo. Dance, instrumental accompaniment, sung poetic competitions, and a plethora of other genres and singing styles were dropped, eventually falling out of use, or were relegated to isolated communities. Women were excluded from public performance.

*Recontextualization and display*: Enactments of heritage take place in new performance contexts, from participatory performances in community settings such as fiestas, rituals, taverns, or homes, to presentational performances on concert stages, in festivals, fairs, among other occasions. While *cante* continues to be an important ingredient in the socialization of Alentejans in private settings, fiestas, and among men in taverns, much of its practice occurs in rehearsals and staged performances within and outside the region.

*Categorization and branding*: Categorizing and branding a musical practice and repertoire as heritage contributes to the construction of a new musical and cultural universe and influences the ways in which musicians, custodians, community members, and listeners perceive and participate in heritage production and in the meaning attributed to heritagized practices. The category of *cante*, designating a performance model (men's choirs) and a heterogeneous repertoire to which it is adapted, brands a new symbolic universe, representing an imagined community through sound.

*Transformation*: Heritagization often results in changes in the meaning ascribed to the repertoire and in performance practices that are often informed by values such as authenticity and modernity. These changes can include the makeup of instrumental and vocal groups, new arrangements, and performance norms. The changes involved in reframing music practices, as heritage can sometimes be radical, transforming the essence of a music practice, or amplifying musical characteristics that collectors and scholars associate with authenticity, such as ornamentation or slow tempo, as in the case of *cante* during the second half of the twentieth century (Moniz, 2007).

The performance model, repertoire, and aesthetics institutionalized and regulated by the authoritarian regime were crystallized and have been maintained up to the present in Alentejo and among its migrants in greater Lisbon. At the same time, participatory performance by men and women was sustained in some domestic settings, private gatherings, fiestas, fairs, and taverns and, up to the last quarter of the twentieth century, by men strolling through the streets arm-in-arm, stopping on street corners to sing in a closed circle (*cantar em redondo*). In fact, informal settings served for learning and "rehearsing" the repertoire, and for recruiting singers for choirs. On the other hand, rehearsals provide moments for socialization and affective bonding among choir members, as I first observed in the rehearsals I attended of the

Grupo Coral Os Ceifeiros de Cuba in August 1986. I witnessed the profound affective involvement of choir members in the act of singing, the zeal with which they attempted to embody their aesthetic ideals and to produce a dense vocal texture where all voices blend, transforming a group of individuals into a whole, united through sound. In a local tavern where men gathered regularly to socialize and drink, I observed how conversation suddenly halted when one of the men broke out into song and was joined by a handful of men, their bodies tightly aligned in a closed circle, creating a shared affective space through sound. In these and other private and public settings, *cante* contributes to the construction and consolidation of friendships, comradeship, political alliances, and a sense of community. It is also a medium for expressing emotion, resisting isolation and oblivion (Castelo-Branco, 2008, 34), and a way of "knowing and being in the world" (Hamil, 2021, p. 115). The resilience of *cante* custodians is also reflected in the creation of new lyrics and melodies by local poets and composers, most of whom initially remained anonymous, as most custodians internalized the idea propagated by folklorists that the authenticity of the repertoire hinges in part on its presumed antiquity and the anonymity of its authors.

The 25th of April revolution and the subsequent establishment of democracy represents a watershed in Portugal's recent history. The political, social, and cultural transformations that followed affected all sectors of life. A new state heritage regime was institutionalized, privileging the preservation of the country's heritage and the promotion of amateur musical activity on the local level as an important factor in the maintenance of social cohesion (Santos et al., 1998). The grassroots associative movement expanded considerably, providing a framework for much local musicking. Sponsorship of amateur folklore groups, wind bands, and choirs active on the local level shifted from central government to municipalities. Regulation, no longer in the hands of central government, was passed on to voluntary associations and to the groups themselves.

Contrary to the expectations of cultural politicians and intellectuals, in democracy, the choir movement of Alentejo and its migrants in greater Lisbon (and the folklore movement more broadly) expanded significantly (Castelo-Branco and Branco, 2003, p. 5). According to a survey conducted by the Ethnomusicology Institute of the Nova University of Lisbon in 1998, more than 75% of active choirs that year were founded following 1975 (Castelo-Branco, Lima, & Neves, 2003). The performance model and much of the repertoire institutionalized by the authoritarian regime were largely maintained, except for the Revolutionary Process between 1974 and 1976, dubbed PREC (*Processo Revolucionário em Curso*) when new politicized lyrics were set to extant melodies, having been abandoned following this politically charged period. Financial and logistical support (rehearsal space, transportation to performances, costumes) shifted to municipalities. Since the late 1970s, women's choirs were formed, modeled after men's choirs, and have increased exponentially in the past two decades. Launching women for the first time in the public arena as representatives of their hometown and region, they revitalized a repertoire heretofore not enacted by men's choirs, and created a new dynamic in the socialization among choirs and community members, especially in informal gatherings following staged performances that inevitably include participatory performances by all those present (Cabeça & Santos, 2010).

A new type of event was configured, the *Encontro de Grupos Corais Alentejanos* (The Meeting of Alentejan Choirs), providing an arena for self-regulation and conviviality among groups and local populations. Hosted on weekends throughout the summer by a choir to celebrate its anniversary, or a secular or religious holiday, and supported by the local municipality, the *Encontro* gathers up to 30 choirs from Alentejo and greater Lisbon. Typically, each choir performs up to three *modas* on a makeshift stage located outdoors, sometimes followed by a *desfile*, a street parade featuring all participating choirs, each forming two or three rows in which the singers are tightly aligned arm-in-arm, singing as they parade. Following these presentational performances, a meal is offered by the host choir, creating a space where choirs and locals socialize and join in informal singing of a shared repertoire. Reciprocity is guaranteed by future invitations to the host choir by the invitees, thus forming a social network based on solidarity among groups that has contributed to *cante*'s sustainability (Simões, 2017, pp. 76–78).

Despite the expansion of the choir movement in democracy, the sustainability of *cante* was threatened by the advanced age of choir members and by rural exodus. According to the above-mentioned survey, in 1998 over 70% of choir members were above the age of 40 (Castelo-Branco, Neves, & Lima, 2003); a similar age profile was reported in this survey's 2013 update (Lima, 2014). Many young people were not inclined to join Alentejan choirs, regarding *cante* as an expression of a rural Alentejo associated with the poverty and hardship of a distant past with which they do not identify. In the 1980s and 1990s, the sustainability of *cante* was a major concern among its custodians. It was also one of the motivations for the organization of the First Congress of Cante in 1997 (Pereira, 2005). A watershed, it provided a pioneering forum where *cante* practitioners and scholars shared their experiences, and debated the problems and future of *cante*. The sustainability of choirs in an Alentejo that is no longer predominantly agrarian and among Alentejan communities in greater Lisbon was the main theme. Debates centered on the value of *cante* as "heritage," the need to assure its "dignification" and "valorization," criteria for authenticity, safeguarding measures, regulation of staged performances, authentication of repertoire, intergenerational transmission, the rejuvenation of choirs, financial support, and the need for an association that represents the choir movement. The Congress created a momentum that contributed to the transformation of a fragmented phenomenon into a grassroots movement, empowering *cante* custodians to debate and decide about their heritage.

The much longed-for association of *cante* choirs, *Moda—Associação do Cante Alentejano* (MACA), was formed in 2000 (www.cantoalentejano. com). Its aims mirrored those of the 1997 Congress: safeguarding, valorizing, rejuvenating, and promoting *cante* as a "living heritage." Its promoters also saw its mission as representing the choir movement, and mediating between choirs, municipal and national governments (www.cantoalentejano.com). MACA has become an important actor in the *cante* scene. It created an institutional space where custodians can exchange experiences and debate current concerns, and where scholars and musicians are sometimes invited to provide perspectives on the issues discussed. It defined what *cante* is, emphasizing its aesthetic and artistic value, and the criteria of the authenticity of repertoire and performance. It established norms for governing choirs, best practices for rehearsals and stage presentations, circumscribed an authenticated repertoire, and defined strategies for the intergenerational transmission of heritage. In addition, MACA promoted the certification of *cante* as "municipal heritage" and its inscription on UNESCO's ICH List. Through its initiatives, MACA has been playing a regulatory role and forging an "authorized heritage discourse" (Smith, 2006) articulated with the state and international heritage regimes.

The sustainability and rejuvenation of *cante* was boosted by the revival of the *viola campaniça* in the municipality of Castro Verde, a process which began in the mid-1980s and developed through 1990s and early 2000s. As mentioned above, although the instrument accompanied sung poetic competitions and dance-songs and solo songs, it was marginalized by the heritagization model that privileged *cante*. As Joana Rodrigues documented

(2017), the revival of the instrument largely corresponds to Livingston's model (2014) and the processes and issues discussed by Hill and Bithell (2014). It was driven by the agency and stewardship of impassioned local cultural activists, most notably Colaço Guerreiro, who was committed to revitalize and sustain Castro Verde's cultural practices. The transmission of performance techniques and construction skills to young people was made possible through the involvement of elderly tradition custodians. In addition, the Municipality's support was indispensable for the institutionalization in the local high school of instruction in the performance and making of the instrument (Rodrigues, 2017).

The seemingly unrelated domains of the *viola campaniça* and *cante* became intertwined through the activities of several young musicians who mastered the instrument, and have been playing a seminal role in rejuvenating and creating the conditions for the sustainability of *cante*. Several have been involved in a program sponsored by Alentejan municipalities to teach *cante* in local primary schools. The *viola campaniça* has been central in their pedagogical strategy, facilitating the repertoire's transmission and guiding the students' collective singing. Furthermore, some of these young musicians devised a new kind of ensemble formed by several of these guitars to perform the repertoire of *cante* with instrumental accompaniment and instrumental adaptations of local repertoire, a formation that is controversial among choirs. Some of the young *viola campaniça* players have also joined established choirs and even assumed the role of rehearsal masters, often using the instrument to accompany *cante* during rehearsals. Pedro Mestre (b. 1983) is the most successful example of an emerging profile of young professional musicians who are dedicated to traditional music in Alentejo. He has been teaching *cante* in several primary schools in the region since 2006. He founded and is a member and rehearsal master of several choirs and instrumental ensembles. He has performed in prestigious concert halls in Portugal and abroad, and his work has been mediatized through commercial recordings and social media. His example has inspired young people to become engaged with Alentejo's traditional music by joining established choirs, and forming new vocal and instrumental ensembles.

## Cante as Intangible Cultural Heritage of Humanity

*Cante* was inscribed on UNESCO's representative List of ICH in November 2014. The preparation of the candidacy was spearheaded by Serpa's municipality, supported by the ERT. In 2011, the municipality hired a consulting firm in culture and tourism to prepare the application. This marked the beginning of a lengthy process, wrought with conflict between different actors and interests, including other municipalities of Alentejo and the Lisbon area who felt left out of the process. Similar situations have been reported in other countries (DeCesari, 2012). In 2013, the application was entrusted to Serpa's Casa do Cante, a municipal institution founded in 2012 to safeguard and promote *cante*.

A systematic study of the impact of *cante*'s inscription on UNESCO's ICH list has not yet been carried out. Here, I offer a few thoughts, drawing on my participation in the final phase of the writing of the application, observations, interviews, and conversations with Alentejan choir singers, as well as the evaluation of other scholars (Branco et al., 2017; Mareco, 2017; Pestana & Barriga, 2019). My preliminary assessment is that UNESCO's certification has had a mixed outcome. On the one hand, it reinforced the symbolic value attributed to *cante* as ICH, raising its prestige and the practitioners' self-esteem. It also provided some choirs with unprecedented national and international visibility. For the first time, especially during the months that followed inscription, choirs from Alentejo were invited to perform in prestigious concert halls in Lisbon, Paris, and New York, among other cities. In Alentejo, several large-scale events featuring *cante* were launched, such as the CanteFest in Serpa. *Cante* also gained a new space on radio, television, and social media, especially during the months following the inscription. In addition, the symbolic value conferred by the inscription stimulated the founding of new groups and the reactivation of older ones. It also motivated the interest of young people, who had previously shunned the genre, to join extant choirs, to found new groups exclusively formed by youth, and to devise alternative performance models with few singers, or a soloist, accompanied by musical instruments, maintaining the core repertoire, but replacing rural costumes with informal attire. These new groups and musicians use social media to communicate and publicize their work, and have attempted to gain a space in the arena of popular music. There was also a rise in the interest of some art and popular music composers to make arrangements of *cante*'s repertoire, to compose new music inspired by the genre, and to mix *cante* with other music styles. Several established popular music singers added *cante* choirs to their performances, as a layer of sound evoking rusticity.

On the other hand, following inscription, the expectations of many choirs to gain national visibility and receive more financial support from municipal or central governments were not met. Some choirs claim that they are receiving less support and are left out of media projection (Pires & Rodrigues, 2017, p. 56) centered on choirs from Serpa. The custodians of other expressive practices in the region, such as sung poetic competitions (e.g., *cante ao baldão*), expressed concern over their increased marginalization (Barriga, 2017, p. 130). Furthermore, some custodians felt left out from the preparation of the application and the safeguarding plan. This problem has been pointed out by several heritage scholars and is partly related to the lack of a definition of "community" and the provision of mechanisms that ensure community participation, an ambiguity that has caused misunderstandings and varied interpretations.

## After Heritage

The resilience of *cante* through different political systems and heritage regimes has many implications for the understanding of the sustainability of music practices. The sustainability of *cante* has not depended so much on the politics of heritage, nor on recent attempts to package it as a value-added product for the tourist market, but rather on its central place in practitioners' lives, and the social intimacy created through the act of collective singing. *Cante* sustains communities and provides a dynamic space for enacting social and political relations and expressing emotions. It is also a medium through which many identify as Alentejans. The sustainability of *cante* has also depended on how practitioners envision its future, and their agency in configuring a strategy toward its continuity. As seen by them, *cante*'s future hinges on intergenerational transmission, a challenge that is being met through the institutionalization of instruction in schools throughout the region, the integration of young singers in choirs, the formation of children's choirs, the increasing involvement of young people in *cante*, and the diversification of its practice. These processes are having profound consequences on *cante*'s ecosystem. *Cante*'s sustainability also depends on securing the necessary financial and logistical conditions for the maintenance of choirs as central spaces for the practice and transmission of its repertoire and aesthetics.

To close, there is a need to rethink the concept of heritage as a fixed model that should be "preserved," and to consider Titon's suggestion that heritage should be conceived as a "trust for present and future generations" (2021, p. 43), a trust that can be approached creatively, as exemplified by the young *viola campaniça* performers. Creativity and change are necessary conditions for a sustainable future in which music practices can respond to contemporary challenges and contribute to fulfilling political, social, cultural, and individual needs.

# References

Aguiar, J. V. (2012). Vidas operárias: A reconstituição etnográfica de contextos históricos em processo de (profunda) erosão social. *Configurações: Revista de Sociologia, 9*, 57–80. https://journals.openedition.org/configuracoes/1114#tocto2n2

Anderson, B. (1983) *Imagined communities: Reflections on the origins and spread of nationalism*. Verso.

Appadurai, A. (1988) Introduction: Place and voice in anthropological theory. *Cultural Anthropology, 3*(1), 16–20.

Balbino, C. (2021). Qui commande le *cante* à Cuba? Uneanalyse des jeux d'autorité et de legitimité autor du *Cante espontâneo*, dans une ville rurale portugaise. Master's thesis, Université Paris Nanterre.

Baptisa, F. O. (2017). Alentejo: Terra, trabalho, património. In M. R. Pestana & L. T.Oliveira (Eds.), *Cantar no Alentejo: A terra, o passado e o presente* (pp. 25–40). Estremoz Editora.

Barriga, M. J. (2017). Cante ao baldão: Uma prática de desafio no Alentejo entre 1980 e a actualidade. In M. R. Pestana & L. T. Oliveira (Eds.), *Cantar no Alentejo: A terra, o passado e o presente* (pp. 89–118). Estremoz Editora.

Bendix, R. et.al. (2012). Introduction: Heritage Regimes and the State. In R. Bendix et al. (Eds.), *Heritage Regimes and the State* (pp. 11–20). The University of Gottingen.

Branco, J. F., et al. (2017). Mesa redonda—O cante: práticas, memórias e património. In M.R. Pestana and L.T.Oliveira (Eds.), *Cantar no Alentejo: A terra, o passado e o presente* (pp. 197–246). Estremoz Editora.

Cabeça, S., & Santos, J. R. (2010) A mulher no cante Alentejano. In S. P. Conde (Ed.), *Actas da Conferencia de tradicion oral: Oralidade e património cultural*, Vol. II (pp. 31–38). Concello de Ourense.

Castelo-Branco, S. E. (2008). The aesthetics and politics of multipart singing in southern Portugal. In A. Ahmedaja & G. Haid (Eds.), *European voices: Multipart singing in the Balkans and the Mediterranean* (pp. 15–37). Bohlau Verlag.

Castelo-Branco, S. E. (2013). The politics of music categorization in Portugal. In P. Bohlman (Ed.), *The Cambridge history of world music* (pp. 661–677). Cambridge University Press.

Castelo-Branco, S. E., & Branco, J. (2003). Folclorização em Portugal: Uma perspectiva. In. S. E. Castelo-Branco & J. F. Branco (Eds.), *Vozes do Povo: A folclorização em Portugal* (pp. 1–21). Celta Editora.

Castelo-Branco, S. E., & Cidra, R. (2010). Música popular. In S. Castelo-Branco (Ed.), *Enciclopédia da Música em Portugal no Século XX*, Vol. III (pp. 875–878). Círculo de Leitores/Temas e Debates.

Castelo-Branco, S. E., Lima, M. J., & Neves, J. (2003). Perfis dos grupos de música tradicional em Portugal em finais do século XX. In S. E. Castelo-Branco & J. F. Branco (Eds.), *Vozes do Povo: A folclorização em Portugal* (pp. 73–141). Celta Editora.

Castelo-Branco, S. E., & Lima, P. (2018). *Cantes* [CD & booklet] 4 vols. A Bela e o Monstro, Edições/Público.

Castelo-Branco, S. E., & Moreno Fernández, S. (2019). *Music in Portugal and Spain: Experiencing music, expressing culture*. Oxford University Press.

Cooley, T. (2019). Sustainability, resilience, advocacy and activism. In T. J. Cooley (Ed.), *Cultural Sustainabilities: Music, media, language, advocacy* (pp. xxxiii–xxxiv). Illinois University Press.

Cutileiro, J. (1971). *A Portuguese rural society*. Oxford University Press.

DeCesari, C. (2012). Thinking through heritage regimes. In R. Bendix, A. Eggert, & A. Pesselman (Eds.), *Heritage regimes and the state* (pp. 399–413). University of Gottingen.

ERT—Entidade Regional de Turismo. (2014–2020). *Documento estratégico turismo do Alentejo, 2014–2020: Visão, prioridades estratégicas e eixos de Intervenção*. https://www.turismodeportugal.pt/SiteCollectionDocuments/estrategia/Estrategi as-Regionais-Alentejo/DOCUMENTO-ESTRATEGICO-TURISMO-Alentejo-2014-2020.pdf.

ERT—Entidade Regional de Turismo. (2015). Plano Operacional para o Património da Humanidade. Apresentação do Relatório, Estratégia e Plano de Acção. https://www.visitalentejo.pt/fotos/editor2/pdfs/atividades/plano_operacional_pha_apresenta cao.pdf.

Feld, S., & Basso, K. (1996). Introduction. In S. Feld & K. Basso (Ed.), *Senses of place* (pp. 3–11). School of American Research Press.

Foucault, M. (1977) *Discipline and punish: The birth of the prison*. Random House.

Foucault, M. (1979) Governmentality. *Ideology & Conscious, 6*, 5–21.

Hamil, C. (2021). The earth is still (our) mother: Traversing Indigenous landscapes through sacred geographies of song. In B. Diamond & S.E. Castelo-Branco (Eds.), *Transforming ethnomusicology*, Vol. II (pp. 115–125). Oxford University Press.

Hellier-Tinoco, R. (2011). *Embodying Mexico: Tourism, nationalism and performance*. Oxford University Press.

Hill, J., & Bithell, C. (2014). An introduction to music revival as concept, cultural process and medium of change. In C. Bithell & J. Hill (Eds.), *The Oxford handbook of music revival* (pp. 3–42). Oxford University Press.

Kirshenblatt-Gimblet, B. (1995). Theorizing heritage. *Ethnomusicology, 39*(3), 367–380.

Leça, A. (1947). *Música popular portuguesa*. Editorial Domingos Barreira.

Leal, J. (2000). *Etnografias Portuguesas (1870–1970): Cultura popular e identidade nacional*. Publicações Dom Quixote.

Lima, M. J. (2014). Cante singing groups: A portrait from two extensive surveys. In M. R. Pestana (Ed.), *The Alentejo: Voices and aesthetics in 1939/40: A critical edition of Armando Leça's sound recordings* (pp. 70–93). Tradisom.

Livingston, T. (2014). An expanded theory of revivals as cosmpolitan participatory music making. In C. Bithell & J. Hill (Eds.), *The Oxford handbook of music revival* (pp. 60–72). Oxford University Press.

Mareco, S. (2017). A nova geração do Cante e as Manifestações sobre o cante alentejano. In M. R. Pestana & L. T. de Oliveira (Eds.), *Cantar no Alentejo: A terra, o passado e o presente*. Estremoz Editora.

Marvão, A. (1955). *Cancioneiro Alentejano: Corais majestosos, coreográficos e religiosos do Baixo Alentejo*. Tipografia da editorial Franciscana.

Marvão, A. (1966). *Origens e características do folclore musical Alentejano*. Author's edition.

Monteiro, N. G., & Pinto, A.C. (2011). Cultural myths and Portuguese national identity. In A. C. Pinto (Ed.), *Contemporary Portugal: Politics, society and culture* (2nd ed.) (pp. 55–72). Boulder: Social Science Monographs.

Moniz, J. (2007). A folclorização do cante alentejano: Um estudo de caso do Grupo Coral Os Ceifeiros de Cuba (1933–2007). Unpublished MA thesis, Nova University of Lisbon, Faculty of Social Sciences and Humanities.

[Pereira, J. F.] (2005). *Que modas? que modos? 1º Congresso do cante: Actas*. FaiAl Alentejo—Organização Cultural.

Pestana, M. R. (2014). Introduction. In M. R. Pestana (Ed.), *The Alentejo: Voices and aesthetics in 1939/40: A critical edition of Armando Leça's sound recordings* (pp. 2–19). Tradisom.

Pestana, M. R. (2015). Introdução: Cantar em Coro em Portugal (1880–2914): Práticas,contextos, ideologias. In M. R. Pestana (Ed.), *Vozes ao alto: Cantar em coro em Portugal—protagonistas, contextos e percursos* (pp. 5–41). Movimento Patrimonial pela Música Portuguesa.

Pestana, M. R., & Barriga, M. J. (2019). "Le patrimoine c'est nous": Voix plurielles autour du cante alentejano. *Transposition: Musiques et Sciences Sociales*, 8, 1–22. http://journ als. openedtion.org/transposition/3353

Picão, J. S. 1903. *Através dos Campos: Usos e costumes agrícolas-Alentejanos*. Reprinted in 1983. Publicações Dom Quixote.

Piçarra, L., & M. D. Nunes (Eds.) (1899–1904). *A Tradição: Revista Mensal d'ethnographia Portugueza*. Facsímile. Câmara Municipal de Serpa.

Rodrigues, J. (2017). *"Pelo toque dav Viola": Um estudo etnomusicológico sobre o revivalismo da viola campaniça em Castro Verde*. Unpublished MA thesis, Nova University of Lisbon, Faculty of Social Sciences and Humanities.

Roque, J. 1940. *Alentejo cem por cento*. Author's edition.

Rose, N., O'Malley, P., & Valverde, M. (2006). Governmentality. *Annual Review of Law and Social Science*, 2, 83–104.

Santos, M. L. L., et. al. (1998). *As políticas culturais em Portugal*. Observatório das Actividades Culturais.

Schippers, H., & Bendrups, D. (2015). Ethnomusicology, ecology and the sustainability of music cultures. *The World of Music New Series*, 4(1), 9–20.

Schippers, H., & Grant, C. (2016). *Sustainable futures for music cultures: An ecological perspective*. Oxford University Press.

Simões, D. (2017) A turistificação do cante alentejano como estratégia de "desenvolvimento": Discursos políticose práticas da cultura. In M. R. Pestana & L. T. Oliveira (Eds.), *Cantar no Alentejo: A terra, o passado e o presente* (pp. 76–78). Estremoz Editora.

Simões, D. (2021). *Práticas da cultura na raia do Baixo Alentejo: utopias, criatividade e formas de reisistência*. Coilbri.

Smith, L. (2006). *Uses of heritage*. Routledge.

Sobral, J. M. 2003. A formação das nações e o nacionalismo: Os paradigmas explicativos e o caso português. *Análise Social*, 37(165), 1093–1126.

Titon, J. T. (2009). Music and sustainability: An ecological viewpoint. *The World of Music*, 51(1), 119–138.

Titon, J. T. (2015). Sustainability, resilience and adaptive management for ethnomusicology. In S. Pettan & J. T. Titon (Eds.), *The Oxford handbook of applied ethnomusicology* (pp. 158–196). Oxford University Press.

Titon, J. T. (2021). A sound economy. In B. Diamond and S.E. Castelo-Branco (Eds.), *Transforming ethnomusicology: Political, social and ecological issues*, vol. II (pp. 26–46). Oxford University Press.

Turino, T. (2008). *Music as social life: The politics of participation*. University of Chicago Press.

# PART III
# THE FUTURE OF MUSIC AS ICH

# 11

# Reading ICH in Cultural Space

## China's National Cultural Ecosystem (Experimental) Conservation Areas

*Gao Shu*

In 2007, the Chinese Ministry of Culture launched a new and experimental ecological approach to safeguarding intangible cultural heritage (ICH): establishing experimental National Cultural Ecosystem Conservation Areas (NCECA), which aim at holistically safeguarding the heritage of areas that abound in ICH items with distinct regional characteristics and well-preserved cultural forms and content. This is a new initiative following the establishment of the well-known system of two lists: the list of Chinese Representative ICH items, with 1,372 national-level Representative ICH items; and the list of Chinese Representative ICH bearers, with 3,068 national-level Representative ICH bearers (see also Xiao Mei and Yang Xiao, Chapter 6 in this volume).

In 2010, the Chinese Ministry of Culture officially issued the "Guidelines for Strengthening the Construction of National Cultural Ecosystem Conservation Areas." In March 2018, China merged the Ministry of Culture and the National Tourism Administration into the Ministry of Culture and Tourism, a department under the State Council. On December 10 of the same year, the Ministry of Culture and Tourism (2019) issued its Gazette No. 1, announcing that the Measures for the Administration of NCECA would come into effect on March 1, 2019. This meant that China declared an end to the "experimental" phase of the project, and would start to carry out its NCECA work nationwide.

In the 12 years between 2007 and 2019, 21 NCECAs, such as Southern Fujian, Huizhou, and Rebgong, had been established in 17 provinces, autonomous regions, and municipalities. Using the same concept and execution, 146 provincial-level Cultural Ecosystem Conservation Areas were also established. The Southern Fujian Cultural Ecosystem Conservation (Experiment)

Gao Shu, *Reading ICH in Cultural Space* In: *Music, Communities, Sustainability*. Edited by: Huib Schippers and Anthony Seeger, Oxford University Press. © Oxford University Press 2022. DOI: 10.1093/oso/9780197609101.003.0011

area, the first of its kind, was founded as early as June 2007, three years before the launch of the first official governmental policy on NCECA. The successful implementation in the southern Fujian area has facilitated the formal development of thinking on NCECA throughout China. In this chapter, I will explain how the concept of NCECA from a Chinese perspective relates to ICH items and contributes to their safeguarding, and how it can be a powerful model for integrated ecological thinking on cultural heritage.

## The Concept of "Cultural Ecosystem" in the Context of Chinese ICH

In 1866, the German scientist E. Haeckel proposed the word "ecology," defined as a science that deals with the relations of organisms to one another and to their physical surroundings. Almost 100 years later, Steward proposed a *cultural* ecology, to study the specific structure and state of the interaction between the total natural and sociocultural environments in which human beings live (Steward, 1955). Influenced by Steward, Georges Henri Rivire, and Hugues de Varine, George proposed the concept of the "eco-museum" in 1971.

Building on their thoughts, and those of ethnomusicologists like Titon (2009) and Allen (2018), Huib Schippers argues that the dynamics of "music as a worldwide phenomenon . . . invite an in-depth exploration of the ecology of music cultures to gain a greater understanding of music sustainability and its mechanics. This, in turn, will provide a basis for making practical insights available to communities around the world, assisting them in forging sound futures on their own terms" (Schippers, 2016, p. 1).

The introduction of the theory of cultural ecology into China has led to further reflection and practice. By the first decade of the twentieth century, 11 eco-museums[1] had appeared in Guangxi Zhuang Autonomous Region, exemplified by the Guangxi Nationalities Museum. While traditional museums move cultural heritage away from their owners and the environment in which they live, into a particular museum building, the concept of an

---

[1] Namely, the Guangxi Nationalities Museum, Nandan Lihu Baiku Yao Eco-Museum, Hezhou Liantang Hakka Walled Village Eco-Museum, Sanjiang Dong Eco-Museum, Jingxi Jiuzhou Zhuang Eco-Museum, Napo Heiyi Zhuang Eco-Museum, Lingchuan County Changgangling Village Ancient Trade Route Eco-Museum, Dongxing Jing Eco-Museum, Rongshui Miao Eco-Museum, Longsheng Longji Zhuang Eco-Museum, Jinxiu Yao Eco-Museum. These museums have been open since 2011.

eco-museum is that cultural heritage should be preserved in its original form and in the communities and environments to which it belongs. Therefore, an eco-museum is not a building or a house, but rather a community. Its connotations are quite different from those of a traditional museum. These eco-museums later became the basis of the NCECA, as well as seven at the autonomous-region level.[2]

In 2003, the concept of regarding not only ICH items, but also people as an integral part of ICH policy officially appeared in Article 15 of the UNESCO Convention for the Safeguarding of the Intangible Cultural Heritage: "Within the framework of its safeguarding activities of the intangible cultural heritage, each State Party shall endeavour to ensure the widest possible participation of communities, groups and, where appropriate, individuals that create, maintain and transmit such heritage, and to involve them actively in its management" (UNESCO, 2003). In March 2005, the General Office of the State Council's "Guidelines for Strengthening the Work of Safeguarding Chinese Intangible Cultural Heritage" went one step further in proposing to "research and explore methods to protect villages or specific areas of relatively intact ecosystems of traditional culture and of special values in dynamic and holistic ways" (2005).

In December of that year, the State Council's "Notice on Strengthening the Safeguarding of Cultural Heritage" advocated to "strengthen the protection of ethnic minority cultural heritage and cultural ecosystem areas. Priority will be given to safeguarding intangible cultural heritage in ethnic minority areas. For areas with rich cultural heritage and relatively intact ecosystems of traditional culture, we shall carry out dynamic and holistic protection with a clear plan. For ethnic minority cultural heritage items and cultural ecosystem areas in need of urgent safeguarding, we shall inscribe them on lists of safeguarding as soon as possible, implementing protective measures and promptly carrying out rescue and protection." By September 2006, "determining 10 national-level ethnic and folk cultural ecosystem conservation areas" (the term later was changed into National Cultural Ecosystem Conservation Area) had been included in the Outline of Cultural Development during the "Eleventh Five-Year Plan" Period.

---

[2] The NCECAs is the Copper Drum Culture (Hechi) NCECA. The provincial-level eco-system conservation areas are the Copper Drum Culture (Hechi), Zhuang Culture (Baise), Miao Culture (Rongshui), Dong Culture (Sanjiang), Yao Culture (Jinxiu), Gui Style Opera and Quyi Culture (Guilin), and Zhuang Gexu Culture (Nanning) eco-system conservation areas.

In 2007, the Southern Fujian Cultural Ecosystem Conservation (Experiment) Area was officially established. In 2010, China completed its four-level system of ICH lists (national, provincial, city, and county levels), while the Ministry of Culture officially promulgated the "Guidelines for Strengthening the Construction of National Cultural Ecosystem Conservation Areas," which defines NCECA as follows:

A National Cultural Ecosystem Conservation Area refers to a specific area designated by the Ministry of Culture for holistic protection of cultural forms with a rich history, healthy state of sustainability, high cultural values, and distinct regional features, with the core aim of safeguarding Intangible Cultural Heritage.[3]

Article 4 of the "Measures for the Administration of National Cultural Ecosystem Conservation Areas" of the Ministry of Culture and Tourism, which came into effect on March 1, 2019, states:

The construction of National Cultural Ecosystem Conservation Areas should adhere to the concepts of prioritizing protection, holistic protection, and "seeing people, seeing items, and seeing life," protecting both intangible cultural heritage and the human and natural environment[s] that foster the development of intangible cultural heritage. The goal is to ensure "rich heritage, strong atmosphere, distinctive features, and benefitting the people."

## Case Study: Puppet Theatre in Southern Fujian

Although music plays a secondary role in the puppet theatre tradition of southern Fujian (it only started to incorporate opera singing and arias since the late Qing Dynasty), it presents a powerful example of how the three levels of "seeing people, seeing items, and seeing life" can form a subecosystem and help to stabilize a bigger cultural ecosystem. The Southern Fujian Cultural Ecosystem Conservation (Experiment) Area stretches from

---

[3] Changed to "designated by the Ministry of Culture and Tourism" in the "Measures for the Administration of National Cultural Ecosystem Conservation Areas," which came into effect on March 1, 2019.

Fujian Province's Quanzhou (11,015 square kilometers), Zhangzhou (12,600 square kilometers), to Xiamen (1,700 square kilometers). Southern Fujian culture refers to the mixed culture formed during people's migration from Central China to the coastal areas of Southeastern Fujian since the Qin, Han, Jin, and Tang dynasties, when the cultures of the Central Plain area, local people of Fujian, and foreign immigrants, including people from the Arabian Peninsula, mingled constantly. The result is a regional culture with characteristics of both agricultural and maritime ways of life, which are displayed through intangible cultural heritage, material cultural heritage, and natural and human ecosystems.

Puppet theatre is an important cultural symbol of southern Fujian, and it is a prominent manifestation of the immigrant culture of the area. The Zhangzhou glove puppet theatre, Quanzhou marionette theatre, Jinjiang glove puppet theatre, Zhangzhou puppet head carving, and Quanzhou puppet head carving have entered China's lists of Representative ICH items and Representative ICH bearers since 2006. Conservation budgets are given to protect both these items and bearers, and related safeguarding projects can also apply for the "National Intangible Cultural Heritage Safeguarding Fund" from the Ministries of Finance and Ministry of Culture and Tourism. However, these safeguarding systems required revision under the holistic safeguarding framework of the ecosystem conservation areas.

While UNESCO divides ICH into five categories in the Convention for the Safeguarding of the Intangible Cultural Heritage, China has divided its ICH items into 10 categories, so that they can be safeguarded specifically: folk literature, traditional music, traditional dance, traditional theatre, *quyi*, traditional sports, games and acrobatics, traditional art, traditional crafts, traditional medicine, and folklore. With puppet theatre, its performance belongs to the category of traditional theatre, while its carving belongs to traditional crafts. They are given specific advice by experts on respective categories. However, as far as the puppet theatre tradition is concerned, it is difficult to understand the overall form and regional characteristics of the tradition without integrating its different parts, which are separated in the ICH system. The establishment of the Southern Fujian NCECA helps to emphasize the existence of and connections between these parts, such as the cultural roles that puppets play in the social life of southern Fujian, and the functions and taboos of puppet theatre in the traditional calendar and religious rituals.

## Inheritance of "People"

Without people, culture may be recorded, but will not be alive. The inheritance of people, who are the first layer of the ecosystem, involves the intergenerational passing of knowledge between people. It is based on human transmission, and is realized jointly by individuals, families, groups, and communities. All ICH items are passed on in this way. The culture bearer is the receiver of inheritance and carrier of the living tradition of specific knowledge of the southern Fujian area. The continuation of the Zhangzhou glove puppet theatre has been guaranteed by its specific master-apprentice education system from generation to generation. Since Chen Wenpu founded the tradition in the early eighteenth century, it has been passed down first within the family, and then in the school and troupe that were established at the beginning of the founding of the People's Republic of China. Until the founding of the Longxi District Art School's puppetry major in 1958, there had been seven generations of bearers of the tradition, and it is still being passed on.

In this layer of the system, there is education both within the family and between the master and apprentice, which helps to maintain the tradition's long-term attraction to the audience. The audience, who accept and identify with the puppet theatre tradition, are also bearers on a social level. The integration of individuals, groups, and communities has facilitated the long-term and dynamic cycle of "people," and the tradition of theatre has also been in operation ever since. When the skills and concepts of puppet theatre work through "people" and become a sustainable ecosystem, they lead to the second layer—the item knowledge system.

## Item Knowledge System

An "item knowledge system" in China refers to an interlocking and self-contained knowledge system around a specific ICH item, including the carrier (materials, implements, etc.), skills, methods, characteristics, customs, and even the experience and cultural concepts of using the materials. For example, the Zhangzhou glove puppet theatre, also known as "play in the palm," is performed by hands with wooden puppets. There is a set of specialized knowledge in how to make the audience believe that these wood figures are "persons" in the play and that human hands can represent those roles vividly.

A puppet is 1.3 chi (尺 , 43 centimeters) long, with the exact dimensions determined by the size of human hands. The performance space is determined by the puppet's costume, which the puppeteer makes according to the shape of his hand. The material of the puppet, eucalyptus wood, is determined by the weight that human hands can tolerate without getting tired for the duration of a performance, as well as the rich local natural supply of eucalyptus. The specific stage, set, and lighting are also closely related to the performance of "puppets" and "hands." This knowledge, born of "hands" and existing because of the puppet theatre, constitutes the ecosystem's second layer that I propose. This set of knowledge is realized through people's mastery and dissemination of it. While the knowledge and "people" make up individual ecosystems, they also cross over to each other.

## Cultural, Natural, and Historical Background

The interaction and inter-influence between local cultural behaviors on one side, and natural environments and historical backgrounds on the other, have determined basic features of regional ecological culture. The materials of puppets are related to nature, while the puppet theatre, which originally consisted of only performances of storytelling, is related to history. The third layer of the ecosystem refers to the continuous interaction among and balance of the three. Schippers writes of musical ecosystems that "[f]or most music cultures, these do not form a neat and static set of characteristics, but a diverse and not necessarily coherent one" (2016, p. 8). We can see this from the differences between local puppet theatre performances.

Generally speaking, the puppet theatre that is popular in southern Fujian can be divided into the northern and southern schools. In Jinjiang, a town subordinate to Quanzhou, the local Nanyin music is influential on the overall musical life that includes the Liyuan opera, Gaojia opera, and puppet theatre. The local glove puppet theatre is mainly composed of "literary plays" that focus on singing and are known as "southern school." Zhangzhou, which is located in southern Fujian but borders with Guangdong, is influenced by southern Fujian, Chaoshan, and Hakka cultures. The music that locals enjoy, like Han opera, Chao opera, Peking opera, and Xiang opera (Gezi opera), are all adapted comfortably to the puppet theatre, and as a result, a "northern school" that is mainly based on actions related to opera has developed there.

Interestingly, in the integrated system of people–item knowledge–natural geographical and historical backgrounds, "people," which is the core, runs through all aspects of knowledge, and natural historical and cultural backgrounds are the final interpreters of these ecological relationships. In the same ecological area, smaller regional units have preserved the differences that reflect the aesthetics of the school, the flow of people, cultural traditions, and group identity. In addition to puppet theatre, many similar ICH items in the area have such a three-layer cultural ecosystem, reflecting different features and balancing the typical characteristics of southern Fujian culture as a whole. If we borrow the Ministry of Culture and Tourism's 2018 slogan, "see people, see items, see life," the embodiment of such a unique local human ecosystem actually constitutes the daily life of local people. Every cultural ecosystem conservation area deserves such an approach.

## The Role of Government and Experimental Status of NCECA

Over a decade of investing heavily in safeguarding ICH has made China a world-recognized giant in its work with ICH. But was its generous funding all that made it a powerful country in ICH safeguarding? There was also a lot of room for reflection and ideas. The construction of ecosystem areas is related not only to survival, but also to idealism. It is proposed under the principle of international cultural heritage protection, and it comes from a direct need in the current phase of protection work and an innovative model that emerged from academia. However, combining the experimental protection of the ecosystem area and local development, national safeguarding rules and local implementation require the implementation of continuous government support, and the special experimental status toward the general goal of the ecosystem areas.

### Government Support

There has always been an emphasis on the government's absolute control over China's ICH safeguarding work through various instruments such as national laws, the representative list system, and financial support. NCECAs and general protection work are also responsibilities of the government, which oversees procedures of application, review, demonstration, and approval under the principle of "smaller quantity, better quality." In fact, the work of NCECAs that involves holistic protection has surpassed the functions of a single department—the Ministry of Culture—and requires the support of various departments, such as the Ministry of Finance, National Development and Reform Commission, the Ministry of Housing and Urban-Rural Development, and State Taxation Administration, as well as the collaboration of local governments of various levels of NCECAs. Without the facilitation of the state through governmental decrees, the establishment and management of NCECAs would have been difficult to achieve.

Therefore, the General Office of the Ministry of Culture writes in its *Notice on Strengthening the Research Work of the Overall Planning of National Cultural Ecosystem Conservation Areas* that "the overall planning of conservation areas should be incorporated into the planning of local economic and social development as well as urban and rural construction, and should correspond to various special plans such as those regarding ecological protection, environmental governance, land use, tourism development, and cultural industry." The Ministry of Culture states in its "Guidelines on Strengthening the Construction of National Cultural Ecosystem Conservation Areas" that it is necessary "to incorporate the construction of cultural ecosystem conservation areas into the local economic and social development planning and inspection objectives of the region's work," and for it "to be included in the construction of the region's public cultural service systems," and "the required funds [should be] included in the financial budget of the regional level" (2019). Favorable conditions have been provided for the work of NCECAs according to the decree. Some NCECAs have established committees led by the deputy provincial governor, the head of publicity of the provincial party committee, and the head of the provincial culture department. The Rebgong NCECA has set up a special management committee and has created jobs with quotas for the personnel. In the Southern Fujian NCECA, the provincial government has created a "Strategy for the Training of Coming Generations of Fujian Puppetry Practitioners," which was selected by UNESCO in 2012 on the Register of Good Safeguarding Practices.

## Experimental Status

It is important to note the term "experiment" in "National Cultural Ecosystem Conservation (Experimental) Area," which an NCECA has always been called in official documents. Its experimental nature has two layers of meaning. On the one hand, it is out of caution. Since 2007, China has established 21 NCECAs. On average, no more than two NCECAs are set up per year, and the oldest NCECA is not yet 12 years old. This "practice" is tentative and is being tested by time. On the other hand, it is exploratory. The NCECA's holistic protection of an area is in line with the tenet of UNESCO's Convention for the Safeguarding of the Intangible Cultural Heritage (2003), and has been seen as an original contribution by UNESCO's Intergovernmental Committee. So far, only China has adopted this practice.

The protection of cultural ecosystems does not exist in a vacuum. The "experimental" area emphasizes the cultural characteristics of the region and encourages the interaction among various cultural resources in the region. It creates more flexibility for the allocation of regional resources. For example, the general level of finger skills in glove puppet theatre is improving. The "southern school," which specializes in literary works, is learning finger skills from the "northern school," which is good at action works. From 2006 to 2016, Chen Yansen (1946–2016), a national bearer of the Zhangzhou glove puppet theatre, taught the glove puppet class (Jinjiang) for 10 years. At the same time, the "northern school" uses the tuition fees it gets from teaching the "southern school" special skills to support the daily operation of the troupes. Based on the NCECA, the traditional performance knowledge, which is the core of puppet theatre, is concentrated in Zhangzhou and Quanzhou. The various factors of southern Fujian puppet theatre complement each other and come together to form a whole, which enhances the visibility of performance skills, of puppet theatre, and of the overall cultural tradition of southern Fujian. Such a mechanism coordinates the needs of various aspects such as the inheritance of puppetry, survival of troupes, and enjoyment of audiences in an ecosystem of its own.

## Conclusion

With the NCECA, China's ICH safeguarding work has entered another stage of development, and has chosen not to stay at the level of simply declaring ICH items and designating individuals as culture bearers. The representative list is a collection of various cultural expressions, while the NCECA is a cultural space aiming at a comprehensive, healthy ecosystem. It breaks through the old evaluation system of ICH items and bearers in which the item and people are separate, and returns them to life. The NCECA emphasizes people and values of their own cultural ecosystems, and examines academically the compromise and interplay between tradition and various other factors, using the real-life experiences of the community, groups, and individuals to approach a geographical area.

In my opinion, the "experimental" nature of the NCECA has been a positive aspect of the government's supportive policies. For the people, this ecosystem has been part of their life for generations. After nearly two decades of China's ICH safeguarding, people have realized that in China's two ICH lists, apart from observances of traditional festivals that are traditions of the entire society, most focus on small traditions that belong to smaller communities and specific groups of people. Although the national ICH lists have given them national recognition, funding, and favorable policies, the sustainability of these traditions still depends on wider support in their specific groups and communities. In this sense, if ICH safeguarding has created an imagined community around the national cultural image, the local cultural ecosystems may be seen as collectives that are closely related to local communities and local people's daily lives. This sense of collectiveness may be intangible, but it actually exists.

The establishment of China's NCECAs is a fascinating and innovative practice of protecting cultural space holistically: a new measure in China's ICH field, and indeed the world. The government act that supports this, which started in 2007, is not just about protection and preservation, but it also points to development and practice. People in the current 21 NCECAs have been given the right to choose their own future. Whether their choices will be consistent with the wishes of their ancestors, researchers, and policymakers, only the future can tell. Of course, the Chinese government's decision to continue this work in 2019 will lead to ongoing discussions on issues of cultural ownership and the demarcation of areas, for instance. However, I believe interesting new perspectives and practices will continue to arise from the current and future steps in China's mechanisms of cultural ecosystem conservation.

# References

Allen, A. S. (2018). One ecology and many ecologies: The problem and opportunity of ecology for music and sound studies. *MUSICultures, 45*(1–2), 1–13.

General Office of the State Council of China (2005, March). Guidelines for Strengthening the Work of Safeguarding Chinese Intangible Cultural Heritage. Retrieved February 27, 2022, from https://www.ihchina.cn/zhengce_details/11571

General Office of the Central Committee of the Communist Party of China, General Office of the State Council. (2006, September). Outline of cultural development during the "Eleventh Five-Year Plan" period. Retrieved April 13, 2021, from http://www.gov.cn/govweb/gongbao/content/2006/content_431834.htm

Ministry of Culture of the People's Republic of China. (2010, July). Guidelines on strengthening the construction of national cultural ecosystem conservation areas. Retrieved April 13, 2021, from http://www.ihchina.cn/Article/Index/detail?id=11580

Ministry of Culture and Tourism of the People's Republic of China. (2019, March). Measures for the Administration of National Cultural Ecosystem Conservation Areas. Retrieved April 13, 2021, from http://www.ihchina.cn/zhengce_details/18424

Schippers, H. (2016). Sound futures: Exploring the ecology of music sustainability. In H. Schippers & C. Grant (Eds.), Sustainable futures for music cultures: An ecological perspective (pp. 1–18). Oxford University Press.

State Council of the People's Republic of China. (2005, March). Notice on strengthening the safeguarding of cultural heritage. Retrieved April 13, 2021, from http://www.gov.cn/zwgk/2005-08/15/content_21681.htm

Steward, Julian H. (1955). Theory of culture change: The methodology of multilinear evolution. University of Illinois Press.

Titon, J. T. (2009). Music and sustainability: An ecological viewpoint. The World of Music, 51(1), 119–138.

UNESCO. (2003, October). Text of the convention for the safeguarding of the intangible cultural heritage. Retrieved October 3, 2019, from http://www.unesco.org/culture/ich/en/convention

General Office of the State Council of China (2005, March). Guidelines for strengthening the work of safeguarding Chinese intangible cultural heritage. Retrieved February 27, 2022, from https://www.ihchina.cn/zhengce_details/11571

# 12

# Archives, Technology, Communities, and Sustainability

## Overcoming the Tragedy of Humpty Dumpty

*Anthony Seeger (summary; full text available on companion website)*

The twenty-first century is seeing a massive growth of community-generated archives that counter hegemonic histories, mobilize communities, and facilitate the sharing of knowledge over long distances.[1] Community archives, sometimes referred to as "DIY (Do It Yourself)" or "DIT (Do it Together)" archives, are growing exponentially as more and more people around the world are able to access the internet via computers and smartphones. Community archives, controlled by the communities that create them, can be pluralist and activist in support of a given cause. They range from Facebook interest groups to stand-alone online resources. There are some physical community archives as well, with legacy analog materials as well as digital formats. The resulting "archival multiverse" can be a wonderful thing for assembling inclusive, multivocal, and enriched materials for sustaining traditions. DIY and DIT archives may be able to supply some of what is missing in little documented audiovisual recordings and enrich the resources available to individuals and communities for safeguarding traditions important to them.

Community archives face their own challenges, however. Preservation for future use is part of the definition of the word "archive," but it can be difficult or impossible for any archive to achieve. The preservation of recordings for future research, instruction, and inspiration is a very serious challenge. The world is about to lose a large percentage of all analog recordings made

---

[1] This is a brief summary of the chapter; the full text appears on the companion website, www.oup.com/us/musiccommunitiessustainability.

Anthony Seeger, *Archives, Technology, Communities, and Sustainability* In: *Music, Communities, Sustainability.* Edited by: Huib Schippers and Anthony Seeger, Oxford University Press. © Oxford University Press 2022. DOI: 10.1093/oso/9780197609101.003.0012

or stored on magnetic tape, as well as tape-based digital recordings, due to deterioration of the media and equipment obsolescence. There may be only a few years left to finish digitizing, and many tapes will not be digitized in time. Whose recorded heritage will be unavailable for future use? What will be saved? Scholars, activists, collectors, performers, and members of communities need to recognize this coming analog "Armageddon" and take steps to ensure that performances important to them are digitized for the future. Even as the world becomes more aware of its ICH, the media on which a vast amount of it is now stored are about to become unplayable.

The importance of this extends far beyond the future of archives themselves. Audiovisual recordings can contribute to safeguarding, reviving, and sustaining music and other forms of intangible cultural heritage (ICH). Orally transmitted ICH is vulnerable to interruptions in transmission when even a single generation fails to transmit its knowledge to the next. Audiovisual recordings of past performances can help communities and individuals to bridge those gaps. Although they can be helpful, a lot of information is lost when only sound and image survive.

The full chapter, available on the website, is structured around what I call the "Tragedy of Humpty Dumpty." I use a nursery rhyme to highlight the shortcomings of existing documentation. In particular, I consider the fragmentation of performances caused by the recording process itself. I reflect on what aspects of performance are and are not recordable and archivable. This is followed by a description of audiovisual archives in terms of six archival functions: institutional affiliation, acquisition, organization, preservation, access, and dissemination. The chapter describes the rapid growth of dissemination and the role of archives in the process of returning archival recordings to the communities that performed them, variously called "repatriation" and "bringing it home." I then turn to the emerging potential of archives to change how the six archival functions are undertaken in the twenty-first century. As stated at the beginning of this summary, the proliferation of "born-digital" (originally recorded in a digital format) collaborative community archives offers opportunities for the improvement, diversity, and democratization of archival holdings. The conclusion returns to the subjects of its title: archives, music, communities, and the victory of Humpty Dumpty: a future of sustaining performing arts in what Anne Gilliland calls an "archival multiverse." This is where we "move from a world constructed in terms of 'the one' and 'the other' to a world of multiple ways of knowing and practicing, of multiple narratives co-existing in one space" (AERI PACG 2011, cited in Gilliland 2018, p. 34).

Online archives face their own preservation challenges. Platform changes and administrative decisions in for-profit companies can result in total data loss. So can malicious hackers, governments, and cyber-warfare. Data loss is a danger for all archives, but it can be swift and arbitrary in cases where the community group does not control the site and does not have a full backup. Increasingly sophisticated technology will probably continue to both enable and endanger audiovisual archives.

There is a large critical literature on archives. They have been criticized for being colonial, hegemonic, and integral parts of the support of existing power structures. Most of the criticisms have been directed at official governmental archives and paper documents, rather than at audiovisual archives. The full chapter on the website discusses this issue and agrees with Miguel Garcia's conclusion in his article "Sound Archives under Suspicion." One of the reasons Garcia places sound archives under suspicion is that "anxiety is always a good starting point for developing fresh perspectives on sound archives" (Garcia 2017, p. 17). I think he is right, and fresh ideas are emerging all over.

Archives do not sustain traditions. People sustain traditions. People often create new art forms from fragments of other ones. Archival recordings, along with photographs, written documents, and community memories, can provide individuals and groups an inspiring vision of a total performance. Increased recognition of the importance of performances for cultural diversity and self-determination, and the use of the "archival multiverse," may help to shape a musical, archival, and sustainable ICH future that is different from our past. But it will require determination, reflection, collaboration, hard work, emotional commitment, and thoughtful reflection to achieve it.

## References

Garcia, M. A. (2017). Sound archives under suspicion. In S. Ziegler, I. Åkesson, G. Lechleitner, & S. Sardo (Eds.), *Historical sources of ethnomusicology in contemporary debate* (pp. 10–20). Cambridge Scholars.

AERI PACG (Archival Education and Research Institute (AERI) Pluralizing the Archival Curriculum Group (PACG). (2011). Educating for the archival multiverse. *The American Archivist*, 74(1), 68–192, cited in Gilliland, A. K. 2018. *Conceptualizing 21st-century archives*. ALA Editions.

# 13

# Mapping Musical Vitality

## A Comparative Approach to Identifying Musical Heritage in Need of Safeguarding

*Catherine Grant*

UNESCO's Convention for the Safeguarding of the Intangible Cultural Heritage (UNESCO, 2003a) precipitated substantial international efforts to identify and support musical and other cultural expressions in need of support. Some 20 years on, we have significantly advanced in scholarly understanding of the dynamics of music sustainability in specific cases (e.g., through the many safeguarding initiatives associated with UNESCO's List of Intangible Cultural Heritage in Need of Urgent Safeguarding, or the nine case studies of music sustainability in Schippers & Grant, 2016a). In general, ethnomusicological research on music sustainability and safeguarding has tended to engage with specific music genres and their communities (e.g., Grant & Chhuon, 2016; Gorlinkski, 2017; Harnish, 2019), as well as matters of theory and policy (e.g. Titon, 2009; Keogh, 2013; Howard, 2016; Seeger, 2009; and chapters by Aikawa-Faure, Ceribašić, Kurin, & Zanten, this volume). It has placed less attention on more generalizing research examining the global dynamics of music sustainability and safeguarding, and it remains difficult to substantiate claims about worldwide trends in music endangerment or vitality.

In this chapter, I weave together discussion of three existing theoretical and practical tools in the area of music sustainability that I developed over the course of a decade of research. I critically examine whether their combined usage could lead to greater scholarly understanding of the global circumstances and trends in music endangerment and vitality, and/ or improved decision-making about the local, national, and/or international allocation of funds and resources for music safeguarding. The three tools are: (1) the *Music Vitality and Endangerment Framework* (MVEF), a tool to gauge, monitor, and evaluate changes in the vitality of music genres

Catherine Grant, *Mapping Musical Vitality* In: *Music, Communities, Sustainability.* Edited by: Huib Schippers and Anthony Seeger, Oxford University Press. © Oxford University Press 2022. DOI: 10.1093/oso/9780197609101.003.0013

(Grant, 2014); (2) the map *Music Endangerment and Vitality*, a key outcome of a project that used a survey methodology based on the MVEF to map 101 music genres across the world (Grant 2015, 2017); and (3) the *Assets, Threats, Solvability* (ATS) Model, a triage system for determining how best to allocate support and resources to support specific genres that may be in need of support (Grant, 2013). The new contribution of this chapter is to consider how these tools could work in tandem to support efforts to safeguard and sustain music genres, and by extension to inform approaches to safeguarding intangible cultural heritage (ICH) at large.

I begin this chapter by providing brief context around comparative approaches to ethnomusicological research, focusing particularly on mapping. I then briefly present the MVEF and map tools, before exploring some challenges, risks, and limitations of using them to evaluate and represent music genres. I close the chapter by critically considering some implications for music safeguarding of this comparative approach to understanding endangerment and vitality. In particular, I reflect on how employing the ATS Model in conjunction with the MVEF and map could strengthen the usefulness and outcomes of all three tools.

## Comparative Ethnomusicology, Mapping, and the Specter of Cantometrics

Since Guido Adler coined the term *comparative musicology* in the late nineteenth century (Adler, 1885), interest and scholarly favor in comparative approaches to musics and culture, including mapping them, has waxed and waned. After a decline from around 1940, interest (and debate) in the topic rejuvenated in the 1960s, in anthropology (Naroll, 1968; Šaraṇa, 1975), as well as ethnomusicology (e.g., Meyer, 1960; Nettl, 1973, 1983; Merriam, 1982; see also Nettl & Bohlman, 1991; Nettl, 2005, pp. 122–137). Some scholars cautioned that comparative approaches tended to take music genres (or other units of comparison) out of context, and when contexts or meanings differ, comparison becomes futile (Merriam, 1982, p. 179). Others disagreed, arguing that such difficulties "can be overcome by a proper definition of the units and the items of comparison and by making clear also the level of abstraction at which one proposes to work" (Sarana, 1975, p. 76). Admitting, in 1982, that comparative ethnomusicological approaches are "basically unpopular, and even disdained" (p. 175), Merriam proposed that "we need to focus considerable attention and energy directly on comparativism in order to search for more feasible ways of making it a useful research tool in ethnomusicology" (p. 174).

Efforts to map music genres are inherently comparative, because meaningful mapping exercises almost always involve more than one mapped "entity" (whether a music genre, community, sound profile, or something else). In *Cantometrics*, probably the most ambitious and controversial scholarly attempt at mapping music, Alan Lomax and colleagues compared and analyzed more than 4,000 songs from over 200 cultures (1968, 1976). Lomax's related effort of the 1960s, the *Global Jukebox* project, similarly attempted to identify and codify features of songs across the world (Lobley, 2014). Lomax's ambitious efforts to compare and map music genres and styles were driven at least in part by his hope for "cultural equity," a "global vision for protecting small-scale cultures in the face of the ravages of centralized corporate power and greedy media and entertainment monoliths" (Baron, 2012, p. 280). As such, they have direct relevance to contemporary scholarly concerns about the sustainability and safeguarding of musical heritage. Lomax's search for the "elusive universals of music" (Hood, 1971, p. 349) has been widely criticized on a number of counts, including for underestimating the degree of intra-cultural musical diversity and the complexities of cross-cultural difference. While largely discredited nowadays, *Cantometrics* continues to resonate in applied spheres: the *Global Jukebox Song Tree*, a progeny of the *Global Jukebox* project, was released in early 2017 as a free and continually evolving online resource with over 5,900 songs from 600 cultures (Association for Cultural Equity, 2015).

Past deficiencies are no grounds to reject comparative approaches to ethnomusicological research in perpetuity, and recently there have been renewed attempts, in various forms, to revive them. One suite of research projects, directly inspired by Lomax's work, has focused on identifying and characterizing stylistic similarities and differences of music within and between cultures, and to map them into "music families," to better understand the historical movements of, and interactions between, human populations (e.g., Savage, Merritt, Rzeszutek, & Brown, 2012; Savage & Brown, 2013, 2014). Instead of assigning a single musical style to one geographic region or cultural group (a key criticism of Lomax's work), Savage and colleagues acknowledge that one area may comprise various styles, thereby presenting "a new type of analysis for comparative musicological studies that permits inter-cultural analysis without ignoring intra-cultural diversity" (2014,

p. 146). Their work has attracted criticism too, however, including in relation to charges of over-ambition, over-claiming, and "grand design" (e.g., Clarke, 2014). Another suite of music-mapping initiatives falls within the wider pursuit of cultural mapping, such as the effort of various national governments to "inventory" cultural heritage as part of their responsibilities as States Parties under the 2003 UNESCO Convention (e.g., Cabral, 2011; Sousa, 2017). These and other broader cultural mapping projects (e.g., Aarden & Huron, 2001; Rawes, 2009) provide useful models for mapping music, and suggest possible pathways toward addressing concerns about cultural inventorying and mapping efforts (explored at more length later this chapter).

One final recent initiative that adopts a comparative approach to evaluating music genres is *Sustainable Futures for Music Cultures* (2009–2014), although its small number of case studies (namely, nine) meant that geographical mapping was not a focus. Its international research team analyzed nine diverse case study music genres against a range of factors that can impact music sustainability across five pre-determined "domains" (Schippers & Grant, 2016a). In contrast with many other comparative endeavors, including those of Savage and Lomax, *Sustainable Futures* did not aim to compare musical *content* (such as styles or repertoires) within or between cultures; rather, it compared various factors affecting music sustainability, and how those factors manifest in specific situations. The editors of the resulting volume (one of whom is also the present writer) acknowledge certain limitations of this comparative approach, including the risk that it be mistakenly interpreted as a "one-size-fits-all" model for music sustainability (Schippers & Grant, 2016b, p. 342). Whether the project signals a return to greater interest in comparative approaches to ethnomusicological research remains to be seen.

## Mapping Music Vitality and Endangerment

In 2014–2015, I carried out a pilot research project that gathered and presented data on the levels of vitality of a small number of music genres around the world. My aims were threefold: (1) to trial the comparative use of a 12-factor evaluation tool for music genres that I had previously developed, called the *Music Vitality and Endangerment Framework* (the MVEF); (2) to evaluate the validity, reliability, and usability of a survey instrument, based on the MVEF, for collecting information about the vitality of music genres;

and (3) to explore whether and how it may be useful to map the vitality of music genres, and the challenges and limitations that arise from doing so.

Since the MVEF is exposed at length elsewhere (Grant, 2014), I present only a very brief overview here, sufficient to provide readers a basis for the discussion that follows. Adapted from UNESCO's Language Vitality and Endangerment Framework (2003b), the MVEF identifies 12 factors in the level of vitality or endangerment of any music genre. (Three random examples are Factor 1, "intergenerational transmission"; Factor 7, "accessibility of infrastructure and resources"; and Factor 12, "documentation of the genre"). The framework permits the user (a musician, community member, researcher, cultural worker, etc.) to carry out an assessment of a given music genre against each factor, comprising a qualitative assessment as well as a quantitative assessment on a scale of 0 (non-vital) to 5 (vital). Taken together, the idea is that these qualitative and quantitative assessments against the 12 factors of the framework can generate an overall picture of the strength of any given genre.

To realize the first two aims of my pilot research project—namely, to employ the MVEF comparatively, and to gauge the potential of a survey instrument to gather data about music vitality—I developed a questionnaire based on the 12 factors of MVEF[1] and disseminated it through professional ethnomusicological organizations.[2] Between May 2014 and March 2015, I received 101 responses from over 80 ethnomusicologists, community workers, community members, and musicians from around the world. In Grant (2017), I report in detail on the process and outcomes, including my conclusions about the survey instrument, advantages and limitations of assessing music genres in this way, and implications for global music sustainability efforts.[3]

It is the third aim of the project that is the primary focus of this chapter: namely, mapping those music genres for which data had been generated through the survey and MVEF evaluation tool. Like the MVEF and the survey methodology, the map takes inspiration from a precedent by

[1] Again, precedent from languages provided a model: from 2006 to 2009, UNESCO used its *Language Vitality and Endangerment Framework* as the basis for a large-scale survey on levels of language vitality across the world (reported upon in UNESCO Cultural Sector, 2011).

[2] Society for Ethnomusicology, International Council for Traditional Music, British Forum for Ethnomusicology, Musicological Society of Australia, and Canadian Society for Traditional Music.

[3] The survey tool, raw survey data, FAQs, and findings are presented on the website www.musicendangerment.com. The National Library of Australia provides long-term, open online access to this website in perpetuity (albeit with some limited functionality) through PANDORA, Australia's Web Archive. My thanks to Ian Kirkland (Geographical Information Specialist, Brisbane, Australia) for assistance with website and interactive map design.

UNESCO: the online and print *Atlas of the World's Languages in Danger*, which makes available data on the situation of the world's endangered languages (Moseley, 2010). Using the free, open-source software Google Maps and Google Fusion Tables, I collaborated with a Geographical Information Systems (GIS) specialist to generate an interactive online map of the 101 music genres and their levels of vitality or endangerment (at www. musicendangerment.com). Each music genre is represented by a pin on the map. Clicking on the pin reveals the name of the genre, and from there the user can click through to the genre "profile page," which presents the full raw survey data for that genre.

The default color of each pin, displayed when the online map is first accessed, represents that survey respondent's perception of the overall *vitality* (current strength) of that music genre, on the MVEF scale of 0–5: from black for non-vital or inactive (0) through to green for very vibrant and viable (5).[4] Using a drop-down menu, users can also choose to style the map according to the survey respondents' perceptions of the overall *viability* (likely strength into the future) of the genres, or by any of the 12 discrete factors of the MVEF (see Figure 13.1). For each of these 14 indicators—vitality, viability, and 12 MVEF factors—the same six-point graded system (0–5) is used to color the pins. Where a respondent left an answer blank, the pin displays as grey. In the very few instances where more than one survey response was received for a single music genre, the individual survey responses were retained as distinct pins on the map, rather than conflated into a single pin. In this way, the map user could compare survey responses for a single genre, and draw conclusions on the validity of the findings.

The map serves several functions. First, it makes available the raw data generated by the project survey, in line with recent calls across many academic disciplines for greater transparency in the research process, and open access of research data (Jefferies & Kember, 2019). Second, maps are a visually appealing, familiar, and engaging way to convey research data to stakeholders and to the public—in this case, information about music vitality. Third, by gathering information on many music genres using the MVEF, this project begins to generate comparable data on music vitality and endangerment across the world. Over time, the collection of a large data set

---

[4] The color scheme for each grade of the scale (see project website) is the same as that used by UNESCO in the Atlas of the World's Languages in Danger. However, the Atlas includes only endangered languages, whereas this map does not exclude any music genres on grounds of vitality. Thus, I added a sixth category to signal "vital" or "vibrant" (represented by the color green).

**Figure 13.1** Map representing levels of vitality of 100 music genres across the world, against the 12 factors of the *Music Vitality and Endangerment Framework*. The first six items in the drop-down "Style by" menu scroll are displayed.
*Source*: www.musicendangerment.com.

could feasibly help build a stronger basis for research, policy, and action on music endangerment. However, the mapping process and outcomes involve various challenges, risks, and limitations that warrant close attention.

## Challenges, Risks, and Limitations of Mapping Music Vitality

Methodologically, this approach to gauging music vitality is inherently comparative, in that it applies a single framework of analysis—the MVEF—across multiple music genres. Visually representing all 101 genres on a single map invites and facilitates comparison between the vitality and viability of those genres. However, in some key ways this project differs from many music-mapping endeavors to date: it does not map musical content, styles, or repertoires per se; it does not attempt to elucidate relationship between music genres and cultural or historical evolution or movement of populations, or between global musical diversity and human biological and cultural diversity; and it makes no claims about the representativeness of a music genre within any one cultural group. In these ways, it appears to avoid some of the vehement and common charges against the comparative mapping endeavor. However, it retains some challenges, risks, and limitations that are inherent in a systematic, positivist framework, including some of those that ethnographers were quick to point out to Lomax some decades ago in relation to the pioneering *Cantometrics* project. I explore some of the key ones here. (They are not considered at any length in previous project outputs.) I argue against some of these charges, while concurring with others: my aim is not to defend the mapping endeavor, but rather to weigh its utility in the context of wide-scale efforts (including those by UNESCO) to support and safeguard music.

First and most obvious, perhaps, is the shortcoming of reducing the complex situation of music genres into a set of factors, a very reasonable charge and limitation that I engage with at length elsewhere (in Grant, 2014, 2017). One argument in defense of mapping music vitality is that in the context of international UNESCO-led efforts to safeguard music (and other intangible cultural expressions), it seems useful to have a reliable and replicable way— even if necessarily reductive—to measure, monitor, evaluate, and compare levels of musical vitality (Grant, 2014, pp. 131–132). However, as Harmon and Loh warn in relation to their *Index of Linguistic Diversity*, any such global measurement system ". . . runs the risk of being irrelevant (or, worse, antithetical) to the needs of indigenous [and minority] communities" unless it is properly qualified and supplemented by data generated by those communities and their culture-bearers (2010, p. 11). Lobley echoes this sentiment in relation to the *Global Jukebox Song Tree*: he writes that whether the resource

> ultimately functions more as another top-down cultural heritage site, or as a genuinely equitable method of sharing insights from performances across cultures, may depend a lot on how the voices and responses of musicians and performers from different traditions can continue to be integrated within archival and online content. (2014, p. 12)

Akagawa and Smith (2019) similarly emphasize the importance of community involvement in safeguarding-related activities. For reasons of relevance, quality, and equity, it seems essential for any wide-scale music-mapping exercise (such as an expansion of the pilot project I describe above) to directly involve musicians and communities.[5] Again, the field of language maintenance provides a possible model for decentralization: the *Endangered Languages Project* and associated website (Endangered Languages Project, 2019), which maps over 3,400 endangered languages, allows language speakers themselves to directly upload data, photos, and other materials relating to their language. Such an approach would be feasible for music genres too.

Second, by their nature, maps can seem official, but they represent the culmination of a long string of choices made by the mapper, as well as the subjective perspectives of the informants. In direct response to the claim of Savage and Brown that "it should be possible to generate a musical map of the world" (2013, p. 158), Clarke appositely asks: "But a map of what kinds of music(king), and what kind of world, exactly? And a map of when?" (2014, p. 8). The official impression maps can give increases the risk of users reading the data, wrongly, as an accurate and/or indisputable representation of the situation of the music genres. This is particularly problematic because maps may be used for political purposes—by governments, researchers, missionaries, or others who have power not only to take actions in *support* of specific music genres, but also to overlook others, or, at worst, even intentionally act against them (as in cases of racism, politics, censorship, and nationalism). Thus, although the music-mapping exercise described above facilitates comparison of (perspectives on) the situation of multiple music genres, and therefore could offer a basis for discussions about the allocation of safeguarding resources, this should not be taken as an unequivocal plus. Maps are open to interpretation, and interpretations will be affected by the ideologies and intentions of those engaging with them.

Third, maps are often inaccurate, incomplete, or entail significant compromises. The project map I generated excludes thousands of music genres, as well as much contextual information that is arguably crucial to a balanced interpretation of the situation of those few genres that it does represent. It is important to remember too that assessments of music vitality, whether generated by insiders or outsiders to the community in question, are necessarily subjective (Coulter, 2011, p. 67). In testing an inventorying methodology for intangible cultural heritage in Portugal, Cabral (2011) observed that that responses by researchers were more comprehensive than

---

[5] This is notwithstanding the challenges of defining and identifying "communities"; see Ceribašić, Tan, and others in this volume.

those by practitioners (concluding that this "point[s] to the importance of awareness-raising activities and to the need for training local mediators"; p. 38)—but even the most comprehensive survey responses only provide that respondent's *perspective* on the situation of a genre. Moreover, how well informants understand the situation of the genre is only one factor determining the quality or accuracy of the answers they give. Among many other factors, political motivations may play a part: for example, a survey respondent may choose to provide a weak vitality assessment for a particular genre in the hope of generating greater support for it.

A specific example of a compromising-involving challenge I faced in this mapping project was the task of identifying a single geographical "focal" point for each music genre, in order to situate its representative pin on the map. The unruly tendency of music genres to mutate, and to migrate even without human bearers (Nettl, 2010, p. 193), complicates the mapping endeavor. Survey respondents were asked to specify the geographical site they were reporting on, and in many cases, they clearly defined that site (e.g., "*Ca trù* as found in Hanoi, Vietnam"). In other cases, however, the respondent nominated a geographical locus that was not easily translatable to a single point on a map (e.g., "Arabic-speaking communities in several countries through South-East Asia"). In those instances, I attempted to choose a pin location that best represented the central locus of the genre being reported upon: an imperfect solution, though all survey respondents were given the opportunity to check and revise my choice. In a few further cases—including *electric music* and *electroacoustic music*—the survey respondent chose not to provide a geographical descriptor for their "genre" at all; doing so may have seemed arbitrary or impossible.[6] Thus, while these four genres appear in the "gallery" of genres on the project website, they are not represented via a pin on the map.

While the limitations of the mapping endeavor are many, so are the possibilities. A significantly larger sample size could be relatively easily achieved by expanding the scope of data collection; a more representative sample could be generated via a more diverse and systematic sampling technique. Improved trustworthiness of data could be achieved by collecting multiple responses on specific music genres from a variety of players both

---

[6] UNESCO met a similar problem in its *Atlas of the World's Languages in Danger*: where is the central locus of Arabic? Of English? *Atlas* Editor Chris Moseley explores this and other cartographic challenges in Moseley (2010), pp. 14–19. My decisions for this project were informed by Moseley's text.

inside and outside the community in question (e.g., musicians, community members, researchers, cultural workers, States Parties representatives) and comparing them for inter-rater reliability, and/or by researchers working collaboratively with musicians and communities to carry out in-depth ethnographic assessments of music vitality (for example, based on the MVEF) (Grant, 2017). These strategies for increasing validity would seem critically important if the map or its associated data are to form the basis for any policy-related, educational, or interventional decisions relating to cultural sustainability, such as those that have emanated from UNESCO's comparable map of endangered languages (2010).

The simplest and most obvious use of the MVEF is to gauge the vitality of a single music genre, to gauge whether it is in need of safeguarding support, or how urgently, or what type of support.[7] Yet using the MVEF to comparatively assess and map music vitality is another potentiality of the tool, notwithstanding the limitations described above. Musicians and communities, fieldworkers and researchers, cultural workers and organizations, government agencies, policymakers, and funding bodies could all find ready uses for the vitality evaluation and mapping endeavor: to build evidence about music endangerment and the local and/or global need for music safeguarding; to track the vitality of certain music genres over time; to develop targeted music sustainability interventions that raise chances of their success; to evaluate the effectiveness of such interventions; to inform policy decisions around strategies for safeguarding; to ensure that resources are directed where they are most likely to be effective; and to support activism and advocacy in support of vibrant and viable musical expressions, among other ways (Grant, 2017).[8]

If the MVEF tool and associated map prove to be useful despite their limitations, a more extensive and accurate interactive map of music genres could be built over time, and as more responses are gathered on the situation of each music genre. UNESCO's *Atlas of the World's Languages in Danger* (Moseley, 2010) shows a possible trajectory: its first edition in 1996 incorporated 600 languages, then 900 in 2001, then over 2,500 languages in 2010. Over the

---

[7] For example, if a community determines that intergenerational transmission for a given genre is weak (Factor 1) and instruments are limited (Factor 7), yet community attitudes to the genre are in favor of its continuity into the future (Factor 10), then the community may be in a better position to take action, and/or to seek external support for targeted and relevant safeguarding initiatives.

[8] In 2015, a comparative MVEF assessment of the vitality of three Cambodian music genres, on which this author collaborated (later published as Grant & Chhuon, 2016), was used by the Cambodian Ministry of Culture and Fine Arts to inform decisions about which musical traditions it would nominate to UNESCO's List of Intangible Cultural Heritage in Need of Urgent Safeguarding.

past quarter-century, the *Atlas* has become "a powerful tool for monitoring the situation of the world's endangered languages, while continuing its proven role as an instrument for raising awareness among policy makers, the media, the general public and especially the speakers of languages in danger" (UNESCO, 2011, p. 10). A similar resource for music genres may inform policies and strategies for music safeguarding, as well as potentially laying groundwork for developing comparable tools and data relating to other forms of intangible cultural heritage.

## A Triage System for Supporting Music Genres in Need of Safeguarding

Although many music genres have received support under the array of strategies, policy instruments, and projects on music sustainability and safeguarding that have arisen since the 2003 UNESCO Convention, resources are finite. Marginalized and economically disadvantaged communities in particular—ironically, those especially likely to be facing challenges to cultural viability—may struggle to find the means to take safeguarding efforts into their own hands. Certain critical global developments since the 2003 UNESCO Convention—among them, the forcible displacement of over 70 million people (UNHCR, 2019) and the advancing climate crisis—seem certain to bring many more music genres (and other intangible cultural expressions) under threat. Targeted safeguarding initiatives often require substantial investment of time, effort, money and other resources, and so setting priorities for supporting music genres is an imperative. Taking into account these realities, how might culture-bearers, communities, governments, international bodies like UNESCO, and other stakeholders effectively determine priorities for supporting music genres? And how might these efforts build on existing theoretical and practical ethnomusicological knowledge and tools, such as the evaluation and mapping tools described above?

In other disciplines, various models have been developed to help stakeholders set priorities for supporting the sustainability of assets. One of these, the *Assets, Threats and Solvability (ATS) Model* (Hajkowicz & McDonald, 2006), is a relatively simple tool that has been used in the environmental sciences to help guide decision-making about which environmental "assets" (things of value) should be most urgently safeguarded. In Grant (2013), I adapt the ATS Model for music, with a view to considering how it may inform music-safeguarding endeavors. In summary, the adapted model encourages consideration of three factors: (1) the perceived value of the music genre in question (*Asset*), (2) the nature and severity of the threat to its viability (*Threat*), and (3) the solvability of the problem (*Solvability*). In principle, priority attention should be given to those music genres that are (i) highly valued (high-asset) in cultural, social, and/or economic terms; (ii) under significant pressure or risk (high-threat) from social and/or economic processes; and (iii) where those threats are easily fixed (high-solvability), measured by the (estimated) rate of change in the vitality of the music genre following investment in sustainability (which could be evaluated using the MVEF). Lowest priority should be those music genres considered to be of low value, that have a low level of threat, and that are difficult or costly to "solve." Since the ATS Model is inherently designed to examine music genres comparatively rather than in isolation, the MVEF and map come into play: the data they generate and make available facilitates comparison of the vitality of music genres, while the ATS Model enables that data to practically assist stakeholders to determine priorities for supporting them, in turn theoretically leading to better deployment of resources and optimal outcomes for effort.

Three steps are involved in implementing the ATS Model in the context of safeguarding efforts (Grant, 2013). The first is to identify the aim of the prioritization exercise.[9] The second step is to evaluate each music genre according to the three constituent parts of the ATS Model, thereby generating a matrix assessing each genre in terms of its assets, threats, and solvability. The third step is to use this data matrix as a basis for making decisions about the distribution of resources for sustaining or supporting the genres in question. It is important to be able to meaningfully compare the genres assessed against each other; depending on the purpose of the evaluation, for example, it could make more sense to set priorities for supporting three music genres within a single geographical region or community of practice, rather than three disparate or geographically dispersed genres.

To illustrate how the application of the ATS Model may unfold, and to consider its relevance specifically to UNESCO's ICH safeguarding endeavors, let

---

[9] Three examples: (1) following an MVEF survey assessment or mapping exercise, a community may decide to assess several of their musical traditions using the ATS Model, to determine where they should best direct their own resources; (2) a government may have a set amount of funding to support traditional genres within a nation-state; and (3) a university team of researchers may wish to determine the most necessary and likely successful target for an applied sustainability initiative.

us assume (as a thought experiment only) that the *Asset* value of all musical elements on UNESCO's *Urgent Safeguarding* list is equally "high," by dint of their inscription to the List,[10] and that therefore only the *Threats* to these genres and the *Solvability* of those threats vary. In analyzing nominations to its *Urgent Safeguarding* list, UNESCO (2019) has identified 46 common *Threats* to intangible cultural heritage, grouped in nine broad categories: *negative attitudes, demographic issues, decontextualization, environmental degradation, cultural globalization, new products and techniques, loss of objects or systems, economic pressures,* and the overarching category of *weakened practice and transmission.* The *Solvability* of those threats varies. For example, *new techniques,* in some cases, relates directly to the production or promotion of the musical instrument or music genre in question, and so could fall at least to some extent within the control of artists to address, with adequate support. By contrast, *environmental degradation* is often a wider issue of social justice and political control that is well beyond the immediate "ecosystem" (Schippers & Grant, 2016b) of the music genre or its community, and may therefore be substantially more difficult to rectify. In conjunction with the MVEF (assessing factors in vitality) and the map (facilitating comparison of MVEF data), the ATS Model could stimulate useful consideration of the value (*Asset*) and challenges (*Threats*) to a given set of music genres, and the likelihood of being able to improve its situation through music sustainability initiatives alone (*Solvability*).

## Closing Reflections

Caution is warranted in applying positivist tools to something as rich, complex, and human as music. In regard to the three tools presented in this chapter: even if further testing of the 12-factor MVEF within and across contexts increased its validity and reliability, the MVEF should always be adapted as necessary to each local context and the assessment purpose at hand (Grant, 2014). Any endeavor to map music vitality should be tackled critically, reflexively, collaboratively (with musicians and communities), and with due acknowledgment of its limitations (Grant, 2017); and the ATS

---

[10] In fact, these music genres are surely not rated equally "high" in the eyes of their respective communities, or national governments, or even UNESCO—a separate discussion. For more on how value might be conceived with regard to music genres, see Clark, Chapter 9 in this volume.

model should only be employed as one instrument in a richer process of decision-making relating to music sustainability, and even then with critical awareness of the role of subjectivities and ideologies of its users (Grant, 2013). Those with political sway should be discouraged from deciding to support—or not support—certain genres on the sole basis of the data these tools generate, without further investigation and consultation with culture-bearers and their communities. Injudicious or uncritical usage of the tools may warrant accusations like those directed against earlier comparative ethnomusicological work, including a failure to sufficiently acknowledge subjectivity in quantitative measurements, a tendency to take ratings and maps as official and trustworthy, the reduction of nuanced systems into gross categories, and an implication of a "grand narrative" to dynamics of music vitality (Grant, 2017, p. 13).

Yet a systematic, wide-scale mapping of data on musical vitality, such as may be enabled through the MVEF and map tools, seems to hold potential to generate a stronger foundation for verifiable claims about global trends in music sustainability and diversity, and a means to better understand the general phenomenon of music endangerment. In turn, in conjunction with the ATS Model, those improved understandings may feed back into improving local (e.g., community-led), national (e.g., States Parties), and international (e.g., UNESCO) efforts to support the safeguarding and sustainability of specific music genres. For these reasons, despite the various concerns and criticisms about comparative ethnomusicological research and the mapping of music genres, my sentiments align with those of Merriam, whose statement of over three decades ago seems as relevant today:

> We need the process of comparison as we need other techniques of analysis, and I suggest that instead of thinking of reasons for discarding it, we need to devote concentrated attention to making comparison a more workable weapon in the ethnomusicological arsenal. (1982, p. 325)

# References

Adler, G. (1885). Umfang, Methode und Ziel der Musikwissenschaft. *Vierteljahresschrift für Musikwissenschaft (1885)*, 1, 5–20.
Aarden, B., & Huron, D. (2001). Mapping European folksong: Geographical localization of musical features. *Computing in Musicology, 12*, 169–183.

Akagawa, N., & Smith, L. (2019). The practices and politics of safeguarding. In N. Akagawa & L. Smith (Eds.), *Safeguarding intangible heritage: Practices and politics* (pp. 1–13). Routledge.

Association for Cultural Equity. (2015). The global jukebox [website]. https://theglobaljukebox.org/

Baron, R. (2012). 'All power to the periphery': The public folklore thought of Alan Lomax. *Journal of Folklore Research, 49*(3), 275–317.

Cabral, C. B. (2011). Collaborative internet-mediated ICH inventories. *International Journal of Intangible Heritage, 6*, 35–43.

Coulter, N. R. (2011). Assessing music shift: Adapting EGIDS for a Papua New Guinea community. *Language Documentation and Description, 10*, 61–81.

Clark, D. (2014). On not losing heart: A response to Savage and Brown's "Toward a new comparative musicology." *Analytical Approaches to World Music, 3*(2), 1–14.

Endangered Languages Project. (2019). [website]. http://www.endangeredlanguages.com/

Gorlinski, G. (2017). Abandonment vs. adaptation: Religiosity and the sustainability of Kenyah traditional vocal performance in central Borneo. *Malaysian Journal of Performing and Visual Arts, 3*, 31–53.

Grant, C. (2013). Developing a triage system for sustaining intangible cultural heritage. *International Journal of Social Sustainability in Economic, Social and Cultural Context, 9*(1), 11–22. http://ijsesc.cgpublisher.com/product/pub.273/prod.48.

Grant, C. (2014). *Music endangerment: How language maintenance can help.* Oxford University Press.

Grant, C. (2015). Music endangerment and vitality [website]. www.musicendangerment.com

Grant, C. (2017). Vital signs: Toward a tool for assessing music vitality and viability. *International Journal for Traditional Arts, 1*(1), 1–19. http://tradartsjournal.ncl.ac.uk/index.php/ijta/article/view/4

Grant, C., & Chhuon S. (2016). Gauging music vitality and viability: Three cases from Cambodia. *Yearbook of the International Council for Traditional Music, 48*, 25–47.

Hajkowicz, S., & G. McDonald (2006). The Assets, Threats and Solvability (ATS) model for setting environmental priorities. *Journal of Environmental Policy and Planning, 8*(1), 87–102. doi: 10.1080/15239080600635182.

Harmon, D., & Loh, J. (2010). The index of linguistic diversity: A new quantitative measure of trends in the status of the world's languages. https://terralingua.org/wp-content/uploads/2015/07/HarmonLoh-Abridged1.pdf.

Harnish, D. (2019). Music education and sustainability in Lombok, Indonesia. *Celt: A Journal of Culture, English Language Teaching & Literature, 19*(1), 1–19.

Hood, M. (1971). *The ethnomusicologist.* McGraw-Hill.

Howard, K. (Ed.). (2016). *Music as intangible cultural heritage: Policy, ideology, and practice in the preservation of East Asian traditions.* Routledge.

Jefferies, J., & Kember, S. (2019). *Whose book is it anyway? A view from elsewhere on publishing, copyright and creativity.* Open Book.

Keogh, B. (2013). On the limitations of music ecology. *Journal of Music Research Online, 4*, 1–10.

Lobley, N. (2014). Musical and sonic sustainability online. *Ethnomusicology Forum, 23*(3), 463–477. doi: 10.1080/17411912.2014.959880

Lomax, A. (1968). *Folk song style and culture.* American Association for the Advancement of Science.

Lomax, A. (Ed.) (1976). *Cantometrics: An approach to the anthropology of music.* University of California Extension Media Center.

Merriam, A. P. (1982). On objections to comparison in ethnomusicology. In R. Falck & T. Rice (Eds.), *Cross-Cultural Perspectives on Music* (pp. 175–189). University of Toronto Press.

Meyer, L. B. (1960). Universalism and relativism in the study of ethnic music. *Ethnomusicology, 4*(10), 49–54.

Moseley, C. (Ed.). (2010.) Atlas of the world's languages in danger (3rd ed). (Online and print versions.) UNESCO. http://www.unesco.org/culture/en/endangeredlanguages/atlas.

Naroll, R. (1968). Some thoughts on comparative method in cultural anthropology. In H. M. Blalock Jr. & A. B. Blalock (Eds.), *Methodology in social research* (pp. 236–277). McGraw Hill.

Nettl, B. (1973). Comparison and comparative method in ethnomusicology. *Inter-American Institute for Musical Research Yearbook, 9*, 148–161.

Nettl, B. (1983). Comparison and comparative method in ethnomusicology. *Yearbook of the Institute of Latin American Studies, 9*, 148–161.

Nettl, B. (2005). *The study of ethnomusicology: Thirty-three discussions* (3rd ed.). University of Illinois Press.

Nettl, B. (2010). *Nettl's elephant: On the history of ethnomusicology.* University of Illinois Press.

Nettl, B., & Bohlman. P. V. (Eds.) (1991). *Comparative musicology and anthropology of music: Essays on the history of ethnomusicology.* University of Chicago Press.

Rawes, I. (2009). London sound survey. https://www.soundsurvey.org.uk/

Śaraṇa, G. (1975). *The methodology of anthropological comparisons: An analysis of comparative methods in social and cultural anthropology.* University of Arizona Press.

Savage, P., & Brown, S. (2013). Toward a new comparative musicology. *Analytical Approaches to World Music, 2*(2), 148–97.

Savage, P., & Brown, S. (2014). Mapping music: Cluster analysis of song-type frequencies within and between cultures. *Ethnomusicology, 58*(1), 133–55.

Savage, P., Merritt, E., Rzeszutek, T., & Brown, S. (2012). CantoCore: A new cross-cultural song classification scheme. *Analytical Approaches to World Music, 2*(1), 87–137.

Schippers, H., & Grant, C. (2016a). Approaching music cultures as ecosystems: A dynamic model for understanding and supporting sustainability. In H. Schippers & C. Grant (Eds.), *Sustainable futures for music cultures: An ecological perspective* (pp. 333–351). Oxford University Press.

Schippers, H., & Grant, C. (Eds.) (2016b). *Sustainable futures for music cultures: An ecological perspective.* Oxford University Press.

Seeger, Anthony (2009). Lessons Learned from the ICTM (NGO) evaluation of nominations for the UNESCO Masterpieces of the Oral and Intangible Heritage of Humanity, 2001–2005. In L. Smith & N. Akagawa (Eds.), *Intangible heritage* (pp. 176–192). Routledge.

Sousa, F. (2017). Map of e-inventories of intangible cultural heritage. *Memoriamedia Review 1*(2017), 1–13. http://review.memoriamedia.net/index.php/map-of-e-inventories-of-intangible-cultural-heritage.

Titon, J. T. (Ed.). (2009). *World of music* [special issue: *Music and Sustainability*], *51*(1). Department of Ethnomusicology, Otto-Friedrich-University.

UNESCO (2003a). Convention for the safeguarding of the intangible cultural heritage. http://www.unesco.org/culture/ich/index.php?pg=00006.

UNESCO (2003b). A methodology for assessing language vitality and endangerment. http://www.unesco.org/new/en/culture/themes/endangered-languages/language-vitality/.

UNESCO (2011). UNESCO project "Atlas of the World's Languages in Danger." https://termcoord.files.wordpress.com/2012/01/unesco-project_en_pdf.pdf.

UNESCO (2019). Living heritage and threats [interactive visual map]. https://ich.unesco.org/en/dive&display=threat#tabs

UNHCR (2019). Figures at a glance. https://www.unhcr.org/en-au/figures-at-a-glance.html.

# 14

# Working Musically Through Crisis

## What Will It Take to Push for a Sound(er) Future for Haiti?

*Rebecca Dirksen*

Contributors to this volume have been invited to reflect on the theory and practice of music as intangible cultural heritage (ICH)—as conceived and enacted through the 2003 UNESCO Convention for the Safeguarding of the Intangible Cultural Heritage—from various vantage points around the world.[1] Moreover, we have been tasked with assessing how efforts toward heritage safeguarding can in turn promote music sustainability, however that might be conceptualized in local contexts. Haiti, while considerably less active in UNESCO initiatives than many other nations (despite notable early engagement and some recent mostly post-2010 earthquake efforts), offers a particularly fruitful location from which to engage with these conversations, in raising several critical challenges to the Convention's mission and to applications of heritage management more generally. Mixed alongside the valid critiques are bright sparks of potential, as UNESCO has encouraged the Haitian state to develop infrastructure to strengthen the nation's *patrimwàn* (patrimony, heritage) and has provided funding through various initiatives. And yet, as theories and praxes around heritage continually shift on the ground, we—encompassing of all who work in support of culture (artists, practitioners, scholars, cultural policy bureaucrats, etc.) in the international community, *including especially Haitians*—will want to observe the many frictions between policies and actions that generally uphold the interests and

[1] I extend my thanks and appreciation to the editors of this volume and to Smithsonian Folkways for organizing the Sound Futures Working Conference in October 2019 that pushed us to further consider the UNESCO ICH Convention and its effects, as well as to the Yale Institute of Sacred Music for granting me the time and a rich intellectual environment for writing through a sabbatical fellowship. Moreover, for years I have been supported by many Haitian colleagues who have fostered a community of learning, exchange, collaboration, and creativity. For this chapter I especially thank Micheline Laudun Denis and her family, Charles Charlesine and his family, and Kendy Vérilus.

Rebecca Dirksen, *Working Musically Through Crisis* In: *Music, Communities, Sustainability*.
Edited by: Huib Schippers and Anthony Seeger, Oxford University Press. © Oxford University Press 2022.
DOI: 10.1093/oso/9780197609101.003.0014

advantages of the key stakeholders and the wider community, and those that, however well-intentioned, may be misguided, counterproductive, and potentially harmful.

Beyond UNESCO-influenced activity in Haiti's cultural sector, however, this Caribbean nation boasts a long and internationally significant (albeit infrequently acknowledged) history of heritage discourse. In fact, Haiti's *patrimwàn kiltirèl imateryèl* (immaterial cultural heritage) has been at the heart of prominent public dialogues over the past century[2]—for example, during the *mouvman endijenis* ("Indigenous" movement) of the 1920s and 1930s; the *mouvman fòlklòrik* (folkloric movement) of the 1940s; the *kanpay rejete* (anti-superstition campaign) of the late 1930s and early 1940s; and the formation of the Bureau national d'ethnologie in 1941. In various ways, these interrelated movements and foundations have represented battles between the promotion of heritage and its active destruction. Equally, several among them emerged as early articulations of radical literary, cultural, and political shifts, which paved the way for and intersected with critical frameworks of transnational Black consciousness, such as Négritude, Pan-Africanism, and Black Power. In other words, culture—heritage, patrimony—was explicitly elevated in the service of anti-colonial and anti-imperial resistance. Subsequent cultural campaigns, such as the *mouvman rasin* (roots movement) of the 1970s to the mid-1990s, have continued this charge.

In this chapter, my objectives in thinking through approaches to ICH safeguarding in Haiti are to (1) cite selected UNESCO-related efforts and observe what has resulted from these missions to date; and (2) consider locally grounded conceptions of patrimony and support for its continuance, particularly as (3) interpreted through two starkly different yet interlinked case studies that reveal certain complexities to this conversation (the case of Haiti's classical music, and the case of Haiti's Vodou drums). With this context established, I reflect more on the political and economic constraints, environmental circumstances, and realities of day-to-day life that make heritage safeguarding urgent yet extremely difficult. I then turn toward broader conceptions of music sustainability and imagine how musically sustainable futures in Haiti—which I reframe in terms of regenerative processes—might be strengthened. While the space allotted here is insufficient to examine in

---

[2] Given space limitations, I restrict this account to a few key periods during the past 100 years, missing important earlier and later heritage conceptions, such as the *mouvman rasin* (roots movement) of the 1970s–1990s.

great detail Haiti's ICH and cultural sustainability issues, I hope this chapter will assist others in launching more in-depth studies.

## UNESCO in Haiti

In 2009, Haiti became the 116th State Party to ratify the 2003 ICH Convention. By the time of its first (and, as of this writing, only available) report to the Intergovernmental Committee in 2016, Haiti's reporting team counted several legislative advancements among the nation's achievements toward the safeguarding of its ICH.[3] These statutes include a 2011 amendment to the 1987 Constitution (Article 215) that extends State protection to archaeological, historical, cultural, folkloric, and architectural heritage; a 2003 government directive that names Vodou as an official religion; a draft Law on Cultural Heritage (2015); and a draft Framework Law for Cultural Policy (2014), all the provisions of which support ICH safeguarding (Garcia, 2016). In September 2019, the Haitian Ministry of Culture and Communication announced that Article 215, together with the Haitian Parliament's ratification of the ICH Convention in February 2019 and Article 4 of the 2005 Decree on Copyright and Neighboring Rights, legally protect the music and dance-related practices of *rara, konpa,* and *kontredans*; the art of tracing *vèvè* (sacred Vodou symbols); the production techniques for the *papier-mâché* carnival masks of Jacmel; and the traditional recipes for several distinct regional foods—all now inscribed on the official national registry of *patrimwàn kiltirèl ayisyen* (Haitian cultural heritage; Staff iciHaïti, 2019).

Institutionally speaking, the Ministry of Culture and Communication has a dedicated Heritage Directorate (est. 2006), which oversees the Bureau national d'ethnologie (est. 1941), the Musée national d'Haïti (est. 1938), the Bibliothèque nationale d'Haïti (est. 1939), and the Institut de sauvegarde du patrimoine national (est. 1979). To date, Haiti has received UNESCO funding for three projects that support capacity-building for ICH management and regulation, including one intended to safeguard sacred songs in Lakou Dereal, a Vodou yard of the Bizonton community in the north near Limonade. The Association haïtienne des professionnels de la musique separately received a grant to conduct a currently underway survey of the Haitian

---

[3] The second periodic report on Haiti's implementation of the Convention was submitted in December 2020 for review by the Committee and was not publicly available as of this writing.

Music Industry, which involves documenting the experiences of 1,500 music professionals (Ayiti Mizik, n.d.). Only in December 2021 was Haiti's first element inscribed on the Representative List, when *soup joumou*—the hearty pumpkin/turban squash, meat, and vegetable-based "freedom soup"—was awarded "protected cultural heritage status."

While the legislative activities accounted for above were mostly confirmed recently, UNESCO-guided cultural development efforts in Haiti date back to the agency's early days, and to Haiti's first actions as a member beginning in 1946. In the wake of World War II, Haitian president Dumarsais Estimé, a pragmatic internationalist, solicited UNESCO's help in implementing a now-noted pilot study in the rural Marbial Valley (1948–early 1950s) to eradicate illiteracy through "fundamental education" and thereby improve living standards (see Boel, 2015, and Verna, 2017, pp. 122–147). Although the project did not accomplish what was hoped, in providing instruction in Kreyòl rather than French (fluently spoken by a minute fraction of the population), it became an important precursor to subsequent critical education programs, such as the STEM-based active learning initiative launched in 2010 via the MIT-Haiti Initiative (see DeGraff, 2020) in connection with the founding of the Akademi Kreyòl Ayisyen (Haitian Kreyòl Academy) in 2011. Moreover, UNESCO has periodically (if somewhat inconsistently) sponsored selected Haitian primary and secondary schools, including at times the École de Musique Dessaix-Baptiste in Jacmel, which offers training in classical music and jazz. (The Dessaix-Baptiste music curriculum has largely focused on canonical Euro/American composers, although it has also fostered the development of several Haitian composers, such as Sabrina Claire Detty Jean Louis.) However, by far the most visible of UNESCO's commitments to Haitian heritage lies with the 1982 inscription of the National History Park—encompassing King Henri Christophe's spectacular Palais Sans-Souci, Site des Ramiers, and Citadelle Laferrière—as a World Heritage Site.

Yet it was really the January 2010 earthquake, which took as many as 300,000 lives and decimated the infrastructure of the capital Port-au-Prince and surrounding areas, that highlighted the fraught state of Haiti's cultural heritage. If 2009—the year Haiti signed on to the ICH Convention—had represented a period of relative stability in recent Haitian history, any optimism came crashing down with the no-longer-avoidable recognition that not only are architectural sites and other tangible heritage items often precariously situated, but so too are countless elements of *patrimwàn imateryèl* and the knowledge bearers and practitioners who keep them going. A period of depression followed the quake as front-line responses to save lives naturally took precedence, but conversations about how best to support cultural production were ultimately renewed and intensified from before, at least for a time. These conversations took place not only among cultural and political leaders in the country, but certain prominent actors within the international arts community leaped to help. Haiti benefited from goodwill efforts to establish international partnerships, such as the Smithsonian's Projè sovtaj patrimwàn kiltirèl ayiti (Haitian Cultural Recovery Project; see Smithsonian Institute/Gouvernement de la République d'Haïti, 2011), which later contributed to establishing the Centre de conservation des biens culturel at the Université Quisqueya. In addition and in coordination with the Smithsonian, the International Committee of the Blue Shield offered its services, aiming to protect cultural property against "threats of all kinds" while declaring that "[h]eritage is fundamental in rebuilding the identity, dignity, and hope of communities after a disaster" (ICBS, 2010).

Within four months of the earthquake, UNESCO's Executive Board established an International Coordination Committee (ICC) for the Safeguarding of Haitian Cultural Heritage, composed of independent experts. Notably, only three of the 10 people appointed to the ICC were Haitian (Staff HaitiLibre, 2011). In April 2011, UNESCO announced a campaign titled "Culture as a motor for reconstruction" (UNESCO, 2011), tapping into the developmentalist discourse that has shaped the Haitian political and economic landscape for decades. These motions led to the adoption of a Strategic Plan for Cultural Development (2012-2020), which was largely premised around a " 'rich culture' defense" against Haiti's persistently touted (and persistently constructed) misfortunes (see Dirksen, 2013, pp. 44-46), with an explicit orientation toward socioeconomic development and tourism. In fact, the leisure tourism sector—which tried to cut a different path from the disaster tourism, medical tourism, and evangelical religious tourism that had exploded in popularity post-quake—received its largest boost since the 1970s, as international travelers were invited to come enjoy Haiti's festivals, arts, cuisine, and beaches. The Ministry of Tourism and collaborating cultural actors advocated to shift the mainstream negative image of Haiti into a vibrant, colorful place teeming with creativity and frenetic energy. Some Haitian scholars began arguing for a substantial deployment of *patrimwàn imateryèl* in the service of tourism, including the reinterpretation, rearticulation, and remodeling of Vodou rituals at Souvnans and *rara* festivals in Léogâne into "creative activities" for visitors to partake in

(Dautruche, 2013). Parallel with UNESCO's "Culture as a motor for recon-struction" campaign, this "mobilizing heritage" stance was posited in capi-talist terms as a means for attaining "sustainable development" (Dautruche, 2013, pp. 158–159).

Post-quake Haiti has benefited from some international interventions in ICH safeguarding by UNESCO and other similarly purposed foreign agencies. Foremost among these benefits have been investments into educa-tion at all levels. In accord with its 2009 ratification of the ICH Convention, the Haitian government began introducing an ICH curriculum into sec-ondary schools, only for the programming to be abruptly interrupted by the earthquake. As schools gradually returned to session, this curric-ulum was revived and expanded with assistance from the Bureau national d'ethnologie (BNE) and the organization Réf-Culture. In conjunction, local heritage experts developed new teaching materials, including the excellent two-volume manual *Inisyasyon nan patrimwàn kiltirèl peyi Dayiti* (Initiation into Haiti's cultural heritage) that introduces secondary school students to tangible cultural heritage (TCH) and ICH through a Haitian lens (Bien-Aimé et al., 2014). The Université d'état d'Haïti (UEH) launched several new heritage-related master's and doctoral degree programs, in large part made possible through a collaboration with the Institut du patrimoine culturel (IPAC) of the Université Laval in Québec. To date this partnership has yielded at least two doctoral degrees, achieved by Joseph Ronald Dautruche (cited above for his article on cultural tourism) and Jean Ronald Augustin for a dissertation on slavery, historical memory, and heritage (2020). Moreover, several current doctoral students are pursuing degrees in ethnologie and patrimoine and in museology.

On a more public-facing front, since 2012 a series of short-term training programs and capacity-building workshops have been held in the cities of Jacmel, Les Cayes, Limonade, and Cap Haïtien, focusing on ICH, cultural tourism, and sustainable development. For a more select group, UNESCO has conducted at least two regional training programs inclusive of Haitian concerns but held in Cuba and the Dominican Republic. Furthermore, in-spired by the 2003 Convention, several efforts have been made toward creating inventories, including the multimedia database Inventaire du patrimoine immatériel d'Haïti administered through UEH and the Ministry of Culture and Communication with assistance from IPAC (http://www.ipimh.org/), and a separate database organized by the BNE on *kontredans* (contredanse) as practiced throughout Haiti's 10 administrative districts.

For all of the benefits of UNESCO-influenced programming, however, there are also significant concerns over how these interventions have been rolled out. The documentation of recent efforts to support ICH in Haiti indicate dedication to the process (see https://ich.unesco.org/en/state/haiti-HT). In reality, though, UNESCO has a limited and circumscribed reach within Haiti, with multiple points of disconnect between the NGO's promoted vision and actual on-the-ground experience. Frankly, the vast majority of the Haitian population has never heard of UNESCO or knowingly been the direct or indirect recipient of any heritage-related support; rather, the collaboration between Haitian and UNESCO experts is still much more an academic venture than anything widely translated beyond specialized circles.

Although surely unintended, inaccessibility and exclusion have been structurally inscribed into the programming—as evidenced through UNESCO's default to French and English in capacity-building workshops and publicly available documentation on the UNESCO website and social media channels. But Haitian Kreyòl is the language of the population, and roughly only 5% of Haitians in Haiti speak French fluently (close to the same percentage who competently speak English or Spanish) (see Saint-Germain, 1997). In the Haitian case, UNESCO and its associates are thus playing right into what creolist linguist Michel DeGraff calls "linguistic apartheid" (DeGraff, 2019), which is as much an urgent contemporary problem as it is a crushing historical legacy. And yet, even as this fundamental error has been repeatedly pointed out, including by DeGraff, who has prominently intervened to urge change with limited success, it would appear that UNESCO's public-facing communications still verge more toward legibility and performance for the rest of the world than toward genuine, sustained connection with the Haitian public. Participation is therefore delimited to a small group of highly educated practitioners already deeply invested in heritage protection, cultural tourism, and the like—a group made even more exclusive when figuring in the additional linguistic and financial requirements of travel to Cuba and the Dominican Republic for regional training sessions, which have been conducted in Spanish.

These observations lead to broader issues of how participation and representation have been handled to date, first with regard to the composition of the UNESCO-appointed International Coordination Committee, wherein only 30% of the members were of Haitian background. While international partnerships and outside expertise extended from a position of respect, egalitarianism, and parity are certainly welcomed and necessary, any international collective operating in Haiti like the ICC must demonstrate a more equitable balance in membership that clearly centers local expertise. This includes the full embrace of Haiti's "citizen scholars," who may not always have university-level training, but who dedicate their lives to independent research and practice. A second matter of participation and representation comes in the portrayals of the extent of community involvement in reporting documents and promotional videos,[4] which at present are generously stated. This may well be a case of leveraging typical developmentalist vocabularies of accountability, with the ideal goal of reaching citizens at all levels of society. Nonetheless, there are reasons to see possibility for deepening connections with a broad public across social, economic, and educational divisions, not least due to the strength and commitment of the local leadership team currently headed by Kesler Bien-Aimé, program specialist for the Commission nationale haïtienne de coopération avec l'UNESCO.

## Haitian Cultural Nationalism and Heritage Movements

UNESCO's activity in Haiti, especially after the earthquake, suggests enthusiasm for shaping cultural heritage policy at the state level within an international framework bolstered by a network of experts around the world. However, conceptions of Haiti's cultural heritage and its management must not begin with or stop at UNESCO's interventions: the country has its own rich history of debate and practice around *patrimwàn*, and associated acts and activities have been found at the heart of major cultural and political movements—in fact, as much heritage movements as anything else—that have transcended Haiti's borders and that still today inform the Haitian cultural landscape.

One such defense of Haitian cultural heritage arose in response to the US Occupation (1915–1934), which, as part of the United States' history of militarized "neighborly" policing throughout the Caribbean and Latin America, brought threats to Haiti's hard-won sovereignty (see Castor, [1971] 1988). This anti-imperialist response was the *mouvman endijenis* ("Indigenist" movement) of the 1920s and 1930s, which pushed for a unified nationalist identity based on a re-evaluation of the African roots of Haitian society.[5]

---

[4] UNESCO-produced/sponsored videos include https://youtu.be/WZ4C2sUOmm8 and https://youtu.be/TCn_craAGcI.
[5] Here "Indigenous" signifies having African roots, rather than referencing the Indigenous Taíno.

Taking cues from the Harlem Renaissance, Pan-Africanism, and Latin American regionalisms, Haitian Indigénisme emerged predominantly as a literary enterprise led by prominent figures such as the poet Carl Brouard and the ethnographer, historian, physician, and diplomat Jean Price-Mars. The latter especially is known for his 1928 collection of lectures on Haitian popular culture titled *Ainsi parla l'oncle* (So Spoke the Uncle). In this now-classic volume, Price-Mars argued for the value of Haiti's oral traditions and Vodou as a valid religion alongside other "world religions," while making a case for studying the folklore of the rural majority. This recentering of the national image around African ancestral heritage stood counter to the Eurocentric nationalism of the elite classes that had contributed to the nation's susceptibility to military intervention. It moreover presented a critical response to the US Marines' modernizing projects (see Lopez, 2015, on "militarized humanitarianism") that aimed to suppress or eliminate local cultural expressions and ways of living while pushing a US-oriented assimilationist agenda. This was a radical stance that anticipated postcolonialism, and Price-Mars would become regarded by Léopold Sédar Senghor as the father of the Negritude movement that subsequently swept the Francophonie (see Joseph, Saint Paul, & Mezilas, 2018).

Price-Mars's scholarly efforts were not merely about encouraging an ontological reorientation to Haitian culture, however. They were also practical political challenges to the long-standing Haitian penal codes that criminalized participation in so-called superstitious practices associated with popular ritual and religious beliefs (Ramsey, 2011, p. 180). The Haitian state had been applying with inconsistent force these laws of prohibition against the performance of cultural patrimony associated predominantly with the rural population over the 150 years during which they remained on the books, from 1835 to 1987. As part of its supposed "civilizing mission," during the Occupation, the US Marines increased the enforcement of Article 405 of the then-in-effect 1864 Code Pénal that banned many gatherings, "spells," "magical works," "fetishisms," and "superstitions" (Ramsey, 2011, p. 181). These activities were legally lumped together as "vagrancy" yet encompassed what might otherwise be inventoried as music, dance, theatre, visual arts, sacred arts, traditional healing arts, and the like. Following the Marines' departure, in 1935 President Sténio Vincent abrogated Article 405 but renewed the Haitian government's commitment to combating "superstitious practices" with a new statutory order, while simultaneously accommodating the rights of the popular classes in the countryside to hold "popular dances" (Ramsey,

2011, pp. 184–185). In some ways, this could be taken as an effort to force-fully "sanitize" these dances from their (African and Vodou) roots and "up-lift" these practices as a national cultural asset.

By 1940, the Roman Catholic Church was using this 1935 *décret-loi* as authorization for its efforts to "purify" the practice of Catholicism in Haiti from "pagan" intrusions into the services that were common in countryside parishes. Concentrated between 1940 and 1942, these efforts became known as the *kanpay rejete* (Fr., *campagne anti-superstitieuse*), which emerged as a ferocious elimination campaign led by the French Catholic clergy, backed with military force by the Haitian government under Vincent's successor Élie Lescot. The principal targets of the anti-superstition campaign were Vodou and its practitioners, although the law was also levied to suppress the rising spread and influence of Protestantism (increasingly viewed as a threat to the Catholic Church) that accompanied US imperialism through US mis-sionary efforts during the Occupation. In accordance with the law, the anti-superstition campaign mandated the destruction of "cabalistic objects," and rural communities in particular were subjected to violent raids that trauma-tized the population while also despoiling sacred drums, altars, and other spiritual objects. From a musical and sacred perspective, among the most devastating consequences of this campaign was the theft and destruction of musical instruments, which led in particular to the near obliteration of the sa-cred *asotò* drum—one of the most significant and highly specialized objects of ritual that is considered to be a divine entity itself (see Roumain, 1943; Fleurant, 1996, p. 41).[6] Moreover, while the Church and State were set about destroying items of tangible culture, the *kanpay rejete* was also very much about rooting out beliefs, practices, and intangible heritage as a modernizing act to move the nation away from perceived "primitivism": this was about stripping people of their core identities and "exorcizing" their "demons," which was a profoundly terrorizing experience (see Métraux, [1959] 1972, pp. 339–351; Roumain, 1942).

One avenue of resistance to the *kanpay rejete* emerged in the *mouvman fòlklòrik* (folkloric movement), which engaged a broader scope of expres-sive mediums—including dance, music, theatre, and visual arts—than had the earlier literary-focused *mouvman endijenis* (see Oriol, Viaud, &

---

[6] Haitian drums confiscated during this period wound up in museums worldwide, including the Smithsonian in Washington, DC, and the Indiana University Mathers Museum of World Cultures in Bloomington, Indiana. Such acquisitions represent an ethically complicated and compromised subject.

Aubourg, 1952). Among the *mouvman fòlklòrik*'s proponents was the ethnographer, writer, and politician Jacques Roumain, who became the first director of the Bureau d'ethnologie d'Haïti (now known as the Bureau national
d'ethnologie), founded in 1941 as a state institution under President Lescot
"to study and defend folk culture," through the inventory, classification, and
conservation of archaeological and ethnological items (see Charlier-Doucet,
2005; Wilcken, 1992a, p. 7). (Indeed, President Lescot both sanctioned the
military force behind the anti-superstition campaign and supported the
development of folklore as a national resource, perhaps in part because he
had been heavily criticized for his role in the violence of the *kanpay rejete*.)
Besides amassing hundreds of objects confiscated during the *rejete* raids
for its collection, the Bureau d'ethnologie became a space for ethnographic
training via the creation of an affiliated Institut d'ethnologie, as well as for
public outreach through lectures and presentations. In addition, it provided
a venue for staging performances of *fòlklò* (folklore, popular and ritual expressive forms) and established its own folkloric choral group.

Beyond the Bureau d'ethnologie, other figures associated with the
*mouvman fòlklòrik* initiated folkloric voice, dance, and drumming
ensembles, while Haitian art composers such as Werner Jaegerhuber and
Lina Mathon Blanchet collected folk songs to arrange into pieces ready for
the concert hall (see Largey, 2006 and 2004; Dauphin, 2014; Dirksen, 2016a).
As performances of folklore stylized for the newly constructed grand stages
of the Rex Théâtre and Théâtre de Verdure became an increasingly popular
form of bourgeois recreation, composers and choreographers alike took up
this task of "translating" culture associated with the popular classes for consumption by more privileged classes—a role Jaegerhuber, for one, warmly
welcomed (Largey, 2006, p. 189). Around the same time, between the 1930s
and 1950s, a number of foreign ethnographers came to Haiti for culture-
based research, including anthropologist-dancer Katherine Dunham (see
Dunham, [1969] 1994), anthropologist-filmmaker Zora Neale Hurston (see
Hurston, [1938] 2008), and ethnomusicologist Alan Lomax (see Lomax,
2009). These researchers and their contemporaries brought with them audiovisual documentation tools, which contributed to a growing sense that certain activities should be recorded and archived and were a valid and valuable
part of Haitian culture and the historical record.

Moreover, this same period saw an emerging tourism industry that drew
visitors to exoticized folkloric presentations of art and artisanry, music, and
even ticketed Vodou "shows"—the latter of which had become a source

of particular fascination following a series of sensationalized (at best) travelogues written and published during the Occupation (i.e., Seabrook, 1929). President Dumarsias Éstime capitalized on this rising energy to launch an ambitious public works campaign and modernization project to draw tourists and boost the economy, which centered around his construction in 1949 of the Cité de l'Exposition, also known as Bisantnè. This world's fair was devised to honor the Bicentennial of Port-au-Prince and placed Haitian "folk culture" at the heart of this effort to rebrand Haiti in a positive light (see St. Hubert, 2018, pp. 99–143). Between the "legitimization" that foreign scholars brought to the subjects of their study, the tourists' eager search for Haiti's "mystique" through the country's cultural offerings, and the increasing interest among middle-class and elite audiences to see popular folklore and ritual performed on stage, the post-Occupation era opened a national dialogue about defining Haiti's national character. Folklore was seen as central to this conversation.

Besides responding to various visitors and influences brought to Haiti, another important outgrowth of these activities was the promotion and valorization of Haitian culture abroad. Namely, folkloric troupes were tapped to become cultural ambassadors, corresponding to a hemisphere-wide resolution to put folklore to use in cultivating Pan-Americanism, as encouraged by Franklin Roosevelt's Good Neighbor Policy. One of the first groups to travel in this capacity was the ensemble Legba Singers, led by Lina Fussman Mathon (later, Mathon Blanchet). In 1941 the ensemble members were sent as official delegates of the Haitian state to the Eighth Annual National Folk Festival in Washington, DC, during which their slate of performances included several at Constitution Hall. In these adapted-for-stage performances of then-still-banned popular ritual practices, which were often presented by performers who had little direct experience with the actual sacred rituals they were supposedly representing, historian Kate Ramsey observes how the process of folkloricization became an explicit nation-building strategy that was tightly controlled by the state (2011, pp. 210–247; see also Ramsey, 2002). From this perspective, the post-Occupation Haitian government employed the modernized and polished "cultural assets" of folklore in demonstration of Haiti's "transcended past," stripped of its "complications" and deserving of renewed consideration in the global eye (Ramsey, 2002, p. 247; cf. Kirshenblatt-Gimblett, 1998, p. 161).

These interrelated cultural, political, and ideological movements of the mid-twentieth century—which laid critical foundations for heritage and cultural policy debates of today—revolved around high-stakes physical battles between loss and active destruction and ardent safeguarding and promotion of cultural heritage. Through these movements, idealized forms of expressive culture were leveraged, politicized, and even weaponized at local, national, and international levels. Of note, each iteration of this dialogue— from Occupation-era persecution and the subsequent anti-superstition campaign to the "Indigenist" and folkloric movements—involved defining Haitian folklore in a narrow, reductionist way: as associated with the nation's rural and low-income Vodou-practicing popular classes, who either required strict policing (or elimination) or valorization. With regard to the latter pairing of pro-culture efforts, *fòlklò* was something "tidied up" and largely stripped of sacred meaning and other context in order to be "appropriate" for enjoyment by urban residents of higher socioeconomic classes and audiences outside of the country.

Yet, simultaneously, both the *mouvman endijenis* and the *mouvman fòlklòrik* critiqued elite hegemony, Western colonialism and imperialism, and the colorist practices that deeply divide Haiti, while identifying the "soul of the nation" (Price-Mars's words) in the darker-skinned majority, their cultural practices, and their spiritual beliefs. These heritage-driven movements may therefore be considered at once in terms of the "expediency of culture" (see Yúdice, 2004) and—perhaps somewhat to the contrary—radical Black liberationism. As we consider more current local perspectives, approaches, and challenges to heritage safeguarding and in turn cultural sustainability in Haiti, we will want to recall these histories and the attendant connections, continuities, frictions, and fissures of debate that have contributed to where Haiti is today with regard to its treatment of tangible and intangible *patrimwàn*.

## Case Studies in Haitian Musical *Patrimwàn*

Two case studies illuminate specifics of evolving heritage discourse in Haiti: one involving *mizik klasik*, or classical music usually associated (though not always correctly) with the bourgeois salon and concert hall, and the other involving *mizik* Vodou, (again, stereotypically) representing a more popular class worldview. While these two settings would seem to implicate different interests and groups of people, there are identifiable points of intersection between these separate avenues toward sustaining *patrimwàn*. Moreover, both involve important articulations of intangible cultural heritage and yet are also tied to tangible heritage: the TCH cannot be separated from the ICH.[7] Both have brought about extended discussions about the value of heritage production, promotion, and maintenance, and both have experienced in turn periods of impasse and energized debates over what to do.

The first study concerns *mizik klasik*. Even in musicology circles, exceedingly few scholars and classical musicians know that Haiti has a highly developed classical music tradition dating back to colonial Saint-Domingue. Among the wealthy white planter and biracial emancipated classes in the mid-1700s, few expenses were spared in creating a flourishing live music scene across the colony's major cities. This involved opulently staging operas by the likes of Rousseau and Gluck, inviting famed vocalists and actors from Europe to perform, and training enough residents (largely those enslaved as "house servants") to play orchestral instruments to enable these grand productions. Saint-Domingan celebrity artists emerged alongside local composers who imitated the then-preferred French and Italianate comedic opera model (see Dauphin, 2014, pp. 181–206; Fouchard, [1955] 1998a and [1955] 1998b). Following the decline in live performance during the 13-year revolution that led to Haitian independence in 1804, King Henri Christophe renewed enthusiasm and support for the arts in his court. His example was emulated by subsequent leaders, including presidents Fabre Geffrard and Paul Magloire, who both founded important national schools of music (Dauphin, 2014, pp. 209–213, 247–249; Dumervé, 1968). Alongside these efforts in music education, the nineteenth century onward has seen many island-born composers rise to national and international acclaim. Among the historical figures with greatest recognition are Occide Jeanty (1860–1936), Ludovic Lamothe (1882–1953), Justin Élie (1883–1931), Frantz Casséus (1919–1993), and Férère Laguerre (1935–1983) (see Largey, 2006, and Dauphin, 2014), as well as Carmen Brouard (1909–2005) (see Dirksen, 2016b). Many of these composers (who often received advanced training in Europe) explicitly sought to create "authentically" Haitian music, and, in accompanying both the "Indigenist" and folkloric movements, found inspiration in Vodou, popular culture, and impressions of Indigenous Taíno practices.

---

[7] Kirshenblatt-Gimblett (2004, p. 60) and others have observed the arbitrariness of separating tangible and intangible heritage.

Of interest in observing how this musical nationalism took shape, several noted composers introduced a serious ethnographic component to their creative process. Beyond the research of American folklorist Harold Courlander, whose book-length monograph *Haiti Singing* (1939) included a compilation of 126 song texts and transcribed melodies from rural Haiti, Werner Jaegerhuber (1900–1953) deemed the music of the *peyizan* ("peasants," rural dwellers) as having the "grandeur of a Handel" and systematically collected and transcribed oral tradition songs (Largey, 2006, p. 189). Jaegerhuber arranged songs for voice and piano, as with his suite *Complaintes Haïtiennes* (1950), and incorporated highly adjusted themes into his *Messe tirée de thèmes vodouesques* (1953) and opera *Naïssa* (date unconfirmed) (Largey, 2006, pp. 186–230). Whereas Jaegerhuber's song-collecting efforts were mostly made by getting singers (often educated middle-class folklore performers outside the tradition) to come to him, his fellow composer and colleague Lina Mathon Blanchet (1903–1994) conducted extensive fieldwork in *lakou* (traditional family compounds) and *ounfò* (Vodou temples and their surrounding sacred complexes). In the 1930s, it was considered outrageous and even revolutionary for an educated woman of her standing to engage in such work, especially when it involved attending Vodou ceremonies. She sometimes took students along on research outings, and this "illicit" activity once even led to her group's arrest (see Dirksen, 2016a). While better known to history as a folklorist and director/choreographer for folkloric performing ensembles, Blanchet composed prolifically, also using her fieldwork transcriptions to inspire her work, including her string quartet *Contes et légendes* (date unconfirmed) and "Essai no. II" for piano (1952).

Likely the primary reason that Blanchet is not well known as a composer, besides the misogyny that clouds historical records, is that the vast majority of her scores have been irretrievably lost. Not only was she reportedly disinterested in keeping records of her completed compositions, but a box of her original manuscripts, arrangements, and other writings—among her few remaining effects known to exist following her passing—was buried under rubble during the 2010 earthquake (Dirksen, 2019a, p. 74). This loss is by no means a rare exception, and it raises an expansive point about musical scores (transcriptions, arrangements, and original compositions) as important heritage documents beyond the particulars of any one person's oeuvre. Namely, today, we as scholars and musicians are not remotely able to assess the totality of even the most prominent Haitian composers' contributions. Nor will we ever know the full scale of loss from environmental, political, and other

threats that have ensured that Haiti's archives remain fragile and in flux—
a situation dramatically compounded because many of the most important
archives in existence are collections held in private homes, where few of the
owner-conservators are well equipped to manage their holdings. While a
few institutions, such as the music archives of the Société de recherche et
de diffusion de la musique haïtienne (SRDMH) in Montreal,[8] have essential
collections mostly outside of Haiti, such infrastructure is sorely lacking in
the country. This has led to the untenable circumstances of hidden archives
and accidental archivists at the heart of safeguarding much of Haiti's classical
music heritage (see Dirksen, 2019a).

Several contemporary parallels to these preservationist-oriented efforts
are found in three notable examples: (1) *Chansons d'enfants en Français et
Créole/Chante Timoun*, a collection of nearly 90 children's songs described
as being "from a time long past" (Educavision N.d.); (2) the two-volume set
*Kandelab* containing 200 "Haitian Folk and Vodou Songs" compiled by choral
music educator Georges Vilson (2013, 2015); and (3) a (likely still growing)
11-volume series of *Chansons d'Haiti* compiled by vocalist Karine Margron
and conductor/composer Julio Racine (2012–2021). The Educavision and
Vilson collections are transcriptions from oral tradition into Western no-
tation, and Vilson cast his mission as essential "musical conservation,"
given that "[i]n spite of the hundreds if not thousands of recorded pieces of
Vodou and other traditional rhythms, books or scores of musical notations
memorializing Haiti's music for posterity were exceedingly rare" (Vilson,
2013). The Margron-Racine collaboration—which, besides thus-described
folkloric and traditional songs, includes classic commercial music hits by
Raoul Guillaume, Candio (August Linstant de Pradines), Ansy Dérose, and
TiCorn—follows a model more aligned with Werner Jaegerhuber's approach
to collecting materials for the purposes of arrangement and composition.
Margron, who coordinated the project, has invoked UNESCO as a source of
definitions and justification for musical heritage and its safeguarding (and
has benefited from UNESCO funding, alongside other sources of support)
(Ladouceur, 2014). She maintains a perspective uncommon among contemporary music and heritage scholars, explaining, "If the traditional Kreyòl
songs of Haiti are very much alive as an oral expression, they remain one of

---

[8] SRDMH was founded in 1977 to research and disseminate Haitian classical music—framed as
"patrimoine ethno-musical haïtien"—by musicologist Claude Dauphin, composer Robert Durand,
and dramaturge Frank Fouché, with participation from composers Carmen Brouard and Édouard
Woolley.

the most fragile parts of the intangible cultural heritage of the country, for lack of tools capable of preserving them in all their authenticity and pass on to future generations" (Margron, 2020, p. 2). Yet Racine (1945–2020) was a composer at heart, and his arrangements in this collection are elaborately developed compositions around the original melodic themes. This extends his prior compositional output based on folkloric and Vodou themes, including *Tangente au Yanvalou* and *Sonate Vodou Jazz*, both for flute and piano (first recorded by flutist Mary Procopio and me, ZAMA, 2007).[9]

Post-quake, there have been concentrated efforts to get such heritage-related educational materials into schools, and the *Chansons d'Haiti* series is now part of the curriculum at Haiti's best-known elementary to post-secondary music institution, École de Musique Sainte Trinité.[10] (Precedence should not be ignored: Racine, for one, was a proponent of studying Haitian-composed music alongside Western canonical literature, dating back to his tenure as conductor of the Orchestre Philharmonique de Sainte Trinité beginning in 1974.) In the United States, advocacy for education on Haitian classical music has been led by university professors such as John Jost (emeritus choral director at Bradley University) and Janet Anthony (emeritus cello professor at Lawrence University), who both have also spent decades involved with the summer music camps for Sainte Trinité and other schools across Haiti. These transnational engagements have in turn brought about the creation of US-based non-profit organizations supporting music education in Haiti and beyond, such as BLUME (www.blumehaiti.org/) and Crossing Borders Music Collective (https://crossingbordersmusic.org/). Moreover, several Haitian-born conductors have risen to prominent positions conducting university orchestras in the United States, where they regularly program pieces by Haitian composers—among them, Jean Montès (Loyola University New Orleans), Jean Rudy Perrault (University of Minnesota Duluth), and Canes Nicolas (Missouri Southern State University). Other educational efforts have entailed a growing number of recordings involving this repertoire (i.e., by Smithsonian Folkways Recordings, ZAMA, Crossing Borders Music Collective, C-Force, David Bontemps, Sydney Guillaume, Daniel Bernard Roumain, Diana Golden, Célimène Daudet,

---

[9] A notable *Chansons d'Haïti* "spinoff" project is the album *Tambour, âme ancestrale* (2018), for which master drummer Welele Doubout (Raymond Noël) performs 10 rhythms in "safeguarding the rhythmic patrimony of Haiti" (Pierre, 2018).

[10] For a parallel discussion, see Eldridge (2015) on the recent carefully limited introduction to *rara* and Vodou alongside classical music instruction at the École de Musique Sainte-Trinité summer music camp.

etc.), and live concerts in Haiti and elsewhere (i.e., in 2014, I organized and performed a high-profile concert with internationally renowned pianist Micheline Laudun Denis, for which I selected manuscripts from Denis's private archive that I then arranged for two pianos; many of these noteworthy pieces from well-known Haitian composers cited above received their long-overdue world premieres at this event, titled "Les Héritage oubliés revisités" [Forgotten heritage revisited, Sérant, 2014][11]).

The second study pertains to *mizik* Vodou. While a detailed discussion of Vodou as an Afro-Haitian metaphysical practice is well beyond the scope of this chapter (see instead Beaubrun, 2013; Dayan, 1995; Rigaud, [1953] 2015, etc.), the focus here is on *tanbou* (drums), their makers, and the process of creation, all in relation to local practices around cultural heritage and national patrimony. The general term *tanbou* describes hand-carved drums of various forms and purposes that often hold sacred significance (see Wilcken, 1992b). In fact, the *tanbou* is frequently invoked as a symbol of Haitian identity, forged when the beating of the drums at a Vodou ceremony in 1791 launched the Haitian Revolution. Moreover, certain *tanbou* are baptized and imbued with a soul, and the voices of the spirits are heard through them; the drums both connect listeners with the ancestral homeland—Ginen (roughly, Africa)—and help practitioners negotiate between the physical and metaphysical experiences (Dirksen, 2019b, p. 51). Perhaps this profound significance is partially why the *tanbou* has sometimes been a persecuted object (or, *being*)—as with the *asòto* drum during the anti-superstition campaign of the 1940s (see earlier, p. 241). Yet the *tanbou* is also venerated, as during rare ceremonies specifically for the *asòto*. Beyond this special ceremony, through different forms (like Dawome and Kongo drums, or Rada and Petwo drums), different rites and rhythms (such as Dawome, Kongo, and Nago), and in different sacred spaces (such as the trio of *lakou* [Vodou yards] Souvnans, Soukri, and Badjo), it's the drums that animate the dancers and invoke the spirits, serving as a call to prayer and communion.[12]

---

[11] Micheline Laudun Denis debuted at Carnegie Hall in 1973, with pieces by Haitian composers Carmen Brouard and Férère Laguerre on the program. Extended program notes that I wrote for the 2014 concert Les Héritages Oubliés Revisités are available: https://www.academia.edu/45120843/ 2014_Dirksen_Rebecca_Complete_program_notes_for_the_classical_music_concert_Les_He_ri tages_Oublie_s_Revisite_s_P%C3%A9tion_Ville_Haiti_January_31_2014_Port_au_Prince_Ban que_de_la_R%C3%A9publique_dHa%C3%AFti.

[12] Dawome, Kongo, and Nago are among the 21 *nanchon* (nations) that indicate ancestral connections to specific geographies and cultures in pre-colonial Africa. Souvnans, Soukri, and Badjo were founded in the Artibonite around the time of the Revolution.

Often unseen and unconsidered, the people who make *tanbou* are keepers of a wisdom that bridges humanity with the divine, making them culture bearers with the weighty responsibility of keeping the rhythm going, through the instruments that sound under the drummers' hands. One craftsman in particular, Charles Charlesine (c. 1934–2019), left an astounding legacy, in provisioning Souvenance, Soukri, and Badjo with most of their *tanbou* for over half a century (see Dirksen, 2019b). This is not insignificant: these *lakou* were designated as official sites of national patrimony during the Michel Martelly administration (2011–2016), following renewed efforts— on Haiti's ratification of the ICH Convention in 2009—to protect Haiti's immaterial heritage, which intensified after the earthquake (see Dautruche, 2010). Beyond serving their local communities year-round, during their respective festival periods these sites receive thousands of spiritual pilgrims from across Haiti and the diaspora, as well as unaffiliated tourists and foreign photojournalists. Besides making instruments for the sacred *lakou*, during the 1970s and 1980s Charlesine found additional business when the *mouvman rasin* (an anti-Duvalierist political/cultural movement focused on revaluing African roots) brought several internationally touring commercial bands from the capital to his door in search of "authentic" instruments (Dirksen, 2019b, p. 65). The aftermath of the 2010 earthquake saw another *rasin* (roots) resurgence, and the band Chouk Bwa Libète descended on the drum-maker's family compound with a European tech team to record a music video and an album.[13]

That Charlesine's drums would move so many people around the world is remarkable: he resided in a village in the foothills of the Artibonite Valley, under conditions more consistent with the eighteenth or nineteenth centuries than with the contemporary experience of life, even within Haiti. From the bustling coastal city of Gonaïves, it takes a 45-minute drive, mostly off-road, to reach Charlesine's home during the dry season, when the route is most passable. There, under the few trees not (yet) harvested on his family plot of land, he built his workshop. Even well into his eighties, Charlesine managed 8–10-hour days of rigorous physical labor under the Caribbean sun to transform trees into *tanbou*, personally managing every step, from hollowing out logs to preparing cow and goat hides for drum heads. While he worked, Charlesine's daughter, grandchildren, and great-grandchildren

---

[13] Chouk Bwa Libète's "Kouzen Zaka" music video is at https://youtu.be/_RKBMeSy7mk; the album *Se nou ki la!* (2015) is on the Buda Musique label.

looked on and would occasionally assist. Sitting for hours to witness this feat was always, for me, both a challenging meditative practice at once about the mundane, day-to-day rhythms of life and something vastly larger, tapping into longer histories across generations and their ties to the divine. Some of this sentiment seems to have been echoed in Charlesine's understanding of how he came to acquire his knowledge about what a drum is and how it is properly made: his expertise was given by the *mistè* (the spirits, the ancestors). One night while he was a young man, the *mistè* came in a dream (*nan dòmi*) to give step-by-step instructions on the process and to compel him to make *tanbou* (Dirksen, 2019b, pp. 65–67). Drum-making was not something he had prior experience with, and although his father was a drum-maker, he passed away while Charlesine was a small child, far too young to understand. This divine intervention was key to the quality of his instruments, and Charlesine recalled that even in the beginning as he was honing his skills, drummers would come to him because they believed in the sanctity of his instruments.

Charlesine's understanding of the *mistè* as the guiding force in his drum-making practice adds a seldom-considered dimension to conversations about ICH and TCH, where the transmission of heritage occurs not through formal apprenticeship or lessons with advanced practitioners, but rather through the spirits. Still, in Charlesine's final years while I knew him, hanging heavy in the air was concern about who would continue his legacy after he transitioned. At the time, his descendants indicated no such interest or inclination: his sole surviving child and his oldest grandchildren, then in late adolescence and early adulthood, are nearly all women with fairly traditional views on gender roles, which places drum-making beyond the scope of acceptable activities for them. His male great-grandchildren, while surely observing, were too young to take up the tools while their great-grandfather was still alive. And although Charlesine was not the only highly skilled and, presumably, divinely appointed drum-maker in Haiti, his influence on the nation's most prominent Vodou *lakou* was immense, even if his name was not widely known, and few other drum-makers in the contemporary era can match his mastery of making sacred instruments. Moreover, as the number of instrument makers alive during the *kanpay rejete* and *mouvman fòlklòrik* dwindles, the profession has been shifting, and younger people who might otherwise take up the craft find that instrument making as a trade is not a viable way to generate sufficient income to live. In truth, it became increasingly less viable with each passing year for Charlesine as well, and he and his family have suffered acute economic challenges.[14] Thus, while Vodouizan leaders reassure that the *lwa* will choose who will next make *tanbou* (Dirksen, 2019b, pp. 70–71), just as they chose Charlesine decades ago, economic realities present stark implications for the longer-term sustainability of sacred experience in the country.

The trajectory of Haiti's economy is not the only existential threat to sacred drums and, by extension, Vodou's sacred communities, arts, and spaces. The *tanbou* itself offers a powerful symbol through which to understand experiences of environmental degradation and climate change, which have dramatically disproportionate impacts on populations such as Haiti's. Exploitation of the land in particular over the past 500 years has had increasingly dire effects. This extractionism includes the aggressive deforestation required to establish Saint-Domingue's productive plantations; extended through a century and a half of lumber exportation that obliterated valuable hardwoods such as oak, walnut, and *acajou* (mahogany) while enriching foreign businesses; and continues today with charcoal production that is for many citizens the only possible option given government failures to make energy accessible to the vast majority (see Bellande, 2015; Dirksen, 2019b, pp. 56–59). Haiti's trees, which once covered nearly all of Hispaniola, serve as a counter-image to the drum; after all, trees are the source material for the *tanbou*. In the Vodou belief system, both the *tanbou* and trees are sacred and central to Haitian culture, and both host spirits who are guardians of the earth and portals between humans and the universe.

As changes in the nation's ecological outlook occur, so too must orientations toward *tanbou* and trees. These shifting understandings in turn impact sacred practices and metaphysical conceptions about the ways the universe works, and demonstrate how humanity, the divine, and the environment intersect in powerful ways. In illustration of these critical connections, I curated an exhibit at the Indiana University (IU) Mathers Museum of World Cultures called *Sacred Drums, Sacred Trees: Haiti's Changing Climate* (January 2019–May 2020), which placed the *tanbou* at the center of these intersections and commemorated Charles Charlesine's contributions to sacred heritage work.[15] To consecrate the exhibit and to

---

[14] Elsewhere, Charlesine might have been declared a living national treasure for his vast cultural contributions and granted an honorary stipend to ensure his ability to comfortably continue his work. Such support does not currently exist in Haiti, and when cultural leaders have been honored, they have largely hailed from the middle and upper classes.

[15] Efforts are underway to bring this exhibit to other venues, including in Haiti, although the volatile political situation and COVID-19 pandemic have presented significant challenges.

offer a memorial service for Charlesine, who passed away within weeks of the opening, I brought Vodou priest Erol Josué, master drummer Beauvois Anilus, and two other Haitian colleagues (Guerchang Bastia and Chrystyan Petit) to IU Bloomington for a residency that featured public performances and classroom visits (Keck, 2019).

For all their differences, these case studies are intertwined. Even if not acknowledged or realized, both involve cultural crossings between socioeconomic classes and other societal divisions. Both play the boundaries between tangible and intangible forms of heritage. And both indicate that there are detrimental long-term effects to weak infrastructural support for cultural sector actors who are key to keeping various forms of heritage going.

## Music Sustainability and Sound(er) Futures

UNESCO-led efforts toward ICH safeguarding and local perspectives on Haiti's *patrimwàn imateryèl* might be glossed in incomplete terms as top-down interventionism versus bottom-up approaches toward the sustainability of musics and other heritage expressions. While still largely unexamined in the Haitian context, ample scholarship exists on heritage regimes and cultural property as technologies of sovereignty around the world (i.e., Bendix, Eggert, & Peselmann, 2013; Hafstein & Skrydstrup, 2020; Smith, 2006), as well as on local implementations of heritage policy related to UNESCO's ICH Convention, including impacts on musical practices (i.e., Akagawa & Smith, 2018; Bigenho & Stobart, 2018; Chocano, 2020; Foster & Gilman, 2015; Howard, 2012). In creating more supportive structures for music sustainability in Haiti, we (invoking the same sense of collectivity as above) need to study the numerous points of friction between internal and external leadership and conceptions about what heritage practices have been, are, and can be.

One starting point may be in observing how UNESCO's internationalist striving toward intergovernmental collaboration and world heritage policy has long served as a globalizing strategy (Kirshenblatt-Gimblett, 2004; Meskell, 2020), counter to the nationalistic objectives and nation-building projects that accompanied the various Haitian heritage movements described above. Relatedly, UNESCO's mediation of ICH has roots in and bears parallels to developmentalist ideology, dating back to the United Nations' post–World War II involvement with reconfiguring world hierarchies toward international peace and stability and modernizing local economies and governance (per stated goals). These ties extend forward through the UN Sustainable Development Goals implemented in 2015 with the 2030 Agenda, with its neoliberal targets and indicators. Given the long history of developmentalist experimentation and humanitarian aid regimes as well as imperialist geopolitics that have shaped their country, many Haitians involved in the culture sector hold reasonable reservations over the potential for UNESCO-led initiatives to become yet another avenue of imperialist interventionism. Moreover, in Haiti, UNESCO, as a specialized agency of the UN, is automatically tainted by ties—however administratively distant they may be—to the UN's "peacekeeping mission" MINUSTAH and subsequent BINUH, which have been experienced less in friendly terms than as a frequently violent military occupation.

A further point of inquiry may be in analyzing the creation and enactment of legislation and administered programs intended to strengthen the cultural sector, but that often do the opposite. While a legalistic stance may be deemed necessary to prevent active destruction of heritage, local efforts may well be inadequately conceived and insufficiently supported. (One hypothetical case: institutions probably cannot enforce laws and cultural policy to protect and manage the *lwa* and their musical articulations, even though the Vodou spirits are surely allied with important *patrimwàn*. Another concrete case: culture bearers seldom receive the recognition or subsidies needed to facilitate their work, and are therefore regularly pressed to make great personal sacrifices to continue their musical or cultural practices.) Inadequate conceptions, distortions, and poor translations in proposals for "urgent safeguarding" are just as pronounced at the international level, despite, for example, UNESCO's stated commitments to local engagement and community-based leadership and to inverting traditional power hierarchies (see Seeger, 2018). Additionally, in better understanding the many frictions that govern heritage processes, there are particular concerns for protecting heritage in the Caribbean, especially with regard to economic development and elevated pressures of neoliberalism (see Siegel & Righter, 2011; Sher, 2011), as well as to climate and environmental matters (see Dirksen, 2019b; Siegel et al., 2013), which all strongly overlap with active discussions in Haiti. Sorting through these complex entanglements is necessary to seeing a fuller picture of actions and priorities around sustainability matters.

Aiming for an apparently less daunting point of departure, even the notion of music sustainability, which might be taken as an urgent if somewhat facile way of describing a constellation of efforts and mechanisms to ensure the continuance of various "at risk" musical practices and performances, is up for debate. Current perspectives often center around *cultural ecosystems* that are seen to be variously flourishing and threatened for a panoply of economic, political, and environmental reasons—a stance influenced by both environmental sustainability discussions and heritage management initiatives, such as the 2003 ICH Convention (i.e., Bendrups, 2019; Schippers & Grant, 2016). Increasingly, scholars see that music sustainability/cultural ecosystems models can only really be envisioned with a view toward advancing social justice (i.e., Lühning, 2013; Silvers, 2018). In addition, "musical vitality and viability" might be strengthened through applied or engaged/activist ethnomusicology frameworks (i.e., Bendrups et al., 2013, p. 155; Pedelty, 2016; Tan, 2021), with sustainability cast as "social action, cultural practice, and relationships with other people, other living beings, and the environment" (Cooley, 2019, p. xxiii). Another prominent line of music sustainability thinking is a sense that a "sound ecological rationality" might be achieved in seeing cultural heritage safeguarding through an ecological lens rather than through an economic lens that values the protection of sound commons and pays greater attention to intersections of sound and naturalism (Titon, 2020).

Critics of these directions argue, however, that appropriating terms from ecological science to explain human musical activity can lead to generalized and politically problematic utopian conceptions (i.e., Keogh & Collinson, 2016), or can superficially extend the metaphor of an ecological perspective while missing opportunities to reach past anthropocentric considerations (Allen, 2017). Beyond music studies circles, the concept of sustainability has been roundly criticized for its diffuseness, anthropocentric framing, insistence on economic growth as the solution, and inextricable links to developmentalist discourse, mostly in relation to extractive capitalist modernity and neoliberalism (see, for example, Escobar, 2008). Thus, as concerns of this volume include defining both music sustainabilities and pathways toward "effective, ethical, sustainable action in the face of threats to specific music practices worldwide," per this volume's editors, I reiterate the call to carefully consider the points of friction raised in these larger interdisciplinary debates. Perhaps in better understanding these multilayered frictions in all their intensity, we can design better collaborative, equity-based action to support ICH.

Yet even if they can be shaped as genuinely collaborative and equity-based, actions toward "music sustainability" in Haiti seem quaint at the moment, given immediate existential threats faced by Haitian citizens on a daily basis. The 2010 earthquake, as suggested above, presented an "opportunity" for an uncountable number of local and international organizations to formulate projects in support of the arts in response to new and newly perceived precarities. However, most of these commitments quickly fizzled once funding dried up and as it became clear how difficult it can be to sustain activities day to day, with other urgent priorities taking precedence. Now, with the perspective of more than a decade, we have firm evidence that many recovery efforts, including some premised on cultural heritage, were profit-driven ventures of non-Haitian partners and the Haitian elite class that allowed for flat-out pillaging of resources.

Moreover, even greater long-term consequences may result from the heightening authoritarian regime and state-sanctioned violence, with the internationally backed budding dictatorship of President Jovenel Moïse.[16] Beginning with Möise's predecessor Michel Martelly and dramatically rising under Möise, the population endured exploding inflation and a rapidly devaluing currency; diminishing access to food, electricity, education, and healthcare; and a recurring gas crisis. Critics of Moïse's administration brought to light a $4 billion embezzlement scandal of Petro-Caribe funds from a Venezuelan oil program intended for development projects, spanning several administrations and ensnaring many political elites. (Government-sponsored) gangs are responsible for a rising tide of kidnapping, rape, and murder used as a political ploy, thereby hindering circulation, and since 2018 several weeks-long rounds of *peyi lòk* (lockdown) have kept millions of people at home (see Dirksen, 2020; Dougé-Prosper & Schuller, 2021).

In the even bigger picture, centuries of extractionism—via plantations, deforestation, and mining—have led to an uncompromising state of environmental degradation that inescapably defines everyday existence. The Haitian government's failure to sufficiently deal with trash, sanitation, and basic public infrastructure has been weaponized against the population. And the Global Climate Risk Index over the past two decades has routinely ranked Haiti among the top three most vulnerable countries to the effects of extreme weather events related to climate change (see Dirksen, 2018 and 2021; Eckstein et al., 2017; Sheller, 2020).

---

[16] On July 7, 2021, after this essay had been submitted in final form, President Moise was assassinated, plunging the country into further political turmoil over leadership and sovereignty.

While resolutions for the current challenges to human rights and civil society are unlikely to be quickly forthcoming, reflecting on this long-and-broad view of history and context is crucial for imagining more sustaining and nourishing practices around heritage matters.[17] We must get beyond the typical prescriptions for "listening locally" and instituting "bottom-up" programs that sound great in theory but that often are little more than platitudes. It is of course essential that leadership be cultivated locally among those closest to the *patrimwàn* in question. It is also frequently helpful to build a trellis of support, selectively weaving in outside resources and expertise where appropriate. In other words, while sovereignty and self-determination are essential qualities for any initiative seeking to create sound(er) futures in Haiti, and even with all the valid critiques about misguided interventionist projects, an isolationist approach is likely not the goal. Rather, paraphrasing one wise young musician, instead of continuing with the standard degrading and demoralizing narratives, this is about defining futures where Haiti stands shoulder to shoulder alongside other nations, in full dignity and respect, as equals (interview Samuel Vicière, September 9, 2015; see Dirksen, 2021, p. 123). This is also about identifying, studying, and managing the many frictions that arise in any encounter over heritage, and beyond.

Moving forward, it may be worth explicitly incorporating practices from transformative justice (i.e., a. brown, 2020; Dixon & Piepzna-Samarasinha, 2020; Rerucha, 2021) and regenerative agriculture (i.e., Anderson, 2019; G. Brown, 2018; Penniman, 2018) into current cultural sustainability initiatives in Haiti. The former offers opportunities for justice-oriented reconciliation and avenues for change when confronting long and ongoing legacies of colonialism and neocolonialism that have profoundly shaped the cultural sector, alongside every other aspect of life. The latter recognizes that sustainability is not enough for viable and vibrant futures, and that even when it comes to matters of heritage, we must focus on regenerative processes that heal and promote healthy life cycles and relations with the environment.

These are not concepts to be imported, however: transformative justice and regenerative agriculture are already core to Haitian experiences and practices of resistance. Reflections of both are evident, for example, in how economics, justice, and conflict resolution are handled within the

---

[17] Yet under current circumstances, all but the most privileged individuals are effectively excluded from participating in substantial discussions and activities around safeguarding ICH.

*lakou* (traditional family compounds; agriculture-based collectives; sacred Vodou yards), as well as in the traditional agrarian practices that farmers are fighting to uphold amidst structural adjustments, "food aid," crop dumping, subsidized imports, and other violences committed against them (i.e., see AlterPresse, 2021).

Even deeper, demands for transformative justice and regenerative acts lie at the founding of the Haitian nation itself. These demands emanate from the legendary expression of resistance that revolutionary leader Toussaint Louverture wrote while freezing to death in a jail cell in France in 1802: "In overthrowing me, you have cut down in Saint-Domingue only the trunk of the tree of liberty of the Black people; it will shoot up again through the roots, for they are deep and numerous" (Madiou, [1904] 1989, p. 327). Along similar lines, Vodou metaphysics—as an ancient belief system that long predates the transatlantic crossing and that found new ontological orientations in this hemisphere—allows for change as an inevitable and continual process but safeguards against complete loss. As Vodouizan Elizabeth Saint-Hilaire once explained to me, even if an element of expressive or material culture were to be lost or destroyed and the creators of that cultural element along with it, the seeds of creation—even a single seed—will always remain, ready to sprout again under more favorable conditions (interview, October 31, 2016; see Dirksen, 2019b, p. 71). From these perspectives, we may find a locally resonant approach emerging for transformative, regenerative practices around music and heritage. Taking these steps may help us to see how, even in fraught times, we can reimagine sound(er) futures.

## References

Akagawa, N., & Smith, L. (Eds.) (2018). *Safeguarding intangible heritage: Practice and politics*. Routledge.

Allen, A. (2017). [Review]: *Sustainable futures for music cultures: An ecological perspective. Ethnomusicology Forum, 26*(3), 400–405.

AlterPresse Staff. (2021, March 18). Agriculture: Colloque, du jeudi 18 au samedi 20 mars 2021, à Papaye, Hinche, sur l'accaparement des terres paysannes en Haïti. *AlterPresse*. https://www.alterpresse.org/spip.php?article26824#.YFPibS2ZO1u.

Anderson, S. (2019). *One size fits none: A farm girl's search for the promise of regenerative agriculture*. University of Nebraska Press.

Augustin, J. R. (2020). *L'esclavage en Haïti. Entrecroisement des mémoires et enjeux de la patrimonialisation*. Unpublished doctoral dissertation, Université Laval, Québec.

Ayiti Mizik. (n.d.). Cartographie de l'industrie haïtienne de la musique. Association haïtienne des professionnels de la musique. http://ayitimizik.net/index.php/carto graphie/.

Beaubrun, M. P. (2013). Nan dòmi: An initiate's journey into Haitian Vodou. Trans. from the French by D. J. Walker. (Originally published in 2010). City Lights Books.

Bellande, A. (2015). Haïti déforestée, paysages remodelés. Les Éditions du CIDIHCA.

Bendrix, R. F., Eggert, A., & Peselmann, A. (Eds.) (2013). Heritage regimes and the state. Göttingen Studies in Cultural Property (Vol. 6). Universitätsverlag Göttingen.

Bendrups, D. (2019). Singing for survival: The music of Easter Island. Oxford University Press.

Bendrups, D, Barney, K., & Grant, C. (Eds.). (2013). Sustainability and ethnomusicology in Australasia. Special issue of Musicology Australia, 35(2).

Bien-Aimé, K., Brusma, D., Josué, E., Lubin, E., Marcelin, D., Paul, R. Arnau, M. P., Chéry, P., Vilson, G., Divers, M., Duquella, A., Millet, E., Paul, E., & Similien, E. (2014). Inisyasyon nan patrimwàn kiltirèl peyi Dayiti: Manyèl pou elèv nouvo segondè (Vols. 1– 2). Réf-Culture.

Bigenho, M., & Stobart, H. (Eds.) (2018). Dossier especial: Música e patrimonio cultural em América Latina. Special issue of TRANS: Revista Transculutral da Música, 21–22. https://www.sibetrans.com/trans/publicacion/24/trans-21-22-2018.

Boel, J. (2015, November 16). Fundamental education: A pioneer concept—Jens Boel explains why. UNESCO. https://en.unesc.o.org/news/fundamental-education-pioneer-concept-jens-boel-explains-why

brown, a. m. (2020). We will not cancel us: And other dreams of transformative justice. AK Press.

Brown, G. (2018). Dirt to soil: One family's journey into regenerative agriculture. Chelsea Green.

Castor, S. (1988). L'occupation américaine d'Haïti (3rd ed. française). (Original work published 1971). CRESFED.

Charlier-Doucet, R. (2005). Anthropologie, politique, et engagement social. Gradhiva, 1, 109–125.

Chocano, R. (2020). Heritage is a struggle: Music, neoliberal logics, and the practice of intangible cultural heritage in Peru. Unpublished doctoral dissertation, Indiana University.

Cooley, T. J. (Ed.). (2019). Cultural sustainabilities: Music, media, language, advocacy. University of Illinois Press.

Courlander, H. (1939). Haiti singing. Cooper Square.

Dauphin, C. (2014). Histoire du style musical d'Haïti. Mémoire d'Encrier.

Dautruche, J. R. (2010). Les festivités vaudou à Souvenance. Indexed in the Inventaire du patrimoine immatériel d'Haïti. http://www.ipimh.org/fiche-les-festivites-vodou-sou venance-3.html.

Dautruche, J. R. (2013). Tourisme culturel et patrimoine remodelé: Dynamique de mise en valeur du patrimoine culturel immatériel en Haïti. Ethnologies, 35(1), 145–161.

Dayan, J. (1995). Haiti, history, and the gods. University of California Press.

DeGraff, M. (2019). Foreword: Against apartheid in education and in linguistics: The case of Haitian Creole in neo-nolonial Haiti. In D. Macedo (Ed.), Decolonizing language education: The misteaching of English and other colonial languages (pp. ix–xxxii). Routledge.

DeGraff, M. (2020). The politics of education in post-colonies: Kreyòl in Haiti as a case study of language as technology for power and liberation. Journal of Postcolonial Linguistics, 3, 89–125.

Dirksen, R. (2013). Surviving material poverty by employing cultural wealth: Putting music in the service of community in Haiti. *Yearbook for Traditional Music, 45*, 43–57.

Dirksen, R. (2016a). Blanchet, Lina Mathon (1903–1994). In H. L. Gates, Jr., F. W. Knight, et al. (Eds.), *Dictionary of Caribbean and Afro-Latin American biography*, Vol. 1 (pp. 343–345). Oxford University Press.

Dirksen, R. (2016b). Brouard, Carmen (1909–2005). In H. L. Gates, Jr., F. W. Knight, et al. (Eds.), *Dictionary of Caribbean and Afro-Latin American biography*, Vol. 1 (pp. 414–415). Oxford University Press.

Dirksen, R. (2018). Haiti, singing for the land, sea, and sky: Cultivating ecological metaphysics and environmental awareness through music. *MUSICultures, 45*(1–2), 112–135.

Dirksen, R. (2019a). Haiti's hidden archives and accidental archivists: A view on the private collections and collectors at the heart of safeguarding the nation's classical music heritage. *Latin American Music Review, 40*(1), 59–88.

Dirksen, R. (2019b). Haiti's drums and trees: Facing loss of the sacred. *Ethnomusicology, 63*(1), 43–77.

Dirksen, R. (2020). *After the dance, the drums are heavy: Carnival, politics, and musical engagement in Haiti*. Oxford University Press.

Dirksen, R. (2021). Zafé fatra (the affair of trash) and the affair of scholarly engagement: Can music (and music scholarship) really clean up the streets of Port-au-Prince? In B. Diamond & S. E. Castelo-Branco (Eds.), *Transforming ethnomusicology: Methodologies, institutional structures, and policies*, Vol. 1 (pp. 110–130). Oxford University Press.

Dixon, E., & Piepzna-Samarasinha, L. L. (2020). *Beyond survival: Strategies and stories from the transformative justice movement*. AK Press.

Dougé-Prosper, M., & Schuller, M. (Eds.). (2021). End of empire? Radical capitalism, forced migration, and state violence in Haiti. Special report in *NACLA Report on the Americas, 53* (1: 1–6 and 32–91).

Dumervé, É. C. E. M. (1968). *Histoire de la musique en Haïti*. Imprimerie des Antilles.

Dunham, K. (1994). *Island possessed*. (Original work published 1969). University of Chicago Press.

Eckstein, D., Künzel, V., & Schäfer, L. (2017). *Global climate risk index 2018: Who suffers most from extreme weather events? Weather-related loss events in 2016 and 1997 to 2016*. Germanwatch e.V. http://germanwatch.org/en/cri.

Educavision. (n.d.). *Chansons d'enfants en français et créole/Chante timoun*. Educavision.

Eldridge (Stewart), L. (2015). (Re)membering Haiti through mizik klasik. *Journal of Haitian Studies, 21*(1), 186–194.

Escobar, A. (2008). *Territories of difference: Place, movements, life, redes*. Duke University Press.

Fleurant, G. (1996). *Dancing spirits: Rhythms and rituals of Haitian Vodun, the rada rite*. Greenwood Press.

Foster, M. D., & Gilman, L. (Eds.). (2015). *UNESCO on the ground: Local perspectives on intangible cultural heritage*. Indiana University Press.

Fouchard, J. (1988a). *Artistes et répertoires des scènes de Saint-Domingue*. Les Éditions Henri Deschamps. (Original work published 1955).

Fouchard, J. (1988b). *Le théâtre à Saint-Domingue*. Les Éditions Henri Deschamps. (Original work published 1955).

Garcia, M. A. (2016). *Report sur la mise en oeuvre de la Convention et sur l'état des éléments qui ont été inscrits sur la Liste representative du patrimoine culturel immatériel de l'humanité.* UNESCO. https://ich.unesco.org/en/state/haiti-HT?info=periodic-reporting.

Hafstein, V. Tr., & Skrydstrup, M. (2020). *Patrimonialities: Heritage vs. property.* Cambridge University Press.

Howard, K. (Ed.). (2012). *Music as intangible cultural heritage: Policy, ideology, and practice in the preservation of East Asian traditions.* (SOAS Musicology Series). Ashgate.

Hurston, Z. N. (2008). *Tell my horse: Voodoo and life in Haiti and Jamaica.* HarperPerennial. (Original work published 1938).

International Committee of the Blue Shield. (2010, January 14). Communiqué Bouclier Bleu Haïti. ICBS.http://ancbs.org/cms/images/15-01-2010_blueshield_statement_ha iti_fr.pdf.

Joseph, C. L., Saint Paul, J. E., & Mezilas, G. (Eds.). (2018). *Between two worlds: Jean Price-Mars, Haiti, and Africa.* Lexington Books.

Keck, M. (2019, May 9). Vodou drums symbolize clash between climate change and the sacred in Haiti. *News at IU Bloomington.* https://news.iu.edu/stories/2019/05/iub/09-vodou-drums-embody-clash-between-climate-change-and-the-sacred.html.

Keogh, B., & Collinson, I. (2016). "A place for everything and everything in its place": The (ab)uses of music ecology. *MUSICultures, 43*(1), 1–15.

Kirshenblatt-Gimblett, B. (1998). *Destination culture: Tourism, museums, and heritage.* University of California Press.

Kirshenblatt-Gimblett, B. (2004). Intangible heritage as metacultural production. *Museum International, 56*(1–2), 52–65.

Ladouceur, R. (2014, September 4). Preserving Haiti's musical heritage. *Le Nouvelliste.* Trans. from the French by A. Galbreath; original no longer accessible. https://lenouvelli ste.com/lenouvelliste/article/135358/Preserving-Haitis-Musical-Heritage.html.

Largey, M. (2004). Ethnographic transcription and music ideology in Haiti: The music of Werner A. Jaegerhuber. *Latin American Music Review, 25*(1), 1–31.

Largey, M. (2006). *Vodou nation: Haitian art music and cultural nationalism.* University of Chicago Press.

Lomax, A. (2009). *Alan Lomax in Haiti, 1936–1937.* Prepared and annotated by G. Averill. Harte Recordings. HR 103.

Lopez, P. J. (2015). Clumsy beginnings: From "modernizing mission" to humanitarianism in the US Occupation of Haiti (1915–34). *Environment and Planning A: Economy and Space, 47*(11), 2240–2256.

Lühning, A. (2013). Sustentabilidade de patrimônios musicais e políticas públicas a partir de experiências e vivências musicais em bairros populares. *Música e cultura: Revista da ABET, 8*(1), 44–58.

Madiou, T. (1989). *Histoire d'Haïti* (Vol. 2). Éditions Henri Deschamps. (Original work published 1904).

Margron, K., & Racine, J. (2012–2021). *Chansons d'Haïti* (Vols. 1–11). Imprimerie Pressmax S.A.

Meskell, L. (2020). *A future in ruins: UNESCO, world heritage, and the dream of peace.* Oxford University Press.

Métraux, A. (1972). *Voodoo in Haiti.* Trans. from the French by H. Carteris. Schocken Books. (Original work published 1959).

Oriol, J., Viaud, L. & Aubourg, M. (1952). *Le mouvement folklorique en Haïti*. Imprimerie de L'État.

Pedelty, M. (2016). *A song to save the Salish Sea: Musical performance as environmental activism*. Indiana University Press.

Penniman, L. (2018). *Farming while black: Soul Fire Farm's practical guide to liberation on the land*. Chelsea Green.

Pierre, E. (2018, October 22). Welele signe "Tambour, âme ancestrale." *Le Nouvelliste*. https://lenouvelliste.com/article/194154/welele-signe-tambour-ame-ancestrale.

Price-Mars, J. (1998). *Ainsi parla l'oncle: Essais d'ethnographie*. Imprimeur II. (Original work published 1928).

Ramsey, K. (2002). Without one ritual note: Folklore performance and the Haitian state, 1935–1946. *Radical History Review, 84*, 7–42.

Ramsey, K. (2011). *The spirits and the law: Vodou and power in Haiti*. University of Chicago Press.

Rerucha, M. Q. (2021). *Beyond the surface of restorative practices: Building a culture of equity, connection, and healing*. Dave Burgess Consulting.

Rigaud, M. (2015). *La tradition voudoo et le Voudoo haïtien (son temple, ses mystères, sa magie)*. Éditions Fardin. (Original work published 1953).

Roumain, J. (1942). *À propos de la campagne "anti-superstitieuse"/Las supersticiones*. Imprimerie de l'État.

Roumain, J. (1943). *Le Sacrifice du tambour-assoto(r)*. Imprimerie de l'État.

Saint-Germain, M. (1997). Problématique linguistique en Haïti et réforme éducative: Quelques constats. *Revue des sciences de l'éducation, 23*(3), 611–42.

Schippers, H., & Grant, C. (Eds.). (2016). *Sustainable future for music cultures: An ecological perspective*. Oxford University Press.

Seabrook, W. B. (1929). *The magic island*. Literary Guild of America.

Seeger, A. (2018). Music and cultural heritage making in Latin America: An afterward. *Dossier especial: Música e patrimonio cultural em América Latina*. Special issue of *TRANS: Revista transculutral da música, 21–22*. https://www.sibetrans.com/trans/pub lic/docs/7d-trans-2018_1.pdf.

Sérant, C. B. (2014, February 3). Les héritages oubliés revisités dans un concert pour deux pianos. *Le Nouvelliste*. https://lenouvelliste.com/public/article/127012/les-heritages-oublies-revisites-dans-un-concert-pour-deux-pianos.

Sheller, Mimi. (2020). *Island futures: Caribbean survival in the Anthropocene*. Duke University Press.

Sher, P. (2011). Heritage tourism in the Caribbean: The politics of culture after neoliberalism. *Bulletin of Latin American Research, 30*(1), 7–20.

Siegel, P., Hofman, C. L., Bérard, B., Murphy, R., Hung, J. U., Rojas, R. V., & White, C. (2013). Confronting Caribbean heritage in an archipelago of diversity: Politics, stakeholders, climate change, natural disasters, tourism, and development. *Journal of Field Archaeology, 38*(4), 376–390.

Siegel, P. E., & Righter, E. (Eds.) (2011). *Protecting heritage in the Caribbean*. University of Alabama Press.

Silvers, M. B. (2018). *Voices of drought: The politics of music and environment in Northeastern Brazil*. University of Illinois Press.

Smith, L. (2006). *Uses of heritage*. Routledge.

Smithsonian Institute and Gouvernement de la République d'Haïti. (2011). *Projet de sauvetage du patrimoine culturel haïtien: Introduction*. Smithsonian Institution. http://haiti.si.edu/index_fr.html.

Staff HaitiLibre. (2011, April 17). Haiti-UNESCO: The importance of culture as a motor for reconstruction. *HaitiLibre*. https://www.haitilibre.com/en/news-2756-haiti-unesco-the-importance-of-culture-as-a-motor-for-reconstruction.html.

Staff iciHaïti. (2019, October 11). Culture: Plusieurs éléments du patrimoine immatériel protégés par la loi. *iciHaïti.com*. https://www.icihaiti.com/article-29228-icihaiti-culture-plusieurs-elements-du-patrimoine-immateriel-proteges-par-la-loi.html.

St. Hubert, H. (2018). *Visions of a modern nation: Haiti at the World's Fairs*. Unpublished doctoral dissertation, University of Miami.

Tan, S. B. (2021). Engaged activist research: Dialogical interventions towards revitalizing the Chinese glove puppet theatre in Penang. In B. Diamond & S. E. Castelo-Branco (Eds.), *Transforming ethnomusicology: Methodologies, institutional structures, and policies*, Vol. 1 (pp. 131–150). Oxford University Press.

Titon, J. T. (2020). *Toward a sound ecology*. Indiana University Press.

UNESCO. (2003, October 17). Convention for the safeguarding of the intangible cultural heritage. MISC/2003/CLT/CH/14. UNESCO. http://unesdoc.unesco.org/images/0013/001325/132540e.pdf.

UNESCO. (2011, April 11). UNESCO for Haiti: Making culture a motor for reconstruction. UNESCO. https://whc.unesco.org/uploads/events/documents/event-725-15.pdf.

Verna, C. F. (2017). *Haiti and the uses of America: Post-U.S. Occupation promises*. Rutgers University Press.

Vilson, G. (2013, 2015). *Kandelab: 102 notated Haitian folk and Vodou songs* (Vols. 1–2). Kandelab Foundation.

Wilcken, L. (1992a). Power, ambivalence, and the remaking of Haitian Vodoun music in New York. *Latin American Music Review, 13*(1), 1–32.

Wilcken, L., with Augustin, F. (1992b). *The drums of Vodou*. White Cliffs Media.

Yúdice, G. (2004). *The expediency of culture: Uses of culture in the global era*. Duke University Press.

Z.A.M.A. (Friends Together for Haitian Music; M. Procopio, R. Dirksen, A. Weaver, & T. Clowes). (2007). *Belle Ayiti*. [n.n.]. Compact disc.

# Index

For the benefit of digital users, indexed terms that span two pages (e.g., 52–53) may, on occasion, appear on only one of those pages.

Note: Tables and figures are indicated by t and f following the page number